Genji Days

Genji Days

EDWARD G. SEIDENSTICKER

KODANSHA INTERNATIONAL LTD.

Distributed in the United States by Kodansha International/USA, Ltd., through Harper & Row, Publishers, Inc., 10 East 53rd Street, New York, New York 10022; in Canada by Fitzhenry & Whiteside Limited, 150 Lesmill Road, Don Mills, Ontario; in Mexico and Central America by HARLA S.A. de C.V., Apartado 30–546, Mexico 4, D.F.; in South America by Harper & Row, International Department; in the United Kingdom by Phaidon Press Ltd., Littlegate House, St. Ebbe's Street, Oxford OX1 1SQ; in Continental Europe by Boxerbooks Inc., Limmatstrasse 111, 8031 Zurich; in Australia and New Zealand by Book Wise (Australia) Pty. Ltd., 104–8 Sussex Street, Sydney 2000; in the Far East by Toppan Company (S) Pte. Ltd., Box 22 Jurong Town Post Office, Jurong, Singapore 22.

Published by Kodansha International Ltd., 2–12–21 Otowa, Bunkyo-ku, Tokyo 112 and Kodansha International/USA, Ltd., 10 East 53rd Street, New York, New York 10022 and 44 Montgomery Street, San Francisco, California 94104. Copyright in Japan, 1977, by Kodansha International Ltd. All rights reserved. Printed in Japan.

LCC 76–44157
ISBN 0–87011–296–1
JBC 1095–785664–2361

First edition, 1977

Preface

This is a book of excerpts from a diary kept continuously since New Year's Day, 1959. They are from the *Genji* years, or some of them, the years when translating *The Tale of Genji* was my principal concern. The first of the really earnest *Genji* years, reference to my diary tells me, in answer to a question frequently asked, was 1966 – although the first three chapters had been done in rough draft at some earlier time. Considerable excerpts from the late sixties have already been published in Japanese, in the magazines *Chūō Kōron* and *Jiyū*. About midway through the *Genji* years there came what might be called the Kawabata interlude, a time of concentration upon Kawabata and his doings and writings. It was the time of the Nobel award and two book-length translations. The *Genji* was neglected. Entries having to do with it are sparse for late 1968 and most of 1969.

It is with the commencement of a new period of earnestness that these excerpts begin. They are from the last five *Genji* years, 1970 through 1974 and into 1975. It had been my intention to publish the last ten chapters – the Uji chapters – first, and most of the work on them had been done before "the Kawabata interlude." Save for a final revision late in 1974, they were completed in the spring of 1971. It was then decided that the first forty-four chapters must be translated before anything was published. The contract for the complete translation was signed in April, 1972. A first draft was finished in September, 1973.

There is in these entries a great deal of jumping back and forth among parts of the *Genji*. To explain each jump would be tedious. It must suffice to say that several things could be going on almost simultaneously: translation in first draft, revision, checking for accuracy against the Waley translation, and readying copy for the lady who checked it against the original. There are also references to seminars at the University of Michigan in which we read extended portions of the *Genji*. If the jumps back and forth are confusing, at least they will have the merit of demonstrating that the translation process was a complex one. It occurred in three settings, Ann Arbor, Tokyo, and Honolulu.

The excerpts already published in Japanese have to do only with the *Genji* and the process of translating it. Early discussions with Kodansha editors looked towards something similar. In making transcripts, however, several times bulkier than this volume, I presently found myself adding material not related to the *Genji*, such material as dreams, with which the diary is studded; and so the entries gathered here are conglomerates, *Genji* matters mixed in with others, as they are in the original diary.

Since the original is reasonably faithful to the name diary in the literal sense, a daily record, it of course contains far more entries than have been collected here. Many of the entries here, moreover, are abbreviations of longer ones. The original contains a great many words which must once have seemed worth setting down, but do no longer.

Sometimes abridgement was so considerable as to leave an entry looking fractured. To avoid that unpleasant appearance, I have sometimes joined one entry to another. Aside from abbreviation and selection, amalgamation has been the most radical device reshaping the original. At no time, however, has it been allowed to give an appearance of prescience or clairvoyance. It would not have been difficult, by combining two entries, to make one of them look uncommonly foresighted, but I hope that nothing of the sort has been allowed to happen.

For the rest, revision has been minimal. Nothing has been added save very brief explanation, and changes, all of them minor, have been in the interests of fluency.

Once a great sheaf of entries from the *Genji* years had been transcribed, the problem of where to begin the final selection asked solution, and it proved troublesome. Had there been a moment of great resolve ("On this day, dear diary, I did undertake to translate *The Tale of Genji*"), that would obviously have been it. But there was none. The undertaking was sidled into. The beginning, early in

1970, of the years of continuous engrossment seemed as good a time as any.

The chapter titles presented another problem. In the original diary they are in Japanese, with few exceptions. To render them immediately into English seemed like the worst sort of cheating, the sort that is easily found out. The process of rendering them into English, sometimes slow and painful, is itself apparent in these excerpts. Save at the very end, therefore, they have been left in Japanese. A list with my translations will be found below.

1. KIRITSUBO – "The Paulownia Court"
2. HAHAKIGI – "The Broom Tree"
3. UTSUSEMI – "The Shell of the Locust"
4. YŪGAO – "Evening Faces" 夕顔 (花) moon flower
5. WAKAMURASAKI – "Lavender" 若紫 light purple
6. SUETSUMUHANA – "The Safflower"
7. MOMIJI NO GA – "An Autumn Excursion" 紅葉
8. HANA NO EN – "The Festival of the Cherry Blossoms" 花
9. AOI – "Heartvine" 葵 hollyhock
10. SAKAKI – "The Sacred Tree" 榊 sacred Shinto tree
11. HANACHIRUSATO – "The Orange Blossoms"
12. SUMA – "Suma"
13. AKASHI – "Akashi"
14. MIOTSUKUSHI – "Channel Buoys"
15. YOMOGIU – "The Wormwood Patch" 蓬生 area overgrown w. weeds yomogi = mugwort
16. SEKIYA – "The Gatehouse" 関屋
17. EAWASE – "A Picture Contest" 絵
18. MATSUKAZE – "The Wind in the Pines" 松風
19. USUGUMO – "A Rack of Cloud" 薄雲 thin (fleecy) clouds
20. ASAGAO – "The Morning Glory" 朝顔
21. OTOME – "The Maiden" 乙女
22. TAMAKAZURA – "The Jeweled Chaplet" 玉
23. HATSUNE – "The First Warbler" 初
24. KOCHŌ – "Butterflies"

3

N.B. The numbers immediately following chapter titles in the diary refer to this list.

1970

Ann Arbor   Saturday, January 17: Slowly, slowly, going back over sentences and passages, in the hour or so before sleep each night (fewer strolls downtown these cold nights when sleep comes more easily), I have been making my way through the life of George Bent that Willie gave me for Christmas. There is much grandeur in the idea of a Colorado with mustangs and Indians and buffalo, and not a single Yankee edifice but Bent's Fort, five hundred miles from "Westport," and nothing between. The Cheyenne, I fear, emerge from the story less as great fighters than as sneak thieves and marauders, their raids upon other tribes having a certain specious, childish quality about them, rather like Japanese student rioting; but these depredations did, I suppose, help keep the plains from being overrun by human beings. Worse than a plague of locusts the Yankees seem as they come flooding up the Platte and the Arkansas, cutting down stands of cottonwood vital to the Indians, driving the grass into the ground. Yet the Cheyenne, with their annuities and their horse-stealing and their tendency to "avoid trouble" when the American cavalry comes in sight, do seem less than heroic. As they head off on another of their raids against the Pawnees, they remind me of the fish at Katakai with other fish in their mouths, swallower and swallowed together in the net.

Snow all day, steady now, not the nasty little spits we have been having. I prefer it this way, bold and muscular. The January thaw, if such it was, did not last long. The temperature has been below freezing all day. Regents Plaza below my window is soft and white, and the cubic sculpture in the middle of it is rather beautiful, rather warming, a sturdy chunk of black in the loneliness of the white.

I worked hard on the *Genji* through the morning and much of the afternoon. I am going back to make a clean copy of "Hashihime"[45] from my messy first revision, in effect doing a second revision as I go along. It is very arduous work, requiring great concentration, and very slow. I get no more than three pages done in an hour, and have to take a few minutes' rest every hour or so. But it has been good to be at honest work through much of a Saturday. When was I last so diligent? As to whether this second revision is any good or not, I cannot say. Once a sheet is out of the typewriter, I find myself afraid to look at it.

Saturday, January 31: Great day – a whole chapter ready to show timidly to whoever will look at it. Descriptions and conversations go much more rapidly (save when conversation contains poems or references to them) than do soliloquies and psychological explora-tion. I do not know whether this is because I feel freer to improvise with the former, or because the vocabulary is so maddeningly lim-ited in the latter. Got to go out and get me a Roget.

In the evening I sort of dreamed my way, not worrying myself about "rapid reading," to the end of the George Bent book. It fades away. How silly and how tragic, that the last fighting should have been over country that we did not want and they did. Just look on your map—the valley of the Powder River is the next thing to uninhabited today. Interesting though it is in its way, the book leaves you dissatisfied, wondering all sorts of things. Wondering chiefly, I suppose, what it was really like to live among the Cheyenne. Here was a man who did, and he doesn't say. How did it smell, how did it sound? Did Indians get bitten by rattlesnakes, which must have been all over the place? How often did they take baths? What did they do on long winter nights, when the coyotes howled and the wind blew free? Did they like Indian paintbrushes?

Tuesday, February 3: Over to the office slightly late, having slept a little too well. I glanced at the good *New York Times* and the bad *Michigan Daily* (how the rebels do take on their own conventions – no one speaks of the Vietnam war as other than "immoral"), and I spent a couple of hours getting ready for my *Genji* class. And then, with the rest of the morning, I worked on my own *Genji*.

I think these days I most enjoy trying to translate the poems. I continue to force everything into two five-accent lines, and think the idea not at all bad, though sometimes a good deal of forcing is needed. For a while I tried a four-beat line, but the effect was a bit too much like the nursery rhyme, "Bah, bah, black sheep, have you any wool?" I was, when I gathered up my scribbles and put them back in the file, almost at the end of "Shiigamoto,"[46] had old Kaoru peeking through the keyhole.

In the mail a propaganda sheet from the Palace Hotel in Tokyo, memorable because it translates Otorisama as "Fair of the Fowl."

Most of the evening I spent on Rackham fellowships, overwhelmingly in European languages and in art and architecture. The art and architecture ones give pause. Sometimes it is because they are couched in such jargon as to make it next to impossible to know what is being proposed – words like "empathic" and "plastic" fly through the air like swarms of bees. Sometimes it is because you want to run off and have a good vomit at the conceit, the sheer arrogance, as when someone tells you that he proposes to use his grant to create a major work of art. Sometimes it is because the proposals are so utterly wacky – you are inclined to let the fellow have his money if he in return will let you go watch. One person in architecture proposes to get a number of graduate students up in a complicated rig of plugs and stops and filters to simulate the senses of the old, and then find their reactions to their "environment" (another of those busy buzzing words).

And sometimes it is because they are damned interesting. One man, a painter in the art department, describes the plight of the provincial artist. Most large annual and biennial exhibits are by invitation, and the invitations are controlled by the New York galleries, and the New York galleries, because of costs and personnel problems, favor New York artists. Makes a person think that it might not be a bad thing for our great republic to fall to pieces.

Still fascinated with the Cheyenne, I moved on, for my bedtime reading, from the life of George Bent to Grinnell's *The Fighting Cheyennes.* I began near the end, with Custer's last battle. Much more the feeling of what it was like to be an Indian, out on the lone prairies, than in the Bent book. A little Indian boy gathering grasshoppers for his brothers to go fishing with, a father and son riding all night upstream and over ridges (coyotes, nighthawks – walks of summer nights in my native Colorado) to join a battle party – it comes across. Indians seem to have liked birds – so maybe they liked paintbrushes too.

Saturday, February 14: Despite the fact that St. Valentine has been dropped from the hagiography, the town has been overflowing with hearts, every shop wearing its heart in its window. I even got a couple myself, both signed "Wendy."

I got a second revision and clean copy made of much of "Shii-gamoto," and so lost myself in it that I quite lost track of time, and failed to be bothered by the silence of the tomb that is the Gunn Building on Saturdays. I made my way through to the Eighth Prince's death and after, and I thought: how much finer a day than ours, that day able to see beauty in old age, and make of it, for artistic purposes, something other than a butt of derision and a source of revulsion. How sadly lacking in our baby-directed culture is litera-ture that takes old age seriously, and sees that it has the melancholy advantage of being able to look back over it all. (How beautiful the Eighth Prince's speech about autumn nights of old – and where among the juvenilia that make up American literature is its equiva-lent?) Back to Confucius! Maybe I, even I, shall be the one to write a Confucian book – we need one far more than we need Alan Watts and his infantile Zen.

In the evening I turned again to my Cheyenne. What a pity and a loss, I kept thinking, that there were no Cheyenne to tell us, with-out benefit of a scribe, what it was like on the plains, with the wind and the coyotes out beyond a thickness of buffalo hide. I am struck, reading Grinnell's report of Cheyenne happenings, with how often they happen at dawn. The twilights are the beautiful times, out on the plains, especially in the summer, when the winds die down for an hour or so and the cottonwoods are still. Little is said about the evening twilights, but the morning twilights seem to have been a time of hope and terror.

Saturday, February 28: Yesterday in the Union the Negroes sought to underline their point, as our dear dedicated *Daily* put it, first disrupting the cafeteria and then stuffing themselves gratis at the buffet, and overturning what they did not choose to stuff themselves with. They will not be disciplined, of course, and so license would seem to reign in the name of idealism.

Today has been still and next to cloudless, and in sheltered, sunny hollows there has been the feel of spring; my amaryllis grew an inch in the course of the day. And I had very amusing dreams last night, perhaps induced by temperance. In one of them I was married to either Marilyn Monroe or Linda Beech, I was not sure, upon awakening, which. Maybe both – when you've known one blonde you've known them all.

It was a hard day's work on the *Genji*, it was, it was. I made my way through a second revision down to midpoint in "Agemaki."[47] What a wonderful tragicomedian Kaoru is as he slams the door of the Uji house forever, and then heads back for Uji on the next bus. I did not have a great many footnotes today, but I managed to get all mixed up on such as I did have, and that was fun. Scholarship *is* fun, perhaps the most fun when it is the most pointless.

A long telephone call from California in the evening. Ruth Lilienthal and Katharine Sansom, the latter back from Honolulu. They were about to set out in the liquid California twilight for Woodside, and were reminded of me. Why? Because they were going to the Village Pub. And why did the Pub remind them of me? Well, because it was there that I was so shaken when Katharine poured her tomato juice in the lampshade.

Tuesday, March 3: It being the Double Three – the third of March, the Doll Festival – I got out my dolls and put them on my file cabinet, and, though no one who came into my office noticed, I felt very happy with them.

It has been a soupy day, fairly warm, foggy and drippy. I got in some hours of concentrated work on *Genji* translation. We approach the end of "Agemaki," the death of dear, silly Oigimi. The last day of the Gosechi is being observed with due gaiety in the city, and at

Uji the winds wail and Oigimi turns her face to the wall and dies; and I kept asking myself what, way back there at the base of my skull, I was being reminded of. Millie Theale of *The Wings of the Dove*, dying in her Venetian palace, and of something more. Then it came to me: the last act of *La Traviata*, Violetta dying while the festival passes beneath her window.

The *Genji* class in the afternoon. We got involved in an interesting discussion of modern Japanese translations – that is, I think, the proper word – of the *Genji*.* The ones that are faithful, if I may summarize our conclusions, are not modern Japanese, and the ones that are in good modern Japanese have transferred the *Genji* to a different world, largely because of the clearer and more frequent nominatives and clearer distinctions between masculine and feminine speech. And so Japanese "translators" face problems which, if perhaps somewhat different in degree, are not different in kind from those faced by us of the blue-eyed persuasion.

Dinner with the Malms, a lovely crab dinner, Joyce's sister having come in from California the day before yesterday, loaded with California crabs. The sister is just as pretty as she can be, one's idea of that Sunkist maid who said don't be late, that's why one can hardly wait, open up your Golden Gate – and what's that last line? Bill was summoned to the hospital this morning to tell a gang of head-healers, including the one who brought him through, of his experiences; and the horror of that last test, when air was pumped into his head, so came back to him that it was as if he were living it again. He talked of it with intense hatred, for he is convinced that sadism lay beneath not the test itself but the way it was administered.

Wednesday, March 4: My amaryllis is now shooting up at the rate of an inch and a half a day. Since it refuses to send up leaves with which to cover that tumescent stalk, it is more and more suggestive of a rutting stallion. I could put a sheet over it, but probably that would only make things worse.

* By, among others, Yosano Akiko, Tanizaki Junichirō, and Enchi Fumiko.

I saw Oigimi to her funeral pyre. The death itself is a scene of wonderful restraint—we know of it only through the attitudes of the bystanders. She is a person, and then she is a thing, to be taken out and burned, and that is that. And the funeral? I found myself asking questions. The similarity to Murasaki's funeral is striking. Almost the same words are used to describe Kaoru's feelings as were used to describe Genji's. Is there an intentional echo, are we to see the contrast, emphasized by parallel description, between the end of a love which, though barren, at least was consummated, and the end of a love that came to nothing at all? Or might it be that both descriptions are conventional, and the author is getting through tiresome things in a hurry?

Friday, March 20: My amaryllis nears the end. Two of its three blossoms are still a glory of cardinal red, over in the corner, but the other one collapsed with weird swiftness a little while ago. Just sort of said good-bye and went away.

Rather better organized than most springs, I went over to the health service first thing in the morning to make a beginning on my summer immunization. "You have to take your life in your hands when you work for this university," said the nurse, with reference to the fact that Hill Auditorium was being picketed by BAM (I have remembered why that little acronym, now signifying Black Action Movement, has sounded so familiar: back in the days when I was young and in the Marine Corps, it designated a member of the she-auxiliary, and meant Broad-assed Marine), and a call for a strike was out, because of the failure of the regents yesterday to compromise and swallow all the BAM demands. The picketing, though evidently it later turned into an attempt to disrupt the honors convocation, was quiet enough both times I passed; but the literature being handed out was very raucous indeed, full of talk about "pigs" and characterizing the "regental" (one of the words these days) resolution as "half-assed." The *Daily* carried on the front page a BAM declaration which characterized it, and if memory serves I reproduce the precise orthography, as "S-H-I-T."

Everything is going to pieces, even the art of rabble-rousing. Tom Paine was a rabble-rouser, as was Patrick Henry; but what style they had compared to these people. Even Hitler, I would imagine, did it with considerably more grace.

Though quickly overcome by my dose of typhoid, and sleepy and heavy-headed throughout the day, I managed to work myself into "Yadorigi,"[49] having finished a first revision of "Sawarabi"[48] earlier in the week. There are rather heavy traces of serialization, so to speak – synoptic passages as of bringing us dear readers up to date. As in the case of Mr. Kawabata and his sleeping beauties, it would have been far better to cut for book publication. Already there are foreshadowings of Ukifune's entrance. Already, at this early stage, Murasaki has realized that there is little to be done with Nakanokimi short of making Niou a complete and utter cad, and that is not the sort of thing she does.

Tokyo   Sunday, June 7: I was tempted to wonder from time to time whether my despondency earlier in the week might have had to do with some sort of prescience, some awareness of the bleakness ahead in comparison with the riches immediately behind. What I did today of "Yadorigi" is very dull, endless mooning by Kaoru and Nakanokimi on how complicated life can be; and at the end (I hope) of the endless, a most clumsy device for introducing a little cheer. Kaoru sends off a lot of clothes, all carefully inventoried, to Nijō. This last device Waley quite cuts, and I fear the world will think him right to have done so. Indeed my gloom, as I made my way through what must be described as protracted evidences of faltering and fumbling, was deeper than the gloom so unconvincingly described: for it might have to do with a suspicion that my labors have been meaningless, giving the world nothing that it will want to read, seeking to change its mind, in a manner all unworthy, about a work the view of which is unchangeable. Yes, Waley's taste is good – I have marked the precise passages he omitted, and how I long to find myself at the point that indicates the end of this particular set of them.

A most pleasant afternoon, out there with the Muramatsus,* beyond the dreary wastes where the intellectuals live and vote for their Socialist governor. We sat eating and drinking the hours away, and butterflies fluttered through foliage rendered luminous by a bright and not oppressive sun, and a pleasant breeze blew through the open house, and students, with whom Professor M. seems to continue to have remarkably good relations despite the troubles, came and went.

He really is a dear man. Beneath his bamboo groves, in a glorious clutter of books and bottles and gimcrackery, he lives the life of the Confucian literatus, reading and writing and painting and drinking, and giving advice to students, and being waited upon by a wife who manages to remain girlish on the near side of old age and who manages to make waiting on him seem like a game. It is the life of Taiga and Buson and their ten pleasures and ten conveniences.

The most amusing of the students who came and went was a young man, now lost in the depths of the Sumitomo Bank, who was captain of the Hitotsubashi crew. I asked whether he had studied under Professor M., and he replied: "Not really. All I did was row a boat." And there was a slightly older person who followed an improbable course: after graduating from Hitotsubashi he went into the Nō, and he is now an actor, in the Kanze school. He brought along a couple of Nō masks, by a modern master. It was the first time I had actually had a good mask in my hands, to turn this way and that; and if generalization were possible from a single such experience, I would generalize thus: the device by which a mask takes on a variety of expressions is really a very simple one, a matter of no more than a protruding lip.

Thursday, June 11: A couple of Interesting and Amusing Things.
There is a Japanese prize-fighter named Cassius Naitō.

These are the names that occur with sufficient frequency to be listed on the cover of the Tokyo telephone directory: Itō, Kobayashi, Satō, Suzuki, Tanaka, Takahashi, Nakamura, Yoshida, and Watanabe.

* Professor Muramatsu Yūji of Hitotsubashi University and Mrs. Muramatsu.

I suppose Kobayashi is the only one that produces a faint twinge of surprise. It continues to be a puzzle why such an unlikely name as Tinklebelltree should be so popular.

I worked really hard on the *Genji*, wanting, before my travels begin again, to get as much of it as possible knocked out and sent off to my typist at Whitmore Lake, Michigan. Afternoon found me some three-quarters of the way through "Yadorigi" – past the title poem, which I don't much like, and past the first mention of Uki-fune, which, I fear, has a somewhat contrived look about it.

A beer at the München, and then out to Roppongi, to a dinner at a Chinese restaurant name of the Fu-ling ("I ain't Fu-ling, I don't know," I kept thinking), given by Lee Chia in honor of Mr. Kawabata and the other people who will be going to Taipei.* Go Sei-gen – how would you pronounce it in Chinese (Wu Ch'ing-yüan, maybe)? – the Go master, was there too, a middle-aging person with a squeaky voice and a bemused look and a Mao jacket. One would not have picked him out of a crowd as a genius, but when one knew that he was, well, he did sort of look the part. His muteness – he talked scarcely at all – made the fact of his being shut up in the make-believe world of Go seem most worthy, and made me once again want to have a try at translating *Meijin*.** It was quite clear that among those present he was the one whom Mr. Kawabata respected most.

As for my own part in the affair, I had too much to drink, and got into a stupid argument with some Chinese, of whom there were numbers present, chiefly diplomats and journalists, on the relative merits of modern Chinese and modern Japanese literature. It is extraordinary the hold which that wispish little Lu Hsün has even on exiled and presumably antirevolutionary Chinese.

Item: there is in Shinjuku, down below the ward office, a cabaret called King of Kings.

Thursday, June 25: Twenty years ago today the Korean War be-

* For a conference of Asian writers.
** *The Master of Go.*

gan. The only notice our *Asahi* took of it was to report Chairman Mao's determination to drive American imperialism from Asia. For the rest, our *Asahi* was filled with self-pity having to do with the textile negotiations and the showing of some movie or other about The Bomb. How, pray, can a country which has so little concern about anyone but itself expect anyone to have much concern about it?

And those were my thoughts on the morning of this day that was a Sunday in 1950. Looking back on it, I have little idea whether or not the Japanese were as concerned as I was – I suspect few of them had the thoughts I had of somehow getting on the last refugee boat. I remember hearing an American friend say in the course of the following week that the invasion had quite finished the Japanese Left. How wrong he was – for they were going into what we hope was their best decade.

This morning, after the series of feints and withdrawals that always accompanies the attempt to put an end to a long period of abstinence from work, I finally did it: I went back to the *Genji*. I seem to have acquired an unerring knack for breaking off at a point where it will be difficult to begin again. This time it was just before the arid festivities (and what is more arid than a grand *Genji* party?) that mark the birth of Niou's son and Kaoru's marriage to the Second Princess, and her removal to Sanjō. (Verily, it is the measure of the greatness of these Uji chapters that soft things, like a brief snatch on a lute on an autumn evening, yes, even the rustle of silk beyond a partition, should echo so much more strongly in the memory than all these noisy banquets.)

A most interesting evening with Robert Guillain. We first had a couple of drinks at the Kagiya,* which has been spared until the end of next year, perhaps has a chance of being spared forever. Then we went for a walk through Negishi. It has some fine, quiet temples, with moldering tombstones and weed-grown gardens, small survivals from Kafū's Negishi. I was shown the house, grand, fortresslike, of the local underworld leader. It is of wood, and three storeys

---

* A drinking place in the Negishi district. At the time of writing it occupied a mid-nineteenth-century building, a very great rarity for Tokyo.

high – and we all know that Tokyo does not permit wooden buildings of more than two storeys.

Then to Kitasenjū, to the last survivor, to G.'s knowledge, among the little neighborhood theaters that used to be scattered around the city; its name is the Kotobukiza. The program was pretty awful, mostly singing and dancing, the former to the dulcet tones of an electric guitar, dominated by a dreadful yawping child name of Baby Mitchi and a simpering female impersonator. The climax, a play, or rather a pantomime to the accompaniment of a strident recording, was about the passion of Tōjin Okichi.* It was patriotic to the point of jingoism, and the audience, sparse and for the most part aging, loved it. "*Sukebei* Harris," the man next to me kept muttering angrily.

And so, all in all, it was not a very satisfying evening at the theater; but one is filled with feelings of sweet melancholy to know that the strolling performer sufficiently devoted to the Edo forms (albeit vulgarized) to go on performing them before rustic and proletarian audiences yet survives. He will not survive much longer, if tonight's performance is a fair example of his prospects.

Finally we had a couple of cups at the Iwateya, which received the highest token of merit, the approval of Robert Guillain. Next to me was a person who begged my pardon but wished to know whether the gentleman on the other side of me might be R.G. No, said I, at the latter's prompting – whereupon we got it as the person's opinion that R.G. is stubborn, unbending, and old-fashioned.

Tuesday, June 30: And so June goes out, and one can no longer deny that the summer is half over. In the morning I got to work on the *Genji* again. I did not make much progress, because the festivities surrounding the removal of Kaoru's bride to Sanjō go on and on, and get more and more maddening. At such times you can almost be tempted to think that the *Genji* as a world classic is Waley's creation, and that Murasaki really is *cette ennuyeuse Scudéry*. But

---

* Said to have been the mistress of Townsend Harris – the first U.S. consul in Japan. *Sukebei*, two sentences below, means something like "lecherer."

courage, courage – Ukifune is heaving in sight, and soon we will be drunk with the greatness of it all again.

Casting about in my mind for somewhere different in which to spend a spare evening, I hit upon Sanya;* and up to Sanya I went, by subway. I did not stay long, however, only until about dark. Sanya, at least the main street, is really rather grim, with drunken or drugged persons lying upon the sidewalks, women crying loudly in their beer, and an extraordinary number of twisted limbs and imperfect or missing eyes. It used to seem bright and cheerful as slums go, and I think the difference is that the population is growing older. The people who have been there all along are of course a year or so older each summer, and young people do not seem to be coming in. But the grimness is limited to a very narrow band along the main street. A few tens of yards back, and the family groups and the shops and the tinkling bells and other appurtenances of summer could be almost anywhere in the lower reaches of the city – which is to say that cheerfulness returns.

A bus coming by for Ueno, I leaped aboard with some relief. In Ueno I had a few drinks. In a nameless place up towards Uguisudani I entered into converse with an amusing and unconventional person. He argued the case for pollution. Why should people be denied, on the grounds that they might not live as long, the things they want? Among our undeniable rights, said he, is the right to live shorter but more comfortable lives. That is sort of the case I would make for alcoholism.

As I was making my way across the lake towards home, shortly after midnight, a most astonishing thing happened, and I must be grateful, indeed am still all a-tremble at the closeness of it, that I did not spend the night in jail. From a passageway, or perhaps arbor would be the better word for it, a rather pleasant face protruded, smiled, and said "*Danna, danna*," exactly as the sellers of dirty pictures, whom I could never resist, did in the days before the Olympics destroyed that sort of thing. Interested, I went in – to find that he was absolutely stark naked, and emphatically tumescent. As I stood expressing silent wonder at this prospect, a policeman

* A working-class district popularly held to be the worst of the Tokyo "slums."

19

came up from the other direction. "Why don't you have any clothes on?" said the policeman. "Because I'm going swimming," said the man. At which point I did the worst thing, hindsight tells me, I could have done: I turned in headlong flight. Had the policeman chosen to come after me, I would not have had an easy time explaining my role in the little drama. But he did not. So I made it home.

Can it be that the good officer had proclivities, which made the pursuit of me seem unimportant?

Oh what an exciting city is ours.

Wednesday, July 1: I neglected to make mention in my last entry of a little happening that seems vaguely noteworthy. In the last place at which I drank, a couple of young men, not unpleasant-looking though with the collarless, loose-sleeved shirts which suggest young men to be less than honorably employed, walked out without paying their bill. The cashier, who I think is either the owner or the son of the owner, mildly pointed out this delinquency to them, and one of them responded by kicking out a panel in the door. Instead of remonstrating with them or threatening to call the police, the cashier became all smiles. Petty extortionists, no doubt. My beloved Ueno is probably not the easiest place in the world in which to run a drinkery.

I worked on the *Genji* in the morning, and managed to push my way beyond matters having to do with Kaoru's royal bride and on to the first appearance of Ukifune; and it was like emerging from a dark, dense forest upon a field of daffodils. Who knows, maybe Murasaki meant it so, and what has seemed to me the infelicity of the passages that have held me up these last days is in fact subtle artistry.

In the afternoon I went over a manuscript sent around for my perusal by the Tokyo University Press, a translation of the *Ugetsu*. It is full of such happy expressions as "he crumpled in a heap of agony" and "the blooming cherries" and "his poor inexcusable behavior." But of course the original is also badly flawed. That it is numbered among the classics is the measure of the poverty of late-Tokugawa literature.

Out in the evening to Sophia University to partake of the monastic life of the fathers. Very pleasant, really. Tonight was the anniversary, the second, of the putting up, the first, of the barricades, and the talk was all of how much quieter things are now – though there is a fear that, come the heady autumn days, the strugglers may start struggling again.

The one girl expelled during the 1968 troubles is named Tokutake Kiyoko. The students call her, said Father Roggendorf, Dokutake Kinoko. Roughly, "Miss Toadstool." The Japanese are very good at this sort of verbal dalliance. The *Kokinshū* spirit.

Thursday, July 2: I was somewhat late in rising, for the good fathers gave me rather too much whisky last night; but once arisen I worked fairly hard on the *Genji* into midafternoon. I am happy to report that, after perhaps three months, I have finished a first revision of "Yadorigi."

It ends beautifully, with one of those so perverse but so effective peeping scenes. Ukifune turns her head for a moment, and it is as if Oigimi were reborn, and the nun appears briefly, and then there is a poem. The end. Really very beautiful. Going rapidly over what I have been about recently, I had to conclude that there is far more art in all that party business than I had been ready to admit – that it serves to delay the entry of Ukifune, which it thus makes more of a thing. And the contrast between all the courtly doings, so elegantly dull, and Ukifune's countrified retinue is very good.

The evening with Mishima Yukio. What an interesting person he is, and I cannot think why I once thought him wanting in humor. He has a richly sardonic sense of humor, and is a very good mimic, with several fine routines, among them a liberal housewife from the western suburbs discussing the educational value of his writings.

And here are some of the subjects upon which he had interesting things to say:

The police. He thinks they are responsible for violent feuding among Leftist student factions. They plant inflammatory rumors.

The government. He had hoped that the rioting last year and into this would stir serious thought of constitutional reform; but the rioters proved too feeble a challenge, and the situation is hopeless. We must live with that awful Peace Constitution.

The literary world. It is corrupt. When you serve on the juries that award the literary prizes, you realize that the jurors make the awards to their friends for all the wrong reasons – and fundamentally by way of serving their own interests. (But after all new people *do* sometimes achieve recognition – so the corruption cannot be absolute.)

Limited warfare. We will always lose a limited war, in which we cannot make use of "the people" as the other side can; and so we should work to do away with the weapons that make all-out war impossible.

His own writing. He worked hardest on the trial scenes of *Runaway Horses*, to make sure that he was right about prewar court procedures. (This seemed to me to demonstrate that he is a very conservative kind of novelist – not that I had not already discerned that fact, behind all the sparkling modishness.) He thinks of ending his tetralogy by having Honda, a very old man, visit Satoko in Nara, where she denies having known such a man. I told him I liked the idea, though I did not quite know what it meant. That life is a dream? He allowed that he did not know either.

Tuesday, July 7: On this day in Hayashi-chō (my old neighborhood), I would see a constant stream of fresh bamboo below my window. On this day in Yushima I saw not a small sign that the meeting of the stars had taken place.* I like my new residence on the whole, but must admit that in certain ways my standard of living has fallen.

Last night, though, there was a delightfully cool breeze blowing in from the south over the pond. It was like one of those days when, after the heat has gone on too long, the first touch of autumn comes

* On Tanabata – the Star Festival, July 7 – two stars, Altair and Vega, are thought to have their annual meeting.

into the air. I sat by the pond for a time and watched the lotuses shiver. It is not good weather for them, poor dears, but it is for me.

And I had lovely dreams. The one that survived most vividly into morning was of being surrounded by fat little pigs that purred like pussycats. Now what, O you specialists in dreams, can that one have meant, save that I was at the moment feeling happy about something or other?

For such reasons, perhaps, I had my best day all summer on the *Genji*, or maybe it was from relief at being finished with "Yadorigi," which should be winging its way across the waters. In any case I plunged enthusiastically into "Azumaya."[50] It begins smoothly, for Murasaki Shikibu obviously knows that she has a good thing in Ukifune – modeled upon someone she knew and liked? The few pages I did are among the freshest in the whole Uji section, those in which the go-between does horrid things to poor Ukifune. Murasaki Shikibu comes to life when she descends to her own class. Yet one is tempted to accuse her of what she accuses the go-between of, fawning. She is very disloyal to her own people, quite plainly is seeking to flatter those on high. (To be sure, she has an occasional sardonic remark to make about them too.)

The afternoon was brightened by a visit from a *Yomiuri* reporter who wished to interview me on a novel subject, *soba* (Japanese noodles). He turned out to be just as cute as he could be, like a shaggy little puppy, and he had a heavy Osaka accent which obviously embarrassed him. I was sorry I could not think of more things to say about *soba*; I learned more from him than he from me. I learned, for instance, that the story of Marco Polo's having introduced *soba* from Europe cannot possibly be true, since the Tartars had it from very ancient times, and it is mentioned in the *Shoku Nihongi*.* I also learned that the Yabu in Kanda is considered the best of all Tokyo *soba* places. Must go there again one of these days, and assure myself that the reputation is deserved.

In the late afternoon I ventured timidly into a barbershop and my! – such treatment as I did get, such an assortment of wetters and driers and steamers and perfumers, all for a thousand yen. I

* Late eighth century.

felt alternately as if I were enthroned and as if I were being guillo-tined. With such attentions to look forward to, how could one pos-sibly become a long-hair?

Then I went on to the Iwateya to have a few drinks, and fear I did not behave as one ought to in so genial a place. For no very good rea-son I had fallen into a surly mood. The person next to me asked all the usual questions, to which I gave not very friendly answers, and when he came to the one about my view of the Japanese character, I said I thought Japan a land of hypocrites and time-servers. He did not take this in very good part, and presently we were shouting at each other; and so I suppose the Iwateya joins the list of nice places I have arranged to make it inadvisable that I visit.

Thursday, July 23: I worked hard on the *Genji* all morning, have a third draft of something like a third of "Azumaya" done. Murasaki may or may not have had a model in mind when she made Kaoru, but her readers must have thought that she did, and thought, further, that they knew who he was. And do you suppose they liked him? Do you suppose they found him a little ridiculous?

Dinner at Makiko's. Much interesting talk about what it is like to be in a big Japanese company. An enormous amount of time is spent on conferences which have as their main purpose keeping everyone in the company happy. Indeed they occupy most of the theoretical working hours, and so the work has to be done after hours. It would seem, then, that the business and trading successes of Japan have to do less with an ability to work as a team than with a willingness to work overtime. And so what will happen when the indulged, pampered youth of the land takes over?

Makiko says that family makes little difference in business any more. The fact that her son is a grandson of a former chairman of Yawata and a great grandson of the founder of Mitsubishi Electric makes no difference at all. It would make a difference were he to marry the daughter of the president, but these benefits do not ex-tend beyond the second generation.

I have been leaving the door open, for the wind to blow through.

Fukuda stopped by and was horrified. "But there is nothing near the door that anyone would want to take," said I. "There is the telephone," said he. Now who would have thought of that?

Ann Arbor   Saturday, September 5: The beautiful weather goes on. I wonder if Miss Y.'s feet still hurt.*

In the morning I went back to the *Genji*, became so absorbed in it, indeed, that I quite forgot an appointment with my friendly dentist. "Kashiwagi"[36] was what I worked on – for my two students decided that, as a piece of one-upmanship, they wished to read a sequence left out by Waley. Returning to an earlier section after years of immersion in the Uji chapters, I find it much easier going. For sentences on end, I needed no help from the commentators at all. Is this accident, or has my reading ability suddenly taken a great leap forward – or might we say that the style and the content are denser in the Uji chapters? If the last is the case, then we would have strong evidence, though of an impressionistic sort, that an an aging and experienced Murasaki Shikibu, and not her schoolgirl daughter, or any other silly Heian woman, for that matter, may be given credit for Uji.

As for the literary quality, I am of two minds. The soliloquy of the failing Kashiwagi with which the chapter opens is studded with poetic references. Is this merely romanticizing, or did the decomposing Heian mind in fact seize upon bits of remembered poetry, fragments shored against its ruins? I do not know.

A very beautiful late-afternoon walk to the Beardsleys', over on the east side, down shaded, cicada-shrilling streets, past dark wooded glens – just as the whole state of Michigan must have looked a hundred fifty years ago. The Beardsleys were offering cocktails.

Much of the talk was of sons and daughters who are out living in communes. They do not want any old humdrum job now that they have graduated; they want something "creative." It is nineteenth-century romanticism pushed to insanity – the romanticism which

* A young lady had given a pain in the foot as her reason for declining a graduate fellowship.

produced the notion of the artist as creator. Earlier centuries had a far saner notion of him and his function. And of course it is the folly of our educational system, which derives from romanticism. Everything must be creative – and so naturally they must go on being creative after they are out of school, and no one wishes to be a shop girl or a yardman. (Which reminds me: a graduate student of some years ago came by the other day. He has been working for a railroad, and has been injured several times. The roadbeds, he says, are in terrible shape, all rotting and wobbly, and trains are constantly being derailed. If one cannot sympathize with the enemies of the system, one sometimes finds it hard to be on the side of the system either.) And behind everything, of course, lies the great American tradition of running away, and the fact that there is nowhere to run away to any more.

Tuesday, September 8: Problems kept coming up having to do with the workings of our tiny department. The most interesting concerned Miss Y. She had a long talk with Charles Hucker, and is now going to drag her sore feet back to California. Charles seemed to think that the chief reason for this retreat is terror at the awful burden we unloaded upon her (one thinks of Harry Truman and his load of hay) in giving her a fellowship. How very difficult are one's relations with the younger generation. "You aren't paying enough attention to me. Now you're paying too *much* attention to me." Maybe a good spanking would strike a happy medium. (I am not sure I put that as well as I might have.)

I did a little more on "Kashiwagi" and then returned to "Ukifune."[51] The former is very touching, the more so, perhaps, for the fact that it makes less overt play for tears than does, say, "Azumaya," and Kashiwagi is altogether less sanctimonious, less self-pitying, than his son. (The great question, of course, is whether or not Murasaki Shikibu *meant* Kaoru to seem sanctimonious.) Kashiwagi's nurse is mentioned frequently; but so far she has been given no name, and I think she gets none through the course of the chapter. Indeed she is scarcely a presence at all. Have we not here evidence that Murasaki had no notion at this point of telling Kaoru's story?

Yes, "Ukifune" is different from "Kashiwagi." In the latter, tragedy is at a distance, so to speak, as if it could be kept there. In "Ukifune" it is palpable, all-encompassing.

In the evening, I did a bit more tidying up of my apartment, taking things out of drawers and closets and placing them upon walls and tables. And then I dug a little farther into the summer accumulation. Mostly I went over book lists. How very cute are the lists of things Japanese available in English – we really do not take the Japanese very seriously, and they do not themselves invite being taken very seriously when they make it appear that their chief contributions to the culture of the world have been the tea ceremony and paper-folding. A little item in the *New York Times*, by chance, adds to the impression that we *will* go on thinking of them as amusing little people. An article on *Hello, Dolly!*, which has just broken some record or other, tells of its successes not only in New York but the whole world over, and informs us that Tokyo just loved "Haro Dori." I suppose that we who seek to teach things Japanese, at least things artistically Japanese, are considered similarly quaint.

Tuesday, September 15: Chilly and rainy in the morning, and all of a sudden muggy in the afternoon, and the skinflints who run my two-hundred-a-month apartment have turned off the air-conditioning.

I had a very amusing dream last night. At a cocktail party a lady came up and introduced herself. "My name is Yellow MacArthur," said she. "A nice name, but a somewhat unusual one," said I. "Yes," said she. "You see, I am the general's daughter by his Oriental cook."

I worked very hard on "Ukifune," am almost at the end of it. While tragedy descends on eminent persons, lesser persons respond in a way that I find most touching, most warming. I like the rustic guards, stung by Kaoru's rebuke, and guarding like mad the whole night through. I like Ukon, pleading with Ukifune to make up her mind, and vowing to stay with her, whichever way she decides to go. In these last chapters, at least, Murasaki Shikibu shows considerable feeling for boys and girls on a lower level than her own. But I am touched in particular because this sense of one's place, this determination to do one's duty, is so absent in our own day. At least in these United States.

Out in the evening with Miss Suh, this being the night of the *meigetsu*, the harvest full moon. It is a big atavistic rite in Korea. People go great distances to visit cemeteries. When we came from dinner, there was the moon, red in the eastern sky, but in the few seconds it took us to get into the car and start east towards Plymouth, clouds had moved in. So we came back to Ann Arbor and went up on the roof here to scan the skies. We did get a glimpse of the moon, and very beautiful it was, too, a Gothic moon, in and out of wildly racing black clouds.

Saturday, September 19: Another beautiful autumn day, bright and clear and crisp. I was up early and off to the farmers' market, which is coming into its best. One of the things I like about it is that its pleasures are such ordinary ones. No highfalutin exotic flowers, no fruits and vegetables that you could not grow in your own yard. Orange, the color of autumn, is all of our own verdant midlands, in tomatoes, squashes, marigolds, dahlias, zinnias. Maybe these are not all native flora, but certainly they have been most comfortably naturalized. It is hard to believe, at the farmers' market, that we are, as everyone says we are, a nation going to pieces. The stall keepers seem so honest and healthy and hard-working, and their children, right in there helping, still seem to preserve the old virtues.

I bought an ample armful of flowers, orange-red zinnias and purple asters (the other color of autumn), and walked to the Gunn Building looking like a Mexican bride.

How interesting the way emperors get pushed into the background by their wives. In "Ukifune," the Rokujō palace – mansion, I call it, to be different from Art Waley – really becomes the court while Her Majesty is in residence there. And in "Kashiwagi," to which I returned late in the afternoon by way of getting ready for tomorrow's class, the former empress is very conspicuous in the celebrations accompanying Kaoru's birth, though she is but distantly related, while the Suzaku emperor, the child's grandfather, is scarcely mentioned at all. No doubt we have here a fairly undistorted reflection of things as they were.

Later in the day, when I took my laundry to the friendly Gold Bond, the lady told me that there has been a sudden increase in the louse population of Ann Arbor. People are always bringing in lousy bedding, and she has to fight constantly to keep from getting infested herself. She blames this new development on "the long-hairs in those tents" – the rent-strikers who have pitched their tents in front of the main library. Perhaps she is right, and as we return to nature, pushed in that direction by the long-haired dears, perhaps new epidemics of typhus will be among the pleasures we may anticipate. I am certain myself that the flea population has gone up (to bring back the pest, perhaps?), for I keep finding fleas in my office, and there is common talk in the elevators of a plague of roaches, which I have escaped, possibly because roaches do not like Metrecal. Well, the upshot of it is that some kinds of life flourish even as Lake Erie dies.

In the evening I read a heap of reviews of *The Sound of the Mountain*. Curious thing: women do not seem to like it as well as men. Woman in the *Boston Herald-Traveler* chides me for calling an *ayu* a trout. Woman in the *Worcester Telegram* makes inquiry: "Is it then the translator who makes the story-telling sound so flat, in spite of the lovely backgrounds and the poetic dreams?" I should point out that the dreams were among the things I disliked most, and so let me modestly disclaim any credit for them, at least.

In the T.L.S., a very nasty review of Earl Miner's "diaries," an approving review of Morris's Waley. In the latter, the secret of Waley's success is offered as simplicity. Well, I do not know what it is, that secret, but at least in the *Genji* simplicity it is not. In the former, the anonymous reviewer sighs that Waley did not see fit to do the Izumi Shikibu diary, for then it might have been done well.

So not only did Waley produce translations which we epigones can never hope to equal, our works must be judged inferior to what he *might* have done, had he chosen to do it. Hagiography is a most intimidating genre.

Saturday, September 26: "To break the green of the autumn dream, beside the autumn window."* Such a day it has been. Fog in the morning, heavy rain in the afternoon. There are black clouds coming down upon us from the black interior of the continent this evening, but no tempestuous noises. Saturday night is not too awful in Ann Arbor, even without alcohol, if you draw the curtains early and pretend that it is some other night.

Up early, I went off into the fog, to the farmers' market. I wanted to buy some more asters, but the aster season seems to be a brief one. Not a specimen in sight. I bought some little orange-red dahlias, which glow like a fire in the night, out of the blackest of my Korean pots, at the darkling entrance to my kitchen.

I worked fairly hard on "Ukifune" through much of the morning and afternoon, and now, save for the notes, have it in shape to send off to the typist. It ends beautifully, and I am inclined to think at the moment that I carry it off rather well. Its success is due in very large measure, I continue to think, to the lower classes. The aging Murasaki saw people for what they were, and we need not think, as perhaps once we did, that she was dazzled by rank. A sort of Goya, perhaps, in her treatment of Kaoru and Niou?

In a dream last night, a memorable line: "Was it you, or was it D. H. Lawrence?" I have no idea what the context was, or to whom I addressed the question.

Saturday, October 3: A cold wind was coming down from the north and west, and there has been winter in the air all day. I like the red-cheeked look, the checkered woolen shirts, that tell of the coming

* From *The Dream of the Red Chamber*.

of winter; but I wish there weren't so God-damned much wild, wild hair to blow in the wind.

After glancing at the papers (huge article on the editorial page of our *Daily* tells us, in several dozen ways, that everybody but homosexuals is sick), I set out for the market. The day for my favorite flowers has passed, and the scene is dominated by chrysanthemums. Numbers of nice things all the same. I like people who stand through the chilly morning to give away excess kittens (I wanted to take them all in, found my own Katzengarten). I like high-school students who keep pumpkin stands. I did not buy much of anything. Only some straggly marigolds. Even when they are not straggly, I like marigolds more for the way they smell, so clean and pungent, than for the way they look.

On my way home in the beginnings of a chill autumn shower, I stood and looked for a time at our best public building, the fire station on Huron Street. Every time I pass, those healthy American boys, the firemen, are to be seen throwing footballs at one another. I do not think I like their way of life much better than that of the pot-smoking students. I remember how, when I was very young, I hated having a football thrown at me. I wonder if I would hate having a frisbee thrown at me.

Back at the office, I got to work on re-revising such of "Kagerō"[52] as I had done in first revision. It flows on from "Ukifune" with little suggestion of hesitation, largely because persons of the lower classes ensure continuity. The flighty Jijū, in a crisis, is every bit as dependable as the dependable Ukon. They are like Faulkner's Negroes. This would be cause enough for designating Murasaki Shikibu a great progressive, a great harbinger of upheavals to come; but I cannot think at the moment of a progressive Japanese critic who makes the case on quite those grounds.

In the evening I violated one of my holiest rules, and the result was a wasted evening, and a renewal of my vows of fidelity to the rule, which is: never go to a French movie. *Lola Montez* was showing in Angell Hall, and I longed to see what the French would do with the California Gold Country, and especially with Lola's declining years in that spooky house in Grass Valley. Well, they did nothing at all with it, that's what they did. And so I had to sit through two and a half boring hours while Lola moved from one repulsive European male to another. No guffaws from the student audience, despite the fact that there were a number of exceedingly specious scenes. In one of them the French ambassador rescues Lola from the Cossacks.

Tuesday, October 6: I got ready for class over the noon hour, and for seventy-five minutes thereafter it met, and an uncommonly jolly little gathering it was, too. What pleasant jokes we did make as Kashiwagi lay dying. Call us callous if you will – but there *is* something ridiculous about a young gentleman lying in bed with his hat on. One of our number made *this* pleasant joke:

> Someone to the Third Princess. "And what color hair did your
>   little boy's father have?"
> Third Princess. "I don't know. He didn't take his hat off."

As I sit by my third-floor window and watch the youth of the land pass up and down Liberty Street, I am sunk in thoughts of things. I think how increasingly alike the sexes are coming to look. They all wear blue jeans and ponchos. The similarity must take much of the joy from life – and so maybe beards do perform a service.

It all, sometimes, seems very ironical. Ten years and less ago I thought that the Japanese were in great danger from their youth and the people who were teaching their youth. Now they seem in far better shape than we. A homogeneous nation with a long tradition of discipline, they will have a far easier time, will not have to be as cruel, keeping youthful lawlessness under control. And of course we will be a horrid example to them, to everyone, save ourselves, because by the time we have become a horrid enough example it will be too late to do anything about ourselves.

One could see all too clearly the causes of the apparent decay in Japan: sentimental liberals, the product of defeat, who had control of the very young. In the general demoralization, there was no one to gainsay them. And what might the causes be here? Rather similar?

There is no politically ardent teachers' union here, to my knowledge, but grade-school and high-school teachers may be as silly, for all I know.

The Japanese decay does seem to have been only "apparent." Maybe ours will prove to have been too. In their case the defeat was the thing that had to be got out of the way. In our case, who knows, maybe it *is* Vietnam. Maybe that is the thing we have to be through with before we can start having some moral fiber again.

The *Times* today informs us that the three she-defendants in the Manson trial were chanting something incomprehensible as they were ordered from court yesterday (disorderly conduct). To me what they were chanting seemed clearly "Nammyōhōrengekyō," badly transcribed or badly articulated. So the Sōkagakkai* has made its first big splash this side of the Pacific. Goody and goody again that it should be in these circumstances.

Wednesday, October 7: Yes, it was indeed the Sōkagakkai, the *Times* informs us this morning. "A practicing Buddhist" told the *Times*, and while he was about it offered what must be one of the most exuberant examples of free translation yet: "Devotion, mystic law of the universe, cause and effect and sound." "Cause and effect" might not be too startling, perhaps, but how did "sound" get into it?

In the afternoon, after class, and after a nap and a can of Metrecal, I got to work on "Kagerō." The scene changes, grief wanes, the First Princess and her good women come on; and I can see how much I disliked it and them, the new scene and the new characters. My prose, always cramped in a first attempt at translation, is far more cramped than usual, and I can see myself pushing grimly ahead, clause by clause. But now as then I persevered (congratulations, Edward), and since there are not too many pages remaining of Kaoru's desultory little lechings here and there, perhaps I shall win through to the refloating of Ukifune without too great an expenditure of time and nerve.

* An evangelical sect of Nichiren Buddhism.

Item: the big moving force in our local Committee of Concerned Asian Scholars is called Cell. Is that not nice? We can speak of our Cell and run no risk at all of being accused of McCarthyism.

Thursday, October 22: I have dreams. Maybe it is because Heian literature so dominates my life these days. Last night I had a singular one, for before the dream was over I found myself already interpreting it. It was about a black, long-haired, round-eyed pussycat all alone in a stopped elevator. As can be the way in dreams, it was all alone, and yet I was observing it. And as I came half-awake in the grayish late-autumn dawn, I was saying to myself, "That was Miss Suh." And as I came further awake I thought it was also Nagara and Katō and the others who have cast their lot with this bad and worsening country, when, like the pussycat with its elevator, they could just as well have stayed away. I know that Nagara has come to find the United States dispiriting (remember the remark about how polite Americans *used* to be) and wonder if the others do not too, and wish they had not fallen victim to the conveniences symbolized by that elevator. Rather an artistic dream, I should say.

Even my long-haired nodder got his midterm paper in on time, and it was nicely written, too. A few were genuinely interesting. One lady pointed out that it would be hard to find a really happy character in the *Genji*. It is true, and now seems so obvious—and yet, you know, I had never really thought of things quite that way. I suppose Niou is happy, for even his bursts of grief have a sort of exhibitionism about them – but who else, save perhaps a person or two of the lower classes?

The evening spent largely completing my revision of "Kagerō." It is done, down to the last poem. "And where is the poetry?" "Well, I don't know, Junior, but what did you expect, now that the only poet among us has passed on?"

Saturday, October 31: It was cold and gray in the morning and again in the afternoon, but in between there were a couple of bright, nippy late-autumn hours that called for going to the market. So I went. The dullness of winter hangs more and more heavily over it. Chrysanthemums and dried flowers and grasses and berries provide the colors, which do not, however, give the sense of ample harvest that was there a month ago. Artsy-craftsy places, sort of as in Carmel, are more conspicuous. Probably they are necessary if the market is to survive, but I do not really like them. Young man wearing the ugly emblem which to me looks like a bomber but which is supposed to signify peace came up with a big bag in his hand and said: "Peanuts for peace?" "I am a warmonger," I replied. I almost thought he was going to hit me, such peace-loving hatred as did shine in his eyes. So I enjoyed the market after all.

In the afternoon I did a clean copy, if you know what I mean – always feel like a fraud calling anything I type "a clean copy" – of as much as I had done in first revision of "Tenarai."[53] The scene in which the spirit possessing Ukifune is exorcised does not bother me as it once did. Indeed I think of those not serious but very frightening fevers I had when I was a child, and wonder if this might not be as convincing a way as any of characterizing a delirium. The suddenness with which my own deliriums would leave was as if something had been possessing me and then let go. Only there were no bishops around demanding that it identify itself. (I like the "bishop" and his sermon about the fishes of the pond and the birds of the hill, and the sinners who are sure to get saved by virtue of having sinned.)

In the evening the streets were of course full of children in long dresses, but they were no part of my life. And Women's Lib, most appropriately, chose this Halloween for a march. One of the slogans that I caught from my window I liked very much:

> Male chauvinist, you'd better be shakin',
> 'Cause today's pig is tomorrow's bacon.

Dinner and pleasant conversation at the Nagaras', until after midnight, Miss Suh being the other guest. Pleasant but sometimes sad. Three of Nagara's high-school classmates in a class of fewer than forty have committed suicide. He thinks the matter has to do with the inability of people who were at their most impressionable when the Pacific War ended to live with the subsequent loss of ideals. He would probably have been killed by the bomb had he been of weak body, like others of his class, and exempted from the schoolboy labor draft.

Monday, November 2: I had a very bad night. I kept dreaming I was in the company of David Eisenhower, and waking up with a stabbing pain in my jaw, and I cannot think what the connection between the two might be.

The afternoon was filled with students. They started coming in at about half-past one, and the last of them left at about four. Some of them were very interesting. Thus there was the lady who served as Matsumoto Seichō's secretary.* A difficult man to work for, she said. One of his best friends is Ikeda Daisaku of the Sōkagakkai, which fact interested me enormously. Perhaps it is common knowledge to the intellies with their elaborate spy networks, but to me it is news; and it confirms my view that the inclinations of the Sōkagakkai are more in the direction of the radical Left than of the radical Right. Or the point may be that the radical Left and the radical Right share a good amount of ground. Doesn't make one much want to welcome avowals of friendship on the part of the Sōkagakkai, in any case.

Then I had a Malaysian student come in and talk about comparative literature. He wants to compare some Malay folk form with *renga*.** I said fine, by all means. He said he thought Japanese literature, and indeed the literature of all Asia, wanting in "intensity." That seemed an odd choice of words, given the bloodiness of a great deal of Oriental literature; but I understood what he meant, and had to agree there too.

Then came the greatest talker of all, and perhaps the most improbable: a Spanish student of naval architecture who is in love with the Japanese. They have been kind to him as apparently Americans

* Matsumoto is a well-known novelist.
** Linked verse, raised to a serious literary genre in the fourteenth century.

never have. He is writing a paper – such things are done, evidently, in engineering – on the Japanese novel, wanted advice. I felt once more the difficulty of talking about Japan to someone who does not already know all about it – which makes it a great puzzle, does it not, to see how anyone gets to "know all about it." He meditated aloud, on and on, about how engineers feel out of step with the societies in which they find themselves, for they move by different signals, and wished to know if Japanese engineers do not feel even more so. I rather doubted it, but was too lazy to seek to explain the wonderful way the Japanese have of keeping their backs to the wall.

I finally got to work on the *Genji* and pushed my way through a few more pages of "Tenarai," which seems not all as delightful as I had expected it to be, not a great deal easier going, indeed, than "Kagerō." I keep myself interested chiefly by avoiding personal names – I think I have not used one yet in the chapter – but it is an undeniable fact that those nuns get awfully confused one with another.

I hate to admit it, but I get sort of jumpy all by myself in the office of an evening. There I am in plain view of Liberty Street, which is populated by uncommonly dangerous-looking sorts, and – well they can see me in my glass cage, and they can see that all the other glass cages are unoccupied, and if one or more of them were to accost me, whatever would I do? Isn't that silly, right in the middle of our Ann Arbor?

Tuesday, November 3: Election day, chill with a bit of rain – the sort of weather that is supposed to favor the Republicans. The Republicans have always been the enemy, but today I halfway joined them, as we shall see – the youth of the land and its strident voice, the *Michigan Daily*, sort of forced me to.

My Karma was distinctly down in the morning. A very pleasant surprise came in the mail, a letter from Harold Strauss at Knopf informing me that he might after all be interested in my *Genji*, and that my *Sound of the Mountain* translation is on the list of things

to which the mysterious powers that make the National Book
Awards have been alerted. The letter should have brought joy. But
my Karma ordered that the effect be the opposite. I started looking
back over the beginnings of some of the *Genji* chapters that are in
theory finished, and found that they made me quite lose confidence.
They seemed so jerky and graceless. Not at all like Waley they
seemed, and in a not at all pleasant sense. Well, what I must do is
try to tell myself that the moment was bad, and go on working; but
it was only late in the afternoon, after a little more work on
"Yokobue,"[37] which, in first draft, seems so much less serious a
business, that I was able to return to "Tenarai."

The *Genji* class was lively, as always, and did a lot to pull me out
of the gloom in which the morning ended. I do most certainly get
along rather well with at least *some* members of the younger generation. But there were feelings of conflict again when I exercised my
democratic rights. I went over to the League and stood in line to
vote. And that sort of did it. All up and down the line were arrogant and exceedingly sloppy young people, and it was all too clear
who *they* were going to vote for. So I found myself going over my
lists and scratching more and more Democrats from it. I ended up
by voting for a Republican governor, congressman, and state senator
and representative – perhaps four times as many Republicans as I
have ever before voted for at any one time.

I should have stayed at home in the evening and tried to get some
some more work done on the *Genji*, but the small effort of the afternoon seemed about all I was up to, and besides, there was showing
under the auspices of the Cinema Guild a movie much loved thirty-
five years ago, maybe, and I felt I had to see how it had borne up
through the decades. *Ruggles of Red Gap*. Charles Laughton overdid
it a bit, I thought, upon surrendering to more-than-temptation, but
the general effect, once I got used to the mannered style, was not
unacceptable. I dreaded the Gettysburg scene and how our "ir-
reverent" audience might be expected to receive it, but it came
through unscathed. Perhaps unabashed sentimentality has a better
chance with the television generation than an attempt at an amount
of restraint.

Here is a small example of the kind of thing that passes in our program notes for sensitive, evocative language: "Like Renoir, McCarey never ever fucks around with flashy technical virtuosity when what interests him is the people in the stories."

Tuesday, November 10: The day of de Gaulle's death – the day of the announcement of it, more precisely. The persons who comment on such things insist upon calling him the last of the giants. I like to think that a giant yet remains from the tumultuous years of my youth: Harry Truman.

I have been making an investigation of modern Japanese translations of the *Genji*, towards putting together the remarks I hope to offer to a breathless Canberra early next year. What I proposed to do was read a single chapter very carefully in several modern versions, and see what turned up; and the obvious chapter to choose was "Kashiwagi."[36] So with much concentration and with microscopic attention to detail, I made my way through "Kashiwagi" in Yosano Akiko's *Genji*, comparing it with Tanizaki's last version and the original.

A. and T. are very different, even though neither can be charged with having made any great number of mistakes. I think the difference is a matter chiefly of two things: the verbal and adjectival forms, and the willingness or reluctance to leave matters ambiguous. Akiko uses honorifics fairly generously, but her manner is brusquer (and this, curiously, despite the fact that she seems to use fewer Chinese characters than Tanizaki), and she almost always ends her sentences with rather brusque verb forms. And while Tanizaki generally chooses to leave things as vague as they are in the original, she comes down solidly for something specific, and explains (though, curiously once more, she is very sparing with her footnotes). So I think I shall have little trouble making my main point: they *are* translators. Despite the advantages they start out with they have to make rather the same choices as do we remote translators. Akiko is a crisp, no-nonsense Waley sort, bringing matters into a clearer and more businesslike world. In a way she is like Harold Strauss and his editors too, very impatient with people who will *not* speak up and say clearly what they are about. I suppose Tanizaki must be called the more faithful translator, in his way, his way being to permit matters to drift indecisively, not demanding clarity of a person whose nature it is to be unclear. Yet "faithful" is such a complex, chameleonlike word. Tanizaki is unfaithful in the sense that he obviously aims at a beautiful style, for him the main consideration; and it is doubtful whether Murasaki really had much nose for style. And of course when it comes to the matter of what she *was* saying, Waley and Akiko, with their clear-flowing stream, are unfaithful, and it is the two extremes of the academics, Tamagami and Yamagishi and the like, on the one hand, and Tanizaki on the other, who are the more faithful. You take your choice – and, as I have said, the Japanese have to take it even as do we far-out Western types. And where am I to be found, having all wobblingly made my choice? Nearer Akiko and Waley, I think, though without Waley's stylistic preoccupations.

But I grew weary from time to time with Akiko – rather frequently, as a matter of fact. Why should I have wearied so frequently? Maybe I was just tired, or maybe Tanizaki's musical vagueness carries you along better than does Akiko's brisk precision. Now the *big* question is, which of the two would the reviewers prefer?

Tuesday, November 17: I went to work on the antipodal article again, and it moved forward expeditiously. I practically have my conclusion written: I prefer the freer translation, be it relatively literal or literary (Tamagami or Akiko), to the more strictly literal. Prefer in the sense of getting through with less resistance, coming upon fewer snags. But it does not follow that the Tanizaki translation is less beautiful, less "literary," than the Akiko translation. And (final, final conclusion) it does not follow that a more literal translation into English must "inevitably" (oh, solemn word) be less beautiful and literary than Waley's.

Class out of the way, I wrote a few letters and pushed yet a little farther along with "Yokobue," well into the nocturnal scene in which Yūgiri gently chides his wife for her superstitious bent. Hard to think, when we have her unkempt and bare-breasted, that she is the daughter of the grandest Fujiwara of them all. How splendid it is, really, and what an advance over the early chapters, that we are made to feel at home with the grand ones, in all their bedroom messiness; and splendid, too, the way Yūgiri is made to emerge as other than a stuffed shirt.

And then, all of a sudden, I felt an impulse to go out into the cold – not to see *My Little Chickadee*, showing in Angell Hall, but to inquire what might be taking place at Hill, where Huey P. was speaking.* There were hordes of people in front, a disproportionate number of them Negroes (which is to say, more than the magic eighteen per cent), but far the larger number white – and of course predominantly young. No one seemed to object to the frisking, and it was announced that the audience would be a captive one, no one, once frisked and inside, being allowed to depart. I had no intention of being frisked myself, and was about to leave when we were informed that a loudspeaker would be put up so that those of us denied the privilege of being frisked would yet have the privilege of hearing Huey P. The frisking went on and on, and finally Huey P. appeared. Thunderous applause. Chants about releasing this person and that person unjustly imprisoned, about killing the Fascist pigs. Then Huey P. started talking. No one could call him a rabble-rouser – indeed he is a very bad speaker, next to inarticulate – but the rabble was there to be roused, and roused it was. No suggestion that anyone took his utterances for what they were, infantile pulings. Roaring evidence that everyone thought them just great.

I did not stay to the end, but cut short my evening with the New Left at perhaps ten. In its essential mindlessness it is very little different from rising Naziism, if the evening gave me a fair introduction to it.

Friday, November 20: A most extraordinary thing, a most worthy thing, with which to begin a new volume of this journal. The Ann

* Newton, the then militant Negro leader.

Arbor telephone directory for December came today, and it contains another Seidensticker! A William Seidensticker. He is a physician, and he lives on Shirley Lane, and I cannot tell you where that is, for it seems to be a bit off the only map I have.

A dark day, a day of Gothic skies and racing clouds. It took a turn for the warmer, and, with a high wind, now from the south and now from the west, one would have thought, had one been near the edge of an ocean, that a hurricane or typhoon or a horrid Bengali cyclone might be coming in. I have enjoyed it.

In the early afternoon I got ready for the *Genji* class, and then moved ahead with "Yokobue." Happy domesticity continues, children tumbling all over the place. Murasaki Shikibu has, in Heian living arrangements, a bit of an advantage over a modern novelist. She can keep her strands completely separated. The matter has to do with one lady, let us say the Third Princess, and the other ladies need not enter into it at all. They are behind blinds, and that is that. I suppose much that I like about "Yokobue" has to do with the fact that so large a part of it is seen from an entirely masculine point of view. What an un-Japanese faculty for standing outside herself our author did have. Perhaps people who really love Japanese literature ought not to like the *Genji* – and perhaps the fact that I have allowed it to occupy so large a part of my life is evidence that I do not really love Japanese literature. (The fact that Waley turned away from things Japanese after he finished the *Genji* may here tell us something.)

Monday, November 23: The temperature went down to ten or so last night, and there were frost flakes in the air this morning, and at intervals through the day there have been flurries of honest snow. Tonight the view from my window is quiet and whitely frozen, and I have been happy with this first real taste of the mid-continental winter.

What grim reading our *New York Times* can be these days, not because of wars and natural disasters, but because of life in New York. This morning it tells all about a New Deal failure, a dream town put up in Brooklyn, now so terrorized that its inhabitants are afraid to unlock their doors even in the daytime. One woman who lives alone says that she cooks all the time, because there is nothing else to do with the awful empty hours. But of course the American Way of Life is such that you don't have to live in a decaying part of Brooklyn to feel trapped. You can have that feeling in what ought to be the pleasantest of places.

Today I got interested in a very unlikely subject, *otogizōshi*,* and so my two pre-class hours sped by. The thing that interested me was a thing I had not paid much attention to before, what an *otogizōshi* actually looks like. Utterly charming – court art made popular without being vulgarized – elegance available to the masses. Verily, I thought, the Japanese are better at things graphic than at things verbal; and verily, I thought again, it is something that would do the world more good than Zen, a lesson in the art of being elegantly vulgar. (I forgot to mention that late Saturday afternoon I paid another visit to our twin pornography marts, over on our version of Fifth Avenue, and thoughts of a similar nature came to me. Why must our pornography be so utterly wanting in grace? I do not compare it only with the great pornography of the Tokugawa period, so delicious with its open-air freshness in the eighteenth century and its indoor opulence and decay in the nineteenth. I speak also of the somewhat indecent things I used to pick up in Asakusa and Ueno and Shinjuku. They were fun to be with, and our own sort of thing is no more fun to be with than the drug habit.)

I did get a little more done on "Yokobue," and each little bit I do makes me like it better. I wonder whether anyone has ever pointed out that it contains high comedy such as we are told only Sei Shōnagon was capable of. Yūgiri looks dubiously at his father, and thinks how quick he is to give advice he would not himself be prepared to act on. My feelings, rather, about Senator Fulbright. And in the most recent passage I did of "Tenarai," there comes from the mouth of the nun Shōshō a remark that Governor Reagan picked up and tailored to his purposes: "When you have seen one Kannon you have seen them all." How very modern our Murasaki is.

* Short fiction of the Muromachi period.

Mrs. Rodd of my *Genji* class informs me that Toyota is putting up a half-million-dollar memorial to people who have died in its cars.

Saturday, December 5: I was suddenly in terror of finding myself as far from abreast of things at the beginning of next week as I was at the beginning of this, and so I turned from "Tenarai" to "Suzumushi."[38] It is getting easier. The midsummer prayer meeting is perhaps supposed to have about it all the sensuousness, the heaviness, of the lotus in full bloom, but I fear the fusion of actor and background does not come off as in the very best of Murasaki – and even if it did, would not a sad, fading autumnal note be more appropriate? And then we move on to the cramming of the warehouses at Sanjō, and may just possibly come to think that nuns did not have it so bad after all. And then we come to Genji's self-pitying recriminations at the poor little girl for having left him and become a nun. They are somewhat better – but would we not prefer a touch of equanimity in a man we know is to die so soon, and a man whose real affections, we know, are elsewhere?

Before returning to "Tenarai," I got off a few letters, chiefly a long one to Harold Strauss explaining all about my Uji chapters, and why they have every right to stand alone.*

Down to Flick's for a couple of fatal glasses of beer. A truly savage wind from the north. Seems there is a big high-pressure zone over Lake Superior. Not a fit place for man or beast, Lake Superior, on a December night.

Monday, December 7: I had dreams last night. I dreamed that I was Noam Chomsky, and that my next big project would be to divide the languages of the world into three great categories, liquid and jellied and powdered. I dreamed, fortunately just before I awoke and moved into the day, that I had been denied a Guggen-

---

* As I explain in my preface, the contract to publish the whole translation was not signed until April, 1972.

heim award, and in a most untactful fashion. I was shown a list of the applicants and a list of the winners, and mine was the single name that was not on both lists.

Over to South University to do some shopping, for Christmas and for a small girl name of Malm who is about to be christened. Really, what repulsive specimens you do have to pass along the way. Anyone who would do it to one of them, I thought to myself, would do it to a pig or a six-week-old corpse. At the corner of South U. and East U. stood a cluster of young Orientals of both sexes, Japanese to judge from the cameras. Very roughly trimmed, all of them, and yet they looked so much cleaner and pleasanter – so much more touchable, withal – than our own youth. Orientals may be shaggy, and certainly these were, but they do seem on the whole – exceptions aplenty are of course to be found in Shinjuku – to avoid looking as if they had just been rubbing cow dung in their hair.

Back to the office, to get bravely to work on "Tenarai." But "Tenarai" simply did not interest me. The figure of Ukifune, busy at her writing practice, just having become a nun, is usually so touching, and today it was not much of anything at all; and her poems, I fear, poor sweet, seemed rather obvious. Perhaps the trouble is that I want too much to finish the thing, the whole Uji thing, before my next Pacific crossing, and have succeeded in blocking myself. It is like being in the doctor's office and knowing that you absolutely *have* to produce a specimen.

The late news has just informed me that today is Pearl Harbor Day. I forgot. Another year and we will have rounded out a full three decades.

1971

Wednesday, January 20: Up in the gray chill at about seven-thirty, and over to the office by not long after eight, ready to get ready for class. We moved from the *Genji* (white, we all know now, and will never forget that fact, will we?) to the *Heike* (red).* It was with pangs as of bidding farewell to an old helpmate that I left the *Genji* behind. The *Heike* is going to be a bore by comparison, I fear: none of the fencing, here, as with an expert and cunning opponent. None of the fascination of trying to guess, as in a good game of bridge or poker, and I can't think when I last played either, what an opponent might be up to. On the very last pages of "Suzumushi," the last *Genji* chapter we are going to read, there are a couple of passages the tone of which changes completely depending upon whether Murasaki had her tongue in her cheek, or only partly there, or at home safely inside her dentures. There are no tongues-in-cheek, by the wildest soaring of the imagination, in the *Heike*.

Anyway, on to the *Heike* we did move. Sadler's translation manages at the same time to be quaint and pedestrian, and I can see no excuse whatsoever for giving only the Japanese readings of Chinese names – unless he wished, as legend has the case to be with Waley, to be more widely read by the Japanese than was his original.

Fukuda called in the evening, from Tokyo. He just wanted to chat. My favorite pigeon is in good health.

Friday, January 22: In the morning and early afternoon I worked on rewriting "Yume no ukihashi"[54] as best I could. It moves easily, and, despite numerous interruptions, I managed almost to finish it. It is a chapter with a difference, straightforward narrative unin- terrupted by poems, requiring almost no footnotes. Is it so because Murasaki Shikibu wished to strike a last memorable blow, or because she was about to launch forth on yet another phase? Who will ever know, this side of the grave, unless of course she deigns to come back and tell us?

The interruptions had to do with fellowships again, and largely

* A reference to a debate over and inquiry into the colors of the banners in the Genji-Heike Wars.

with a disagreement over who is eligible for them there "Rackham prize fellowships." In the course of the "hassle," I believe the fashionable word for it is, I gave forth once more with my frequently expressed views on the uses of adversity. I said we were going back to the days of my youth, when students didn't *expect* to be richly subsidized. Ah, yes, replied Royston, but back in those days it was possible to get a job that would pay tuition and board. Now, it isn't. He is right, I suppose. The rise in affluence has had the curious effect of putting the basics out of reach of us the middle class. Prices rise, unemployment rises, even as it becomes more and more difficult to find anyone to do anything. The times seem a bit worse than out ,of joint. But I am so naive in matters economic that I can but tell myself that someone must be keeping something from me, and have another beer.

On turning on WUOM* for the late news, I got instead a partial rebroadcast of the President's speech to Congress. It should have been inspiring, but it left me feeling sort of heavy and downcast. For one thing, his manner is so unctuous, as if he were delivering a eulogy for someone he loathes. And then I suppose I am more and more of a pessimist in these matters, feeling, however much I may seek to tell myself that the prospect is more cheerful, that nothing will change, or rather, that changes in the structure of government, shifts of power, will make no difference. The bureaucratic monster that is Washington was put together because local government seemed so incompetent. Now the monster has been diagnosed as incompetent, and the time has come for local government to have its turn at incompetence again. And of course even if something could be done, nothing will, for a paleolithic Congress stands in the way.

And so cheerily to bed.

Monday, January 25: Preparation for the pedagogic day began at noon. The morning was mine own, and I put a good part of it into giving "Yume no ukihashi" a last going over. The process left me

* The University of Michigan radio station.

feeling once again, and I think that it has been the dominant feeling over the years, that it stands at the beginning rather than at the end of something. An altogether drier, more laconic story should follow – and that it does not is, once again, a strong argument for the theory of single authorship. Only Murasaki herself had come far enough to be up to it, and when she faltered, there was, as with Genji, no one to take her place.

Some Kafū in the modern-literature class – it was the little "Fox" sketch we read. His evocations of early childhood must be among the most beautiful ever written; and is that not enough to make him a great writer? The trouble is that such writing falls between genres; it does not fit into the categories our formalistic minds insist upon imposing. But when an experience remembered with such deep emotion is communicated with such immediacy, do we not have poetry? It takes a singular talent, in any case, to make one feel, right there against the skin, the afterglow of Edo. What is nicest, perhaps, among a great many nice things is the way the underlings, the nurse who loves Edo picture books, the gardener who burns snakes, the houseboy who bravely sets out to confront the fox, are brought to life – as Kafū was not able, in his later and more ambitious attempts, to bring his characters to life.

Sunday, January 31: It was just above zero, one degree above, said the indicator in front of the bank, when I arrived at the office, at shortly after nine. I have liked it, the cold. It has been company of a sort, and this has been an uncommonly companionless day. I exchanged words with no one at all, and there were scarcely even any passersby in Liberty Street. I especially liked the crunching and squeaking of the snow when I went out for a walk. There were few automobiles to compete with that most wintry of sounds, and when I closed my eyes I could imagine that I was walking over the hills of home, with the Peak turning red in the freezing twilight. Colorado has been rather a lot on my mind of late.

At the office, I first read a page or two of the *Heike*, largely by way of dawdling, for I did not really want to start going over "Agemaki."[47]

But presently I did, and got through perhaps two-thirds of it. I had my reasons, other than weekend despondency, for not wanting to begin it. The beginning is as nearly unacceptable as anything in the Uji chapters, fussy and contrived, when the situation, the first anniversary of the Eighth Prince's death, could be so compelling. It is in such passages that the temptation to "improve" is strongest. But once it is past, things are all right again.

In midafternoon I turned to the Mishima article,* and it quite ran away with me. In my efforts to establish the line of fanatical sincerity in which I would place him, I managed to bring in Wang Yang-ming, Mencius, Yoshida Shōin, and Robert Louis Stevenson. So here I am with the allotted number of words banged out, and I have said not a word about the most interesting matter of all, his sexual proclivities, nor much of a word either about a less interesting but still unavoidable matter, his novels. I have a sort of suspicion that, as in the novels of the fifties which I so dislike, he is being merely eloquent and clever in Isao's peroration in *Runaway Horses*, in his own final declaration, the one distributed to the troops, and even in his essays on the February 26 Incident; and that the only real honesty may be in his masochism and exhibitionism and fear of growing old and ugly. If so, then a massive cynicism encompasses his whole work and takes on a grandeur of its own, and the novels of the fifties become not just so many potboilers and so many facile displays of rhetoric, but part of a huge joke at the expense of us all, and most particularly, perhaps, at least on this side of the water, at the expense of the Zen Society of America.

Tuesday, February 2: "Agemaki" is now finished, and I have passed another millstone – and that is really what it feels like.

After lunch, as I made my way back to the Gunn Building through a freezing fall of snow, I passed a young man shouting at the top of his voice, "Fuck society, fuck society." Being true to himself, no doubt. Not allowing convention to warp his personality.

* A magazine article. It appeared in *The Hudson Review*.

Monday, February 8: I dreamed last night that I was on a special mission from the Vatican, escorting a priceless collection of Rembrandts to some museum in the United States. The collection arrived safely despite the efforts of the airlines to lose it, but when it was opened it proved to consist entirely of Tokugawa pornography. Everyone was very surprised, and I laughed hysterically.

Back to work again. Cloudy and cold again. Flurries of snow again. In the morning I debated whether to get my driver's license renewed, or start rewriting the Mishima article, or do some more on the *Genji*. The last had the highest priority by far, I concluded, and so I began reworking "Yadorigi."[49] It is a chapter that has in the past much annoyed me, because of Kaoru's weepiness, and because of the suddenness with which it takes its new turn, makes its surprise announcement. Today, however, it seemed rather more subtle. Though with not such subtlety as to allow a strong argument that it was known far in advance, Ukifune's appearance *is* adumbrated, in, for instance, the mention of "a certain bishop." (Of course if that is admitted as evidence, it must also be admitted as evidence that Murasaki Shikibu had Ukifune's reappearance planned before her disappearance.)

Over a can of Metrecal I got ready for my evening class. Then it met, with a special attraction awaiting it: Nagara came to play my Heikyoku tape,* made for me by Bill Malm, on the department's machine, said to be so eccentric that only Nagara understands it. Actually not even he seemed to. For much of the performance the Ohara episode was playing forwards while the Chikubushima episode was playing backwards. The backward playing (backward flaying) was in some ways more interesting than the forward. It showed clearly, by having the plunks at the end and all the aftertones in advance of them, how great a variety of plunks is possible. The two singers, one from Nagoya and one from Sendai, said to be the only surviving masters of Heikyoku, so differ from each other in the joining of music and narrative as to make you think that Heikyoku can be just about what you want it to be.

* *The Tale of the Heike*, sung to the accompaniment of a lute.

Wednesday, February 17: Another full day of classes, with preparation before and in between (think of that, O *Daily*, when you are busy telling the world that professors only work six hours a week). They went well. We barely began our first Kawabata story, "Song of Italy," but after Kafū, how violently alive, how almost shocking, Kawabata does seem. And how very remarkable his cold withdrawal from his material appears after Kafū's irritable involvement in *his*. "He burned very well." Hemingway without the sentimentality. I think it annoyed Kawabata to be honored by the Swedish Academy as a staunch defender of Japanese prettiness. Though of course a Kawabata who showed annoyance would no longer be Kawabata.

In the morning and early afternoon I finished putting the final touches to "Ukifune"[51] and all its notes. The last section goes exceedingly well, I think, as the crisis approaches. Towards the end of the chapter, with Ukon begging Ukifune to make up her mind, we would seem to have one of Waley's favorite passages, since he sorted it out for purposes of sincere self-reflection in his remarks somewhere. He cannot, I believe he says, think of a way in which he could have bettered his rendering of it. Everyone, which is to say the half dozen who care on this side of the Pacific and several thousand Japanese, is sure to compare his version and mine; and yet I refused to have another look at his, lest I be too obviously influenced by him – or perhaps because I was afraid?

There came from the registrar's office an instruction sheet to be distributed to students who wish to register early. It is next to incomprehensible, at least to me, and it contains the following extraordinary sentence, to show how advanced is the decay: "A printout of course elections for those students who advance classified and early registered will be mailed in early August to the student's permanent address on file with the Registrar's office at that time." Oh, what a passion for the rectification of names that does arouse in Confucians like myself.

In the mail came a postcard from Bob Gillette, who has been in Japan. He describes himself as upset at the impossibility of getting at Japanese culture short of embracing the whole of it. Very perceptive, I should say, compared to the lyrical outpourings one gets from most voyagers to Wagakuni.* Of course there is implicit in what he says an assumption that it is possible ever to get "inside" Japan; but I think I know what he means. I think of myself standing on the outside of a festival, back maybe fifteen years ago, and thinking how nice to be a genuine card-carrying member, as if that sort of thing were possible for us blue-eyed ones.

Saturday, February 20: We seem to have had a nuclear alarm last night, and neither I nor anyone else at the party knew anything about it. If we were to be really in danger, I suppose my non-electronic way of life is such that I would know nothing until we were all wiped out or until the danger had passed. I never watch television and rarely listen to the radio save for the late-night news, and I don't suppose anyone would call me (no one seems to have tried last night) even if telephone calls were, in a real emergency, possible. I think I would like it better that way, not knowing what happened to me, not knowing of these little crises until they are over. I shall live and I shall die the non-electronic way.

It has been colder again, there is again ice on the sidewalks, and we have not seen the sun the whole day. I was told last night that Michigan has a bad climate even as Midwestern climates go. The presence of lakes on virtually every side seems to contribute to a winter cloudiness more extreme than in other parts of the region. Far from depressing me, this information makes me feel proud, for myself and for Michigan.

Today I finished "Kagerō"[52] and all its notes. It went very rapidly. It would have gone even more rapidly had I not come upon a couple of footnotes which made no sense at all. Tracing them back to my very earliest draft, I found they had reference to passages that got lost along the way. Alarming, for two reasons: they, the footnotes, cannot have made sense in intermediate drafts, and I did not notice the fact; and other passages must be absent as well, and lacking in dutiful footnotes to alert me to their absence. I have been less than wholly attentive.

* "Our country."

In the afternoon, I read on in the *Heike*. I read Sanemori's famous apostrophe about the warriors of the east, and it brought to mind all the wrong things. It made me think of a dear little piece of Japanese pornography I read once years and years ago, I have no idea where. I do not remember the plot. What I do recall is a scene in which phalluses are measured exactly as Sanemori tells us arrows are by the eastern warriors. Such are the edifying associations that were called up by Sanemori, so soon to die, so heroically.

Dinner and drinking at the Nagaras'. The other guest from outside was Miss Suh, and the Nagaras have with them a most uncommonly nice man, about my age, though he looks several generations younger, named Kazamura. He is a teacher of physical education at Hiroshima University, and he knows all about baseball, having been a trainer for the Hiroshima Carps and the Nankai Hawks. He offered pleasant tidings: that the invincible Giants are about to be conquered, most probably by the Whales. Also unpleasant tidings: that Hirose of the Hawks is not a Korean. Hirose has always been one of my favorites, and my chief reason has always been that he seemed so Korean in his pugnacity.

Saturday, March 27: The day began brightly and ended with snow and rain and falling temperatures. Winter dies slowly.

I had a hard time getting myself launched on the day's work, for the weekend seemed to loom altogether too silently ahead. I got myself to the office in midmorning, and dawdled over the *New York Times*, reading of the disturbances in Pakistan with a fascination I find it quite impossible to muster up for Vietnam. It is cruel and inhuman of me, I know – but I sort of enjoy a war for which I cannot remotely be held responsible, either by doctrines of collective responsibility or by doctrines of individual responsibility.

Late in the morning I turned to my introduction to the Uji chapters. It moved ahead with astonishing speed. I had expected to be stalled over it for days and days, but by midafternoon I had a first draft finished! Such facts as can be mustered up I had mustered well in advance – and the speculating upon them is something I have lived with the last two or three years as I have not lived with another literary problem. It was with great exhilaration that I came gliding in at the end. All that I had to do, really, was let myself go.

I then spent an hour or so trying to decipher the most recent letter, enchantingly illegible, I have had from Mr. Kawabata. Concluding that he was expressing pleasure at my willingness to translate *Meijin*, I answered accordingly.

I then came home and got my laundry started, and went out for a walk. First I went to the porno mills. They are asking a fifty-cent entrance fee, however, and hardly seemed worth it. So I walked to the river in search of traces of spring, which I found only in the willow trees. On the way back I spent a pleasant half hour in the mineral-and-gem shop on Washington Street, and bought myself some cufflinks, of the Michigan state stone, the Potosky stone. Potosky stone was formed, it seems, from coral which grew in warm Michigan waters some hundreds of millions of years ago.

The driers in our basement being occupied, I took my laundry to a drier in a laundromat a few steps down William Street. I asked a bearded young man how long the drying cycle might be. "I don't know," he said, not looking up from his newspaper. He *must* have known, since he had been waiting for one cycle to finish and had just put in his dime for a second. He wasn't giving out any information to a middle-aged fag.

Sunday, March 28: I was at the office early, not dreading the day as I had dreaded yesterday. Company in store for the evening and amusing things to occupy the remainder of the time of silence and solitude. And I had amusing dreams last night to send me smiling on my way. In the best of them Queen Elizabeth was seeing me off at a railway station, but I couldn't really pay much attention to her because I had lost all my baggage. Presently someone came staggering up a flight of stairs with a huge overstuffed chair, and said, "Here is your baggage." And that was the end of the dream. My dreams tend to be of frustration, and it was nice to have one end on such a successful note.

The most amusing thing I had to look forward to was the drawing up of genealogical tables for my *Genji*. Really, I should be in the employ of Burke's Peerage, such pleasure do I get from this sort of thing, from figuring out where everyone belongs and squeezing everyone in. And it is fun making the tables look sort of balanced – with no talent whatsoever for drawing or draftsmanship, I think I find in making a genealogical table look nice an outlet for my graphic urges.

Monday, March 29: In the absence of the *New York Times*, which never gets in on Monday mornings, I turned to a final version of my genealogical tables. I thought I was going to have more fun, but I didn't. After about the fifth unsuccessful attempt to get the imperial family into attractive and balanced shape, I felt like a perfect fool. Names kept bumping into each other, and popping up where lines ought to be – it was like trying to assemble all those curious little parts into one carbine back in my Marine training days. But in the belief that putting it off for another day would only get me all uptight again, I persevered, and by noon had them finished. And rather pretty genealogical tables too, I must say.

Tuesday, March 30: It has been a bright, springlike day again; and it has been a day to be memorialized, but I have had no one to tell what makes it memorable. What it is is this: I FINISHED MY UJI CHAPTERS. I made a clean copy of the introduction and I went over my genealogical charts carefully, and I even typed out a pretty title page; and all that remains is to separate the three copies and wrap two of them and put them in the mail. I have been trying to think when I first went to work on "Hashihime,"[45] and cannot; but I know that I was intensively at work on the Uji chapters when I went out to Japan on my year's leave, in the spring of 1968. Things happened to slow me down that year, notably Kawabata's Nobel Prize* and the selling of my house. Still, these have been three

* I went with him to Stockholm for the celebrations.

years of hard work; and so do I have six years of hard work to look forward to before I finish the rest?

But let us not think about that. Let us exhilarate. Something big is finished. After lunch, I said to myself that something really must be done by way of celebration, so I went and made my reservations out to Japan. I have myself leaving for Denver on April 25 and arriving in Tokyo on hooray, hooray, the First of May.

Thursday, April 1: Well, it is in the hands of the gods now, which is to say, Harold Strauss and the postal authorities. Now that "it" – my Uji chapters, of course – has been sent forth into the world, I feel the deepest apprehension. I feel next to certain, indeed, that the gods will not be kind to it, poor little thing (poor little hundred-fifty-thousand-word thing), and that it will die aborning. I must get immersed in something else. As if by clairvoyance, a book came in the mail from Mr. Kawabata, all about Go and especially the great match that is the matter of *Meijin*, my next translation. I could get immersed in that. Tomorrow, maybe.

Tokyo Monday, May 31: I had a bad night. This building is full of strange noises, of things that go boom and hiss and splash in the night. And then I awoke feeling rather depressed, about something that must not have bothered me much last night, else it would have been mentioned in yesterday's entry. A gentleman from the Liberal Democratic Party with whom I had a conversation in the Suehiro knew the names of certain of my colleagues, but did not recognize mine when I informed him of it. It is not fun to have what small store of note one has accumulated dissipate itself so quickly. But I suppose it is some comfort to think that in a hundred years most of us will be forgotten. "It is a terrible thing, to seek to be remembered a hundred years," Mr. Kawabata once remarked. In a thousand years not a half dozen people now alive will be remembered. Assuming, of course that there is anyone to remember. Or *is* it such a comfort?

Much of the morning went into Harper's dissertation, on *Genji* criticism. Extremely interesting if not entirely persuasive. It is very well to say that Buddhist interpretations of the *Genji* tended to assign it a didactic function, but quite another to seem to say that Buddhism *demanded* such an interpretation. There must have been something innately puritanical and perhaps masochistic in the Japanese that made them demand of Buddhism a straitjacket which it did not insist upon imposing.

Down to Nihombashi at noon to meet Mr. Kawabata. A gallery is having an exhibit of his calligraphy, which is striking but not beautiful, though of course I would love to own a few frameable specimens. It hardly seems possible that he could be more fragile and birdlike each year. But he is, and his voice becomes more thinly reedlike. We had lunch at a very good *sushi* place, name of Sushiden, I believe. It was for me a difficult meal. A pile driver was madly at work outside (is there anywhere in the world a city of more madly working pile drivers?), and I caught very far from everything he said in that reedlike voice. I gather that he does not approve of Mishima's last writing, thinks the ending to my volume (*my* volume) of the tetralogy altogether too abrupt. On the subject of the municipal elections he waxed suddenly and uncharacteristically ardent. The burden of his remarks seemed to be less that the conservative candidate is outstandingly good than that the Socialist one – Minobe – is impossible, both incompetent and unprincipled. To see that serene, otherworldly man become suddenly, ardently political was fascinating and in a way disturbing.

Fukuda came by and we went down to the Jūgoban to have a glass of beer and a look at the *sumō* on television. He was in one of his moods, sunk in silence. Everywhere else I looked I saw the most evil-faced of persons examining racing forms. I kept wondering how they managed to acquire so uniformly those narrow piglike eyes. By long practice in front of a mirror? By natural strengthening of certain muscles through constant sneering? Or is it that people with piglike eyes, denied employment elsewhere, turn to gambling and extortion? I remember awakening from a dream and smiling to myself at the sentence that was running through my mind: "I like hams and I like yeggs." However I may feel about hams, I do not really think I like yeggs.

And I am reminded to record that I awoke one morning, a week or so ago, singing the following mentally, to the tune of "Yellow Submarine":

> When the moon begins to flicker
> And the stars begin to die,
> Then it's time for we to snicker,
> Time for you, and time for I.

Yesterday morning, I think it was, or perhaps the day before, I dreamed I was in a shop with great arrays of lamps and lanterns and chandeliers hanging from the ceiling. "Let me have a look at the gurkinbustable one, please," I said to the girl. She knew exactly what I meant, and took the gurkinbustable one down.

Then there was the morning when I found myself singing this mentally, to a tune, I think, of my own making:

> He's so lovable, so shovable,
> So livable, so civible,
> That old dog of ours,
> That old dog of ours.

Ann Arbor Monday, November 8: Last night I dreamed I was called in by Pope Paul. He offered to make me archbishop of Denver, but I replied: "No, thank you, I couldn't possibly live in that city." And I don't think I could, either.

I found Mishima keeping me awake last night after I had had my late news and settled down in bed. There came thoughts of things that were said over sherry after I had finished that eloquent lecture in Pittsburgh. I thought of a person, Japanese, who kept saying, and would not stop for an answer, that Mishima was a complete nihilist, and that his espousal of nation and emperor was wildly derisive, the act of someone who, not believing in anything, emphasized that fact by professing to believe in the utterly unbelievable. It may be so – who knows? It may be that he was fooling us and lying to us to the very end. But somehow I cannot quite agree. The eroticism is very genuine, and it takes him back to nation and emperor not in any literal sense, not in a way that suggests any specific person or group or program, but as a symbol of what he found wanting in this our day, the day of pale, desiccated libbies.

I took care of my Monday chores on Monday this time, and was over on Liberty Street early of a cold, clear morning. Thence almost immediately to St. Joe's to have another inning with the medical profession. Dr. Magielski, my ear person, had referred me to an allergy person. This transfer seemed to me quite senseless, for there can be very little in the way of a necessary relationship between an infection and an allergy; but I meekly went through a series of tests, had my left arm all punctured like a pin cushion. The results again seemed quite senseless, for they showed me to be allergic to *most* things, including things not at all of a seasonal nature, such as feathers. Well, if I was not aware of being allergic before, I am sure that I shall be now, and that my sleep will be badly disturbed by my pillow. (Another thing seems calculated to interfere with my sleep. The other night a lady was victim, just in front of this Maynard House, of a bullet thought to have been shot from the parking structure up Maynard Street. The lights from same parking structure shine cheerfully upon me as I sleep.) The tests were sort of fun, though. "And here," the doctor would say with great gusto, as if coming up with a new taste treat, "are feathers. And here – my, look at it, would you? – about the size of Maine – is ragweed." (Sibley's translation the other day of Suzaku's note of condolence I thought rather good: "Since your mother was such a damned hypochondriac, I hadn't worried a great deal.")

In the afternoon I finally made myself get down to revising my *Genji* introduction, as urged by Harold Strauss. The main thing he wishes is to convince the world that a new translation is necessary. I do not have much heart for the work, and am inclined to think it futile. Too much protesting is too much protesting, and if the translation cannot be its own defense, there is very little that an introduction can do for it.

Thursday, November 11: It has been a lovely day again, quiet and warm and sunny, and I have through most of it been feeling happy, risen from the depths of last week, already in something like the spirit that should go with the approach of Christmas and the migration westwards. I even enjoyed being up a half hour before sunrise, and watching the columns of steam from the power plants turn rose, and Burton Tower catch the first rays, and then, at eight or so, the sun itself emerge over the Hatcher Library, its most formidable obstacle up and down the eastern skies.

At the office, I did a few pages of "Yūgiri"[39] in first draft, for my *Genji* class has come within snapping distance of me once more. The interview between Yūgiri and his father is very deftly done, with each party quite proper and deferential, and Yūgiri in the end not giving Genji the smallest sniff of what he is after. Yūgiri is a rather wonderful character, entering upon no one else's domain (save the poor princess's, of course), and coolly guarding his own against intrusion. He is more successful, I should say, than Genji.

A couple of students came in to talk about end-of-term papers. One of them had another problem: Waley has "the Colonel," the son-in-law of the younger of the Ono nuns, "making love" to Ukifune. "But he *doesn't* make love to her," protested the student, a young lady. I thought this very interesting. While most words and phrases of whose changing meaning one is aware in these sad latter days of ours have become broader and broader until they mean nothing at all, the realm defined by "making love" has narrowed and narrowed until it refers to a single physical act.

Thursday, November 18: A couple of little verbal treats. Arriving at Liberty Street earlier than usual, I went into the beanery next door to the Gunn Building for a cup of coffee. Beside me was a policeman who remarked of someone that he belonged to the "Five W Club." And what, asked the young lady across the counter, might the Five W Club be? "We won't work, will we," replied the policeman. The *Daily* informs us this morning that "women march on abortion." A pretty picture.

I should have been able to get a great deal done on the *Genji*, for there did not seem, as I approached this Thursday, a great deal else to do. But I did not. All of a sudden I remembered I had a dental appointment. I made it, just in time. The dentist put in a couple of minor fillings, but mostly he did again the cleaning I had done a couple of weeks ago. It made me think of how, back in high school, we had to have the same American history course over and over again. As he laboriously did each tooth, all the tiredness came back of having to face that Manifest Destiny stuff yet another time. He kept telling me of the amusing things I said on my last visit. I must have been drunk. It is not my habit to be amusing in the dental chair.

Back in the office I did get a little done on "Yūgiri," and again I was overcome at how deftly the characterization of Yūgiri himself is done. The passage in which he sits outside the princess's closet and thinks of home and wife is genuinely delicious.

Friday, November 19: I understand that after I left the meeting yesterday there was a small thunderbolt: the department, said a lady graduate student, and particularly the Japanese side of it, is "sexually unbalanced." Bob Brower later in the day attended a meeting in the dean's office during which the chairman of the curriculum committee reported on a troublesome new course. It is to be concerned with the function of women in the revolutionary movement, and no men are to be admitted. The furies are loosed upon us.

In the afternoon I got ready for the *Genji* class. It was fun again. The encounter in which Kumoinokari tells Yūgiri to drop dead is delightful (a faculty colleague who sat in on the seminar translated it even thus, and was not at all far from the original); and Waley leaves it out.

In the evening I went to the Mendelssohn Theater for the student production of *The Magic Flute*. It was beyond their range, naturally. The Queen of the Night had trouble with her high notes and Sarastro had trouble with his low notes, and Pamina seemed so awed by it all that she could scarcely open her mouth. It was in English, so that the silliness stood fully exposed. The audience laughed heartily as the priests, trumpets pointing every which way, sounded the triple chord and Sarastro replied "Thank you." It *was* ridiculous. I laughed heartily too. Some of the rhymes were rather wonderful: "complete" to rhyme with "need," "happy" to rhyme with "shabby." Herr Blatt seems to have some sort of Korean trouble with his voiced and unvoiced consonants. But it was fun. I am sure Mozart would have loved it.

Dean Haber sat behind me but did not recognize me. To listen to him, I would have thought him a Jersey City barkeep.

Thursday, December 2: It was a bright morning again, and since I overslept a little I was still here when the sun emerged, this time at an angle from the south side of the library – the first time it has gone so far. Fascinated to see what it will do next, I awaken with eagerness each morning. Each clear morning, of course – it clouded over today in midmorning, and has remained so all day, and the moon, so icily bright last night (to remind me of Mr. Kawabata in Stockholm), is not out tonight, and so I fear I have little to look forward to.

In the morning I returned to the *Genji*, not given much attention in recent days. It is good that I was feeling alert and alive, for I faced the most trying sort of passage, the sort in which obscure material objects of no very great account follow one another in quick succession. All those women of the Second Princess's change clothes, so that the scene as she receives Yūgiri may be neither too mournful nor yet too gay. One wonders whether the commentators might not be outdoing themselves by a good deal. Can Murasaki have thought so precisely not only of the outside but of the inside of each robe brought from the mothballs? Might she be speaking as imprecisely as I when I say in this document that an autumn landscape is all russets and golds? I would like to think that we work in harmony in these little matters, Murasaki and I.

In the evening I browsed some more in my Meiji guide to notable Tokyo places. Hongō is astonishingly unchanged this half century and more – there are scenes that I recognized immediately. Yet it is utterly changed, for the pictures show it to be, in liveliness, second only to Asakusa, and today it is, like Asakusa, stagnant and seedy. Much of Komagome looks, in the fortieth year of Meiji or thereabouts, as jerry-built and ramshackle as the outer reaches of Nerima do today – one understands what Kafū was complaining about. And such a tangle of wires you never saw. Much of Koishikawa is positively pastoral, though the rise on which I lived for upwards of a decade seems already, in Meiji forty or so, to have had a generous coating of barracklike row houses – *nagaya* is the word I seek to translate. There were gracefully arched bridges across the Edogawa, and people went boating at night to view the cherries lining its banks. At Sakashita-machi there was a special cemetery for Confucian scholars in the service of the Shogunate. I wonder where they were moved to.

Saturday, December 4: Last night I dreamed I was a Jesuit and the food was very bad.

I got myself to the office in midmorning, and was informed by the *Daily* that the United States supports military dictatorships the whole world over. What China is doing in the case of the Indo-Pakistan conflict somehow escapes comment.

Settling down to work I finished, in first draft, of course, my translation of "Yūgiri." Strange that things should be left so in the air – one sort of feels that Murasaki Shikibu meant to say more sometime, and then the death of the other Murasaki in the next chapter proved to have such overwhelming finality that she had to turn to quite new material, and only as she groped for it remembered that things did need to be tidied up a bit. It is always possible, to add to the puzzle, that someone else in fact wrote "Kōbai,"[43] where the tidying up occurs. (A letter from Miss Ibuki the other day said that a woman putting herself in the position of the Second Princess becomes exceedingly fretful and impatient that Yūgiri is not more decisive. Somehow the matter had never affected me that way.)

After a sandwich, I got started on something I have not done before, reading over extended portions of my diary. The reason is this: I think, given the Japanese fondness for diaries and their willingness to accept anything that goes by the name, that I will make a piece I am doing for *Chūō Kōron* something in the nature of "A Genji Diary." And so I have chosen the year of my leave in Japan – the year of the Nobel Prize, though that is neither here nor there – and I shall go through and transcribe entries having to do with the *Genji*. So I read through a volume, for part of March and all of April and May, 1968. Things that I note in thus going rapidly through considerable expanses: (1) What a great deal of time I do waste. Only a tenth or so of my hours go into things which now, from a distance of three and a half years, seem productive. (2) How little of it all I actually set down. What I did set down does frequently bring memories of how things were, but it is the merest shadow of the substance, not likely to say much of anything to anyone else (and I do not know whether the thought brings relief or disappointment). (3) What a great deal of talking we did in those days of the race problem. We really do not talk about it as much as we used to. We do not, I am sure, feel any more sanguine about it than we used to, nor is there much likelihood that it will go away. I suppose we just manage to live with it, as with the prospect of death.

Tuesday, December 7: I am right, am I not, in thinking that Pearl Harbor was just thirty years ago today? Not a word has been said about the anniversary. And of course the day of the dropping of the bomb on Hiroshima is never forgotten. Perhaps I am out of step, wrong in thinking the earlier of the two days the more important.

I spent several hours in the morning and afternoon copying out *Genji* things from my diary. I am once again, alas, impressed at how much time I waste – had I really worked on the *Genji* and not enjoyed Tokyo so, I would, I almost believe, have the whole of it out of the way by now. Enjoy Tokyo I certainly did, and, far from being chastened, I am getting ready to enjoy it some more. "In the evening I drank at Ueno. . . . In the evening I drank at Shinjuku. . . ." I fear I want to do more of the same. I copied out one rather long passage that has nothing to do with the *Genji*, unless I think of a gimmick wherewith to attach it somehow. It is a description of a meeting with Mishima in June, 1968, and I am startled at how clearly, though I did not know it at the time, and, curiously, did not remember when the big event came, he told me what he was going to do.*

* The entry for June 7, 1968, says in part: "The evening with Mishima Yukio at a Nishi Ginza restaurant, very Kansai, called the Izui; and a fascinating evening it was. Initially we were alone, and we talked of his hatred for democracy and his fellow men of letters, and of violence and suicide, the conjunction of which he considers to be the essence of the Japanese, and in his fascination with which I think he is being honest. . . . Of the recent troubles in America, he said in effect: splendid, splendid, a sign that America is not dead. England and Sweden are dead. Just you wait – we are going to have plenty of assassinations in Japan. He means to do something dramatic before he is fifty, and clearly he does not mean something literary. Just what, was not made clear; but his belief in the efficacy of violence would seem to be very deep. . . . He said at one point that he wished to accomplish at least as much as Nakano Seigō accomplished. What that means, once again, I do not really know."

1972

Tokyo   Friday, February 11: Much of my fifty-first birthday was silent and solitary. I did not mind. Fifty-first birthdays should be treated with silence and solitude. The silence was first broken when, in the afternoon, Bill and Joyce Malm called to wish me a happy birthday. I picked up the receiver and there they were, singing the birthday song. I had not realized that it was possible to get across the Pacific without the intervention of those harsh-voiced operators.

My first good *Genji* day since perhaps November or early December, and it was on "Minori"[40] that I worked. Usually descriptions of festivals and ritual observances are a bore, but the central presence of Murasaki, who amid all the noise and color knows she must be the first to go, makes the ceremony that gives the chapter its title very beautiful. Very beautiful too are the little touches harkening back to her good days, cherry blossoms through the mist and the like.

To Ichigaya in the late afternoon to have a few drinks with Charles Terry, who prospers. He says that Tokyo is without question the printing capital of the world: as much printing is going on here at any one time as in all of Western Europe. His staff is taking English lessons. He chanced to pass the door of the classroom a day or so ago, and heard this remark: "How much is your wife?"

Back to Ueno for a few more drinks, first at the Iwateya, and then when it closed, at nine, at the Suehiro, and when it closed, at ten, at the Taishō. Holidays are not what they used to be: now, apparently, things just shut down.

Saturday, February 12: I worked hard on the *Genji* through the morning and much of the afternoon, and have brought myself up to almost the pace I would like to maintain, five to six pages of the Iwanami text every day.

The important things one has to learn for oneself – all that schooling, and there is no one to teach them. Among the important things is how to work on a translation of the *Genji* so that it is all-engrossing and there is no time for visions and revisions. One must have the day's task precisely fit the time allotted. Thus: I finish shaving my chin and getting angry with my *Yomiuri*, and it is eight-thirty when I settle down with, say, "Minori." When I have read over the day's allotment of pages, and seen what problems they are going to present, and done what is to be done by way of solving them in advance, it is about ten. There then remains the banging out of three typewritten pages, elite, very narrow margins, and this can be counted on to take almost exactly three hours, since the proportion of text to typewritten page falls as the problems increase, more space being taken up with queries and speculations and explanations. And so by lunch time and nap time in the early afternoon I have my five or six Iwanami pages finished. It is so efficient a routine that I hate to give it up, and think I would like to go on and translate some late-Heian thing when I have finished the *Genji*, allowing myself much license, "improving," perhaps.

I did that most moving of passages, Murasaki's death and the days preceding. How lovely the fabric that is woven, harkening back to Murasaki's youth, looking ahead to the time after her death. How beautifully everyone behaves: little Niou, gazing up at her and then running off lest he weep (one sees already, this early, that he is essentially a nicer person than Kaoru); Yūgiri, treating his father with the utmost courtesy and deference, and yet making bold to look at the corpse; Murasaki herself, putting on no airs, allowing herself no histrionics. One sees why she did not die in that earlier crisis. She had to have a chapter of her own. Is there anything in the Chinese novel to equal the quiet pathos of it all?

Happily exhausted from seeing Murasaki to extinction, I went out in the warm, still afternoon to look at the plums at the shrine. They are at what I suppose might be called their best, though I like them better when the first blossoms are coming out. They are fine old trees, in any case, the little dots of white against the twisting trunks far finer than the expanse of color that is the cherry in bloom. Of the flowering trees, it is the only one that is beautiful when not in bloom. Well, the magnolia and the camellia are beautiful too, I suppose, but with them it is for the dark glow of the leaves, while with the plum it is for the shape, as of a powerful piece of calligraphy. A pity that the blue sky is shut off on almost every side by ugly buildings. Only looking off to the east does one have what must have been on all sides, a century or so ago, a sky open but for black-tiled roofs which do not seem to climb into and obstruct the sky but rather to sweep downwards from sky to earth. Flocks of pigeons turning suddenly to silver, like fish scales, just as they wheel overhead.

Tuesday, February 15: It has been a bright day, with a sharp wind coming down from the north – the sort of day on which you feel snug and smug when your exposure is southern – and you do not live in the sort of Japanese house, mine for so long, which gives a groan as of the end of the world at each new gust. My crocuses thrive. My geranium is about to come into bloom. And who cares, save only I? Therein lies much of the pleasure – as of presiding over the Creation.

In the morning I got to work on the *Genji* again, pushed ahead with "Maboroshi."[41] I got through the final review of Genji's ladies, and it really does have a finality about it, as if Murasaki Shikibu knew that they, and Genji too, would be gone at the beginning of the next chapter, and as if she were bringing us full circle with an altogether subtler version of "the rainy night's discussion," to sum up and recall the chapters between, and show what they have done for her and for us.

Lunch at the Imperial with Professor Hisamatsu and Miss Odagiri. They were my guests. It was awful. The place was very noisy, and the table arrangement, about which I could do nothing, had me a half dozen feet or so removed from Professor Hisamatsu, and I could literally not hear, much less understand, a thing he said. At one point I nodded, and he thrust a Kabuki ticket into my hand. Thank heavens it is for a day when I am not otherwise occupied – and so I find that I am invited to the Kabuki on Saturday.

Saturday, March 4: My departed parents' fifty-third wedding anniversary, I am aware only now as I set the date down.

I worked very hard on the *Genji* through the morning and on into the afternoon. I approach the end of "Maboroshi." It is very moving. Murasaki Shikibu seems to have made up her mind, Genji must be done in. The silly business about Chūjō was but a moment's wavering – though one might wish that she had gone back and cut it. (Did she ever cut much of anything? I sort of doubt it, all the solemn scholarly evidence about rejected chapters to the contrary.) The burning of the letters and with it the harkening back to Genji's youth is especially affecting.

In the evening there was a gathering in honor of Hasegawa Izumi and his huge Ogai work. There were large numbers of speeches, through most of which the room roared with conversation. I was among the victims, though I think I was treated better than most. The decibel count dropped noticeably when I began, said Val Viglielmo, who was also among the victims. Mr. Kawabata was there, looking dreadful, as if the flicker were about to go out. And several hundred other people were there, each of them having contributed twenty-five hundred yen.

Tuesday, March 7: I did the last few lines of "Maboroshi," and then I went back to the beginning of the whole long translation, not looked at in perhaps half a decade. I seem to have got three chapters, and three only, out of the way in my faltering Stanford years (1966 and before), and so "Yūgao"[4] is next, and upon "Yūgao" I started today. The opening passages are uneven. The glimpse we get of the other side of the tracks, so to speak, is very vivid, and so is the haughtiness with which Genji's man steps into another's garden (peace, peace, O Ogden Nash) and breaks off an "evening face." But I could do without the tearful interview between Genji and his nurse.

Mr. Yanagita of *Chūō Kōron* came around in the afternoon with a Go board and stones, and for perhaps three hours went through the great match for me.* It was a wondrous performance. At critical

---

* I was then translating Kawabata's *The Master of Go.*

junctures he would show me the ways in which the game might have gone, and then, without consulting a chart, remove stones illustrating plays that were not made, and proceed with plays that were, the course of the game as clear in his mind, apparently, as a slide projected upon a screen. I watched and listened in admiring incomprehension. I did understand one thing well enough, however: that Mr. Kawabata's account of the match is in a way fictional, shaped to dramatic effect. He makes a thing of White 130 as the great climax, the turning point. The outcome was fairly clear by the hundredth move, however, says Mr. Y., since the Master played badly from about the eightieth play, not, he says further, that his opponent was playing terribly well. An irony: had the game been played today the Master would have won, for as White he would have had a handicap.

Thursday, March 23: The dismembering of the two-storey house two houses to the south goes on apace, and tomorrow or the next day it should disappear from sight. The earthly remains are each day piled neatly on a truck and taken away, no doubt to be burned in someone's public bath. Such a process, far more civilized and less wasteful than our own, will probably one day become economically impractical. It will be as in the United States: cheaper to abandon a building than to tear it down. A Japanese house, I can see, is a most wispily constructed thing. Only the roof seems solid. It is odd that in a country of earthquakes people should have chosen to live under so much weight so precariously supported.

It was a great day for the *Genji*, one of the best days yet, perhaps because of the solemn grandeur of the material I had to work with, the death of the lady of the evening faces and the dark, silent hours that follow, and the transporting of the body. The terror and loneliness of Genji's watch, before the arrival of Koremitsu, are palpably real. Koremitsu is an amusing fellow, so energetic a lover that he has no fixed abode, but he has certain unlikable traits too. His notion of duty looks only upwards, and towards the weak and humble he is brutal. He advises keeping the people at Gojō in ignorance of what has happened – and no attempt is made to ascertain whether or not the lady has relatives.

In the evening I went off to Asakusa again. Sad and even bedraggled though the old place may be, it yet has the power to draw me. I suppose the knowledge of what it once was has something to do with the matter. Would I be so attracted if I knew nothing of its past? – the past which I myself was witness to, and perhaps even more the great day of Meiji. Kafū's movie alley is rapidly becoming, I fear, a bowling-alley alley.

Wednesday, March 29: Spring has come. Today I saw for the first time short sleeves and bare arms.

I have finished "Yūgao" and moved into "Wakamurasaki"[5] (Wacky Murasacky, as Dave Osborn used to call her). Yes, there is a change, from fall to spring, of course, on the most obvious level; but the feeling is less of moving ahead into a later spring, as the compilers of chronologies tell us we do, than of moving back into an earlier spring. Things are more carefree, more open, less complicated. The change is not all for the good. There is something rough and heedless about the way in which the narrative rushes ahead and the characters are all brought on stage immediately.

"Yūgao" ends rather densely, with some editorializing that I for one could do without. But the way in which we are brought back to the beginning of "Hahakigi"[2] and reminded that Genji is guilty of youthful derelictions suggests greater maturity than "Wakamurasaki," in which he is grandeur itself, albeit a stripling, and people bathe in the radiant clouds he trails behind him.

To Ted Cohen's in the evening, for my first experience of a Passover *seder*, a grandly ritualistic dinner. Most of the other guests, of course, were Jews, a dozen or so of them. I found it very moving, for it was an affair of the extended family, conveying a sense of the tribal, atavistic loyalty that has held the Jews together and made it possible for them to survive these thousands of years. The smaller Rubinfien girl was a delight as she read responses in Hebrew, and Ted most erudite and rabbinical as he explained the symbolism. I felt a little uncomfortable eating with a hat on, but that was all right.

Thursday, March 30: Spring is most definitely with us (and is not "spring" a nice word? – it speaks to us immediately, as *haru* does not). The cherries are in full bloom over beyond the pond. The row of zelkovas over towards the Yushima Tenjin is a delicate mist of pale green, and in the night the loquats with their new shoots are like magnolias in full bloom.

I had another good day with "Wakamurasaki," which continues to seem much the most youthfully openhearted and at the same time romantic chapter I have done. The way in which situations repeat themselves continues to strike me. Genji pleading that he is not like other men, that he is just a poor orphan boy, is very much like Kaoru doing the same thing some forty chapters later. It is possible, I suppose, to argue that cyclical recurrence is evidence of a want of imagination, but I prefer to think that it is purposeful, that Murasaki thought of the world and life as cyclical, and set out to demonstrate the workings in the flesh. When nearly identical situations are found in later chapters, they are more subtle. Here, we are merely told that Genji is a lonely boy who misses his mother. In the case of Kaoru we really feel, as when the old woman gives him Kashiwagi's letters, the anguish of one who has never had a father and suspects that there are darkly hidden facts about his birth – we are sorry for him even though we cannot bring ourselves to like him very much.

Down to Ueno in the evening. It was, as was to be expected, full of noisy, reeling drunks.

Monday, April 3: I had great trouble with my young gromwell (Kenkyūsha's translation for *murasaki* – what could be more unfortunate?), both because I was suffering from too much weekend and because I did not much like what I was translating. The affair between Genji and Fujitsubo is altogether too fleeting and casual and offhand. Fujitsubo is not enough of a presence to make us feel that anything of moment has happened, certainly not anything of sufficient moment to haunt Genji through all his years. We are not even told how the affair took shape, whereas we are later told in polite and careful detail how Niou made it with the second Uji princess. Might Murasaki Shikibu have had an actual instance in mind, and felt reticent about, and no very great need for, the details? The contrast between Fujitsubo and Ukifune is striking. Both are silent, but Ukifune is a real presence, and Fujitsubo is not. All in all, one senses a novelist not yet in full command of her art. It is as if she were writing an outline for someone else to fill in.

With many a rest and many an urge to throw the book out the window, I did by evening succeed in turning out a full day's quota.

A letter came from Harold Strauss. He is having a contract drawn up. My deadline is to be the first of July, nineteen hundred and seventy-five. I think I can make it, granted I have not by then ruined my liver.

In the evening I thought of going out again to view the cherries. Deciding that I was not in the mood, I had a few drinks down at the foot of the hill.

Tuesday, April 18: I had pretty well decided to turn this extended document into a record of my work, in the hope that it might stimulate that work. It has not, this diary, served what I think was its original purpose, to stimulate me to another kind of work, "creative writing." And of course there is the sad possibility of having to destroy it, or the tiresome one of having to go through it and ink out passages, one of these days. And then I grow old, and the events of my unremarkable life seem less and less worth recording. But I must say something of happenings since Sunday night.

It is strange, but I was feeling terribly bleak, my lowest in what had been a very low week, on Sunday evening, and it must have been just at about that time that Mr. Kawabata was doing it.* I pulled myself together and went down for a few drinks at the Jūgoban. The television was on, and everyone tells me that it was over television that the first word came. If it came over our channel, I did

* Kawabata Yasunari died, probably a suicide, on April 16.

not notice, nor did it create any perceptible stir among the other patrons.

It was when I came back up the hill, at about eleven, that I had my first news. The telephone was ringing as I came in. It was a *Sankei* reporter. Needless to say the shock was considerable. Mishima had given us plenty of inklings; Kawabata gave us, so far as I was aware, not a one.

Japanese journalism is a remarkable institution. I was on the telephone until one in the morning, and reporters have been after me all the hours since, as sticky and persistent as Canberran flies. In the initial agitation I said yes to everything I was asked to write, and afterwards I had great trouble remembering what all the things might be. In any event they have occupied all my spare hours since, and destroyed a good part of my sleep as well.

On Sunday night I got no sleep at all. Among the journalists who called was Miss Ibuki. She had a car, she said, and was going down to Kamakura, and she suggested that it would be a good idea if I were to go too. So she came by for me, and we were in Kamakura at two in the morning. The lane leading into the Kawabata house was jammed, and there must have been a hundred automobiles parked out on the main street. The flashing of bulbs and the thrusting of microphones were horrendous, and the television lights were so bright that it was next to impossible to avoid mud puddles.

Within the gates, all was quiet. Numbers of people had gathered, and discussion of the funeral arrangements was in progress. When first I offered incense there was a towel over the face. When, an hour or more later, I was invited to say farewell, the towel had been taken away. The face was calm, there seemed no discoloration. I would be tempted to say that he looked as if he were asleep but for the fact that I never saw him asleep, and the fact that the absence of those extraordinary eyes made the face very different from the one I had known. Mrs. Kawabata was dry-eyed. She said over and over again: "I don't understand it. I just don't understand it."

Back in Tokyo in the dawn, I wrote the first of the promised manuscripts. Then I was off for a television panel – my first television appearance in years and years. Afterwards I wrote another article, which was a bit of a triumph, for it made the front page of the *Tokyo Shimbun*. Then, sleepless since Sunday morning, down to Kamakura again, again with Miss Ibuki, this time to attend the wake.

The wake, at which vast numbers of celebrated persons were, naturally, present, was very different from the Tanizaki wake. That was almost fun. This was hushed and stiff, with everyone keeping to himself. There were Buddhist services. The Buddhism of our day is not very elegant. The priests, though from one of the grander Buddhist centers, seemed rustic and uncouth. And oh, the photographers! If reporters are unpleasant fellows, photographers are worse, refusing even to dress as a sad and solemn occasion demands, looking as if they were recent graduates of an extortionist gang.

To sleep, finally, at about midnight.

This morning it was a discussion with Saeki Shōichi, for the *Shūkan Shōsetsu*. Back at Yushima in the early afternoon, I frantically pounded out yet another article, this one for the *Shūkan Sankei*. It would be easy to say that I could have left the telephone off the receiver immediately upon having the news. Or that I could have said no a few times. The latter I have never been good at doing, and the former I could not bring myself to do either. Partly, no doubt, the inability had to do with unworthy feelings of gratification, mixed in with the sadness and shock, at having the attention of the journalists again; but partly too it had to do with a wish, out of respect, to have my say about the old gentleman.

The question everyone is asking, of course, is why he did it. Some say it was because of illness, some because of Mishima, some because of the Nobel Prize. To me the most likely explanation is that he was very tired and could not sleep. But probably, in the final analysis, the only thing one can say is: "I don't understand it. I just don't understand it."*

Seeking to resume work upon the *Genji*, I glanced back over the pages done on April 6 and at the diary entry for that day, interrupted in mid-sentence. I was troubled by a disparity. I think it must have been between what we are supposed to think of Genji and what his behavior

---

* Recent "disclosures" about his fondness for young girls, such as the Usui Yoshimi story, seem to me to explain nothing at all.

forces us to think. He does not hesitate to kidnap Murasaki, knowing that Prince Hyōbu means to come for her the very next day. We have good evidence, in any case, of how little regard there was for the feelings of imperial princes. I'll bet Genji would not have stolen her out from under the nose of an important Fujiwara. Admittedly, he did keep Tamakazura a secret from her important Fujiwara father – but the fact that Tō no Chūjō had lost track of her is crucial.

Sunday, May 7: I have thought I have understood, these last few days, why aging people commit suicide in the spring. Below my window all is life. The zelkovas over beyond the Iwasaki house are, with the wind riffling through them, a wonderfully fresh spring green. Over in the second lot to the south of me, where recently the tearing down of a house fascinated me, the putting up of a house has been equally interesting. The way in which the carpenters seem to go each his way, with no consultation and no cooperation, and yet a house emerges, is very interesting indeed; but above all it is a scene of great vitality. I have thought how nice it would be to find purpose in squatting half naked in the spring sun and banging nails into a roof.

And that is the thing: to feel life all around you, and to feel none in yourself. At least I have my *Genji* to go back to. Apparently, to judge from a letter Harold Strauss recently had from him, Mr. Kawabata did not have even that much. He had kept his royalties in the United States, expecting to go there again; but in the letter, written perhaps two or three weeks before his suicide, he asked to have them sent to Japan, because, he said, he was too tired to think of going abroad again, and indeed too tired to think that he would ever do any more writing.

I think I understand the suicide better: in sum, my original view, spontaneous and so I suppose instinctive, finds support. An aged gentleman was very tired and longed for sleep. There was an interesting article in the *Asahi* this morning on the relationship – indirect – between sleeping medicine and suicide. Sleeping medicine can lead to addiction and change of personality, and present-ly to desperation. Might it not be that the awful stuff, no longer strong enough to put him to sleep, contributed to the diminution of his powers? I am glad that my addiction is to alcohol – which *does* put me to sleep.

Today I went back to the *Genji*, and a great delight it was – and at the same time there have been strong feelings of regret and re-morse for all the days in which that half-typed page of "Waka-murasaki" lay untouched. Anyway, I finished the chapter. It ends gracefully enough, but there is something very uncourtly, something indecent, almost, as of incest, in the way in which Genji plays with this little doll whom he means one day to make carnally his own. The "one day" must have come as a great shock to the poor girl, as if she were being raped by her own father.

Lunch with Fukuda and his friend Keiko. Leaving them, I walked on to Asakusa. Very sad – the Shinsekai, setting for the nice little Mishima piece I translated, the one with the million-dollar, I mean yen, title, is being torn down, probably to be replaced by a bowling alley. I remember so well how, in the late fifties, we looked for-ward to its completion. It was to be the center for a new, revital-ized Asakusa. When I came back from Europe in 1959 it was one of the first places I went to look at. But construction had stopped. There were endless difficulties before finally it was finished, in the early sixties, and of course Asakusa has gone downhill ever since.

I think that the district to the west of the Kokusai Theater and behind the Jintan Tower may be showing faint signs of new life, however. The Kikusui is selling burned chicken once more.

I looked in on the porny movies. The police would seem to have said something. The women are still stark naked, but the men clothed from the waist down. Two weeks ago both were stark naked. Sexism is what it is. Another sign of it: there is plenty of female homosexuality, not a trace of male.

Tuesday, May 9: Every morning a crow comes by, or maybe it is a different crow every morning, and looks in under the eaves

for little doves to eat; and all the big doves can do is flee, and observe from afar. Here we have one of the better reasons for not
being a dove.

I sped ahead with "Suetsumuhana,"[6] back in full stride for the
first time since Mr. Kawabata's death. I cannot help thinking that
the narrative technique shows considerably more sophistication
than in "Wakamurasaki." The affair with Fujitsubo takes place in
a manner so casual that it is scarcely believable, and preparations
for the encounter with the safflower princess are elaborate, keeping us in suspense, on and on; and the former is one of the central
events of the book, while the latter is fleeting and comical. Does this
not suggest that Murasaki Shikibu has come a considerable distance
from the tenth-century spinner of yarns towards her own mature
self?

I see that the problem of when, if ever, to give the princess a
name is going to be a difficult one. Dare I try to get by without
calling her anything ever, save "the safflower lady" or "Prince
Hitachi's daughter"? With her something of the sort might be
possible, but not with Murasaki, in whose case, too, I have failed
to solve the problem. I long to peek and see how Waley solved it,
but have resisted the temptation.

I may have remarked elsewhere on the curiously wavering line
between dialogue and non-dialogue. There are passages of osten-
sible quotation that cannot possibly be put between quotation marks
("such-and-such a person, my lady, has come calling"); nor can
the chatty quality of the narration, as of someone right there before
you, talking interminably, produced largely by honorifics, be dupli-
cated in English, unless one is prepared to have the results sound
like *Huckleberry Finn* or *The Catcher in the Rye*. I suppose I have been
wrong in saying that a modern Japanese translation is as far from the
original as a modern English translation, since something of the
same quality is easy to reproduce in modern Japanese.

The overlapping of time, with "Suetsumuhana" beginning earlier than "Wakamurasaki" – is it a matter of conscious technique,
or does it suggest that when "Suetsumuhana" was written the narrative had already moved ahead, and there was nowhere to tuck

it in? I think the latter, in view of the fact that "Wakamurasaki" moves easily into "Momiji no ga,"[7] and because the minor affair with the Hitachi princess is handled so much more carefully than the altogether more important affair with Fujitsubo.

Dinner at Makiko's. There was talk of many things. Of the tyranny of the banks, for instance. Said someone: "A bank does its *sumō* with another man's *fundoshi*."* And of the Crown Prince, his arbitrary ways, and his unpopularity. The feeling in this conservative house seems to be that the imperial institution itself may come to an end with the death of the present emperor.

Wednesday, June 7: Back to Tokyo. It was cloudy all the way from Seoul, which was just as well, since a hyperactive Korean child kept popping up between me and the window.

After Kimpo airport, everything at Haneda seemed so quiet, so efficient. I had a chatty taxi driver who asked me to buy him a pistol. Why, I asked, not unnaturally. Because he just loves the sound of a pistol, replied he.

I unpacked and read the papers, particularly to see what they might make of the Tel Aviv incident, not at all well reported in Korea (though one would expect the Koreans to be delighted with every gruesome, anti-Japanese detail).** On the surface, of course, the *Asahi* condemns the three, but underneath runs a current of sympathy. The survivor is a confused but basically nice boy, worried about home and father. The girl, who is said to have been training with the Palestine guerrillas, liked hydrangeas, which fact, apparently, makes her basically a nice girl. And in the letters to the editors is the usual crap about how society and the Satō government are at fault.

I meant to bring a thing from the Chosun Hotel, and, damn it, forgot to. It is a sheet of helpful hints for guests: they must not let strangers know of their plans for being out of the hotel, they

* Loincloth.
** Three Japanese terrorists fired indiscriminately on passengers in Lod airport. All but one of the terrorists, Okamoto Kōzō, were killed.

must not admit strangers to their rooms, they must have all persons who announce themselves as repairmen certified by an assistant manager. And so on and so on – perhaps a dozen injunctions in all. And at the end: "Relax and enjoy your stay." The list of things to be on one's guard against does not include inspection of one's room and belongings by the police and intelligence gentlemen.

My diary informs me that it has been almost exactly a month since last I did work on the *Genji*. A perfect scandal. Anyway, to-day I got started again. I moved on towards the end of "Suetsumu-hana." Tomorrow, with luck, I should finish it.

A reason for thinking that it must have been written fairly soon after "Utsusemi"[3]: when Genji thinks of other ladies, it is of the governor's wife and daughter, and not of Fujitsubo, who, given the chronology, ought to be most on his mind. These are for him tragic days, as far as the Fujitsubo narrative is concerned; but there is little suggestion of tragedy. Indeed Genji seems bright and cheer-ful, always ready to give forth with a cruel little joke at the red-nosed lady's expense.

The evening with Robert Guillain. We met at the Imperial, and then, coming back over much of the course I had traveled to meet him, got off at the Sendagi subway stop and took a long walk, with a pause for beer, through Yanaka and on to Nippori. He showed me a couple of remarkable little shops, one a seller of paper wares, the other a seller of basket wares, and then we walked from temple to temple. The best of them are deeply shaded, mossy places, heavy with the sensuousness of the approach of high summer. So must much of Edo and Meiji have been – one remembers Chamber-lain's description of the view from Atagoyama as richly green. But even in the temples they are cutting down trees to make room for automobiles, and leaving the moss to scorch.

Monday, June 12: A day of fierce winds and rains once more. Because of too much weekending, I was very slow in getting started on "Momiji no ga" – but the fact that I was able to get started at all made it a better Monday than most. After "Suetsumuhana," "Momiji no ga" is, quite as I expected it to be, dull. I feel thrown back to an earlier age, and in the hands of an altogether less mature writer. The mooning over Genji suggests a lovesick adolescent, and the affair between Genji and Fujitsubo continues to have a strange insubstantiality about it. Might not an older and more mature Murasaki Shikibu have looked back on these early chapters, and found them wanting, and pasted "Suetsumuhana" over the cracks between "Wakamurasaki" and "Momiji no ga," to give them a somewhat less ramshackle appearance? But why did she not rewrite them? Such was not her method, one feels – a chapter, once written and offered for circulation, was left pretty much as it stood, and another superimposed upon it if need be.

Thursday, June 15: We had a fire in the early morning hours. Two houses in the row that separates us from the university were gutted, and a third badly damaged. Since it began in a building under construction, the theory is that a pair of lovers had wandered up from the lake and occupied it, and either set it afire on purpose or been careless with matches. A fire in the night is like a coral snake, a beautiful and frightening thing. This was a minor fire, several yards away, and yet it bent our roof drains and balcony railings. It is easy to see that there would be scarcely any escaping the sort of fire likely to ensue upon an earthquake.

The other happy news of the day is that I have picked up lice somewhere.

In doing my day's quota of "Momiji no ga," I came across one of those stories that lead nowhere, of the affair between Genji and the elderly Naishi. One feels that such stories are there because they are based on actual happenings and because Murasaki's imagination has momentarily faltered; and one is reminded of the *Tales of Ise* and feels that Murasaki has not yet advanced a great distance from its world.

Wednesday, July 26: In the evening, down to Yokohama, with Nakamaru Kaoru. She interviewed me along the way, for that horrid magazine *Weekly Post*. The purpose of our going to Yokohama was to attend a bon-voyage party for Sol Sanders, aboard the *Cleveland*, on which he departed for Hong Kong.

Kaoru and I then made our way back to Tokyo. We had some *sushi*, and then she took me to a most extraordinary place, a "host club." A host club is the reverse of a Ginza bar. The clientele is female, and its needs are seen to by boys. The clientele, this particular evening, consisted of rather frowsy ladies of a certain age. The boys were all excessively pretty, and their masochism seemed quite open – and I suspected many of them to be boys from the band. I was fascinated, and at the same time repelled, and I suppose the most curious thing is that I felt nothing in the least erotic about the scene before me. The bill, after about an hour of observing and perhaps six whiskies, was just under fifteen thousand yen, or about fifty dollars.

Earlier in the day I got back to work on the *Genji*. I finished "Momiji no ga," which should have been finished way back around the middle of June. I said, when last in this document I referred to the chapter, that in it Murasaki Shikibu has not advanced much beyond the *Tales of Ise*. In a formal sense this is true. It is fragmented and disjointed, and the episode about the old lady stands quite apart from the rest; and even as regards content it can have been influenced by the *Ise*. And yet how very different is Murasaki's story from anything in the *Ise*. Her narrative has flesh and blood. It is as if she were writing a story the plot for which the author or authors of the *Ise* had but sketched in. He avers (or they aver), she demonstrates.

Ann Arbor Wednesday, August 30: Today, for the first time in I hate to think how many weeks, I returned to the *Genji*. "Aoi."[9] The scene of the clashing oxcarts. Memory – which of course means memory of the Waley translation – had promised me something very exciting, and I had not remembered the narrative to be other than clear. In fact it is very confused, and the commentators are not at all agreed on who is doing and thinking what. Myself, I kept thinking of a review I recently read somewhere by Aoki Haruo of Bernard St. Jacques's book on the Japanese language. It is argued, by either Aoki or St. Jacques, that Japanese verbs are not without subjects. The subjects are buried deep in the verbs themselves. I doubt that this is entirely true of the modern language, even – witness the number of occasions on which, in conversation, a person is asked to supply a subject. And the Heian language? Murasaki must have been called upon countless times to explain herself. The pity is that her answers were not preserved.

Lunch with a most interesting man from Tel Aviv University, a political scientist named Harari. He was the interpreter in Lod airport on the night of the slaughter. I was greatly astonished to detect what seemed like an undercurrent of admiration for Okamoto, the survivor among the three slaughterers. Okamoto, he said, was completely in control of himself, indeed the only person in the airport who retained a measure of self-control. (Well, why shouldn't he have, after all? He was the only one who had known what was going to happen.) He broke down and started talking only after being taken to identify the bodies of his two accomplices. Israeli opinion is divided on the sentence of life imprisonment, some thinking (as I do) that it was the best possible, others arguing that it will encourage similar incidents in the future. The Israeli government would be happy to have him off its hands.

As, seeking to go to sleep, I lie with my good ear against the pillow and my bad ear elevated, I seem to hear a shrilling of cicadas, "min-min-min-min-min." I must be homesick. Most of the birds, save pigeons, sparrows, and crows, have left my part of Tokyo, but on hot summer days the cicadas shrill as lustily as ever.

Friday, September 1: Up bright and early of a sunny day that in its late stages turned to thunder showers. I got to the office similarly bright and early, and, after assuring myself that all is disorder in the McGovern camp and that Bobby is certain to win the chess championship, settled down with "Aoi." It is a good chapter. There is too much praise of the radiant Genji, of course, but the description of the festivities is not heavy and cluttered, as such descriptions so often are. The crowds come to life, you feel the festive pack, and you come away knowing that it was a truly lovely day. The brevity of the visit to Rokujō is good too. There are no tears, there is no pouting. There is but a muttered complaint about the uncooperative ladies of the harem. Our Murasaki is finding her stride.

She must have been young when she wrote it, and yet in terms of what might be called understanding of the weaknesses and foibles of the human race, it is next to miraculous. The Rokujō lady is not evil, merely unhappy and sadly mistreated. Aoi, in her proud aloofness and her apparent acceptance of what her servants do to the Rokujō lady's oxcart (how would my readers react, I wonder, if I were to call it just that?), comes the nearer to being evil.

I like the idea of having possessive spirits handed down in a family from generation to generation. You take them with you.

The late-night news brought us a long and detailed report on highway conditions, for we are at the beginning of a three-day weekend. What a silly way of life. The town will be dead for the duration, and everyone will be out in his little iron box, iron box jammed in against iron box, all up and down the highways. It is a way of life that permits of no community.

Saturday, September 2: A rainy day, with the touch of autumn in the air. I spent it in utter solitude, speaking only to Brower, briefly, over the telephone, and to the lady who let me into the Frieze Building, which contains my office.

Ah, but I forget – I paid my first visit this year to the farmers' market before going to the office, and there was privileged to speak to numbers of people not seen since before Christmas, including Tinka Bear, who has her bread stand once more. The market was nice, but not yet its autumnal best. No cider, for instance, and without cider it cannot be said that Michigan has entered autumn. Seas of chrysanthemums, which we shall tire of before autumn is over, and seas of asters as well, to vanish long before we have even had a good look at them.

Anyway, I was back in the Frieze Building by midmorning, looking out over the green that separates us from Rackham. There are advantages in the deadness that comes with an American holiday (or Anglo-Saxon? – remember Christchurch on New Year's Day). Usually the green is infested with hairy creatures, human and canine; but today it was silent and softly verdant, like the Kokedera* back in the days before the tourists found out about it.

Though slow in getting started on "Aoi" and rather dreamy and badly collected in the pursuit of it, I had by the end of the afternoon made my way through the largest number of pages for any day thus far since my return. Though not, as we have seen, without its complications, "Aoi" is on the whole straightforward. The death of Aoi, which was as far as I got, is a marvel of laconic, no-nonsense presentation, of getting on with the story. Low-keyed horror is the most horrifying – and what low-keyed horror there is as the dying Aoi suddenly becomes a languorous, wheedling Rokujō lady.

Murasaki must have seen death – else she would have tried to color it up a bit. And did she see dying ladies subject to possession? Perhaps. Perhaps we who doubt are at fault, having seen so much evil that we are insensitive to subtle forms of it shooting through the air like radio waves.

Wednesday, September 6: I moved ahead with "Aoi," and am very near the end – this in just over a week, a fact to show the whole world what a horrid waste those last weeks in Tokyo were.

I did the scene I have found so objectionable in the past, the defloration of Murasaki. I continue to find the material revolting, both for what Genji does to Murasaki without having prepared her – could he not at least have allowed her a somewhat more normal girlhood, perhaps by sending her back for a time to her father? – and for what he does to her father, to whom revelation of the secret can only come as an intolerable insult. Yet revolting material can be

* The Saihōji, or "Moss Temple," in Kyoto.

delicately treated, and the treatment here is delicacy itself, scarcely a trace of the erotic.

One wishes: (1) that Murasaki Shikibu had foregone physical description of her characters (all so closely related to one another, they must all have looked very much alike, and the few adjectives she has at her disposal are all very much alike too); (2) that she were not so explicit in telling us the manner in which speeches of a pronounced tone are delivered (" 'I hate you, I hate you,' he said resentfully"); (3) that there had not, over the centuries, been so much scholarly energy devoted to hunting up poetic allusions. Allusions are constantly being averred when they are not at all necessary, and indeed something of a hindrance.

Saturday, September 9: A crisp, rather chilly day. Autumn has come. There was cider at the market. The asters seem to have almost passed, already. Very beautiful, the market, predominantly oranges and reds, with a touch here and there of somber russet to give us a foretaste of the sere and wintry. Lots of acquaintances – well, for *me*, lots of them, I have not many – were there.

I presently wandered over to Frieze, and, with Frieze all to myself the whole day long, worked on "Sakaki."[10] I got as far as the old emperor's death. How quietly Murasaki Shikibu treats death, and how circumspectly. It just happens – and in this instance we are not even present – it interrupts Kokiden's hesitations and deliberations. And how clamorous, by contrast, is the treatment of grief. Is there a Shinto influence – a defilement brought on by even writing of death, to be cleansed by elaborate rituals? Or does the matter have to do rather with the writing process itself? Having with a quick thrust (one admires her bravery) killed one of her characters, Murasaki perhaps needs a period of tears to decide what should come next.

Although the treatment of death is uniformly subdued, some die in agony, others serenely. The aged – the old emperor, the Eighth Prince – merely fade away. There is a time for dying, and if one but perseveres, it will come pleasantly.

Sunday, September 10: Professor Konishi has offered it as the chief characteristic of the *monogatari** that it includes everything and sprawls all over the place, whereas the novel is a result of careful selecting and shaping. Insofar as the novel is the shapelier of the two forms, no doubt he is right; but one is struck by how much is left out of the *Genji*. We do not witness, and what fun it would have been to witness, the scene in which Prince Hyōbu learns of Murasaki's whereabouts. Nor are we told in any specific detail of the indignities to which Genji is subjected after his father's death. There is a good bit of canny political reporting even so, by suggestion rather than by direct statement. In particular, we are given an immediate sense of what it must have been like to be a member of the imperial family with marauding Fujiwara all about. Poor old young Suzaku, so well-meaning and so impotent.

Dinner at the Malms'. I was their only guest, and the food was solidly, splendidly Mexican. Before dinner Bill and I went out into the giant vegetable garden that occupies the center of the block, to pick tomatoes and corn. Forever safe from developers, one hopes, by virtue of being quite closed off from the streets, it is very quiet and very green and bosky, and very American, with its corn and tomatoes and pumpkins. One could imagine that a hard-pressed Indian tribe had abandoned it but a day or two ago. Only I seem to remember having read somewhere that Indians did not like tomatoes.

Thursday, September 14: What was it that kept the Fujiwara within bounds? Did they really believe in the divinity of that one line unbroken for all ages? It would be so easy, one would think, for the Minister of the Right to get rid of the crown prince once he has control of the emperor; yet there is no indication that the thought ever occurs to him, or that the thought ever occurred to Murasaki Shikibu that the thought might have occurred to him. Here we have a little item arguing for the independence of the Japanese from Chinese influences. They read their *Shih-chi*, but declined to follow its example.

* Usually translated as "tale" or "romance."

I was given a rather surprising little jolt when the morning mail came in. It contained a letter from Fukuda. At my behest he has been reading the *Genji* (whether in the original or in a modernization he did not say). He says that he finds the early chapters in "schoolgirlish taste" (*shōjo shumi*). I know what he means, and suppose I shall feel constrained, as I move into the work of revision, to make it cooler, brisker, more brittle.

The remark was much with me as I moved two-thirds of the way through "Sakaki." The point is, I found myself thinking, that Murasaki may be considered a pessimist, and indeed commonly is by the Japanese, for her views on the decline of Buddhism, and, by implication at least, the decay of the court aristocracy; but she is an optimist in her view of human nature. Even when people, in spite of themselves, work evil, they strive to be good: the outstanding example, of course, is the Rokujō lady. The nasty woman, in the early chapters, after which nasty women pretty well disappear, is Kokiden; but she is kept at a distance, an abstractly malign influence, an existence that we must recognize, but not physically present.

And so I thought: how fortunate Murasaki was to write at a time when an awareness of the complexities of human nature was developing, but when it was still possible to take the sunny view. It is becoming nearer and nearer impossible today – hence, I should think, Fukuda's views on the schoolgirlishness. Who in America today takes the sunny view? Saul Bellow, perhaps, sometimes – he at least sees the possibility of a moral order. And who in Japan? Inferior novelists like Mushakōji, I suppose, and – and who else? Maybe, in a twisted way, Mishima, with his belief in the purity of action; but of course Mishima spent his time making his big point by indirection, running through the list of perversions and perversities that enshroud the nothing-at-all of our day.

Sunday, September 17: A rationale came to me for leaving out a number of the exaggerations and the redundancies. Murasaki Shikibu had no punctuation marks and wrote a language that urged the omission of subjects, and so needed a verb to indicate the fact that someone had spoken and to indicate as well the level of the speaker; and she saw fit to play elegant variations upon the verb "to say." We who are blessed with punctuation and are in the habit of making explicit the subjects of our verbs have no need for the elegant variations. Such, in any case, is the rationale for the cuts I feel more and more strongly inclined to make.

I was chauffeured to Jerry Bergwin's for dinner. It was a somewhat dramaturgic evening. One of the guests kept saying: "Florence, Florence, ah Florence! You can have the rest of Italy, but Florence, ah Florence!" We had dinner on the terrace. There were mosquitoes, but there were also broad lawns dotted with fruit trees, and presently there was thunder and lightning, and so we withdrew inside.

Over dinner, new horror stories about the youth of the land. It is dangerous, it seems, for nice young people to give parties at home these days, because word gets around, and those who have not been invited come and ransack the house. Nice young girls at Pioneer High School are afraid to go into the ladies' room. Is one to call it the end of the American dream, or the return of the wild frontier, to keep the dream going?

Saturday, September 23: It has been a remarkable day, perhaps the only day in my life in the course of which I shall bang out a draft translation of a whole chapter of the *Genji*. I finished "Sakaki" and went through "Hanachirusato"[11] and began "Suma."[12] I was wrong in thinking that Kokiden never says anything. She makes a long, angry speech just at the end of "Sakaki." It is a very good speech, and she comes forward not as a paragon of evil (if such there can be), but as a strong-minded person capable of expressing herself forcefully and with a strong sense of wrongs done to herself and people near her. I found myself sympathizing. Genji did behave towards her in a manner next to openly insulting, and he deserves the spanking (conceited young person) that he is about to get.

"Hanachirusato." Why does it exist? Everything about it is so vague, so abstract. Is it another example of what we might call writing backwards? When at last Genji assembles all his women at Rokujō, an orange-blossom lady becomes necessary, an uncomplaining person who does not mean much to Genji and is utterly dependent upon him.

And "Suma." It is nice to know that Genji has a safe-deposit box off there somewhere, in which he keeps the deeds to his property. One would have feared that he had as little knowledge of his holdings as I have of mine. It is interesting that a woman should be called upon to watch over them. Something of a masterpiece, the Japanese woman, then as now: competent but not aggressive, confident that things will come her way if she but waits. And if they don't? Well, she hasn't waited long enough.

Tuesday, September 26: Gray and muggy. Since Sunday the air has had rather the feel of Tokyo in June about it.

I devoted myself to "Suma" through much of the day. I am almost at the halfway point, and only just have Genji out of the city. His last day is spent in quiet converse with Murasaki. One suspects that he might have spent it rather in quiet slumber – there is no indication that he has had any sleep for maybe three or four nights. The *Genji* is not, in every respect, realistic.

The play between realism and want of realism is most curious, and I am of two minds about it. Does it give the book variety, and a certain tension by virtue of the way in which it is pulled in opposite directions – or does it merely give unevenness?

The relationship between the imperial family and the Fujiwara is very interesting indeed, and here Murasaki does give us a taste of politics as they were. The old emperor, Genji's father, clearly hoped to work a sort of imperial restoration through Genji. Genji is not a son of the grand Fujiwara, and he is spared the disability of being a prince of the blood, that he may have room to maneuver against them. And the restraint with which the Kokiden people behave is astonishing. They have the crown prince, Genji's chief hope, in their hands, and they do nothing to dispose of him. Why? Because they would not dream of laying hands on the Sun Goddess's duly appointed heir.

On the other hand a great deal is left out, and there is unmistakable romanticizing. What are the Kokiden people doing all the while Genji is making his farewells? We do not know. We have our one glimpse of politics, we go with Genji on the rounds – but all the while it is as if we were in the women's quarters, listening and observing through dense layers of curtain. Is it possible to believe that Genji *really* interceded with his father on behalf of all comers? Such is not the way in which the successful Heian politician worked. Probably Murasaki is dreaming about how nice things would be if there really *were* a Genji chancellor.

Of the journey to Suma we learn little, save that it called forth poetry and thoughts of poetry; and that is disappointing, though excusable, probably, in that Murasaki herself may never have made the trip. I think of Isabella Bird, whom I have been reading by snatches in the evenings. Isabella's case is less excusable. She visits places, and then declines to describe them, when we are hungry for any small detail of early Meiji Japan. She says that the regions east of the Sumida are an uninteresting collection of canals and warehouses – those regions which a score of years later were still able to delight Kafū. How one would have loved a tour through them. But Isabella, fixed in her predispositions, refuses to look at them. The cities into which foreigners have intruded are spoiled, and that is that.

In the evening I went over to the library and read the *Asahi*. So far as I could discover, only a single letter to the editor has been carried on the subject of the Munich massacre. It is from a person who announces himself as a university lecturer, and whose name is Samukawa Michio, Mr. Cold-river Road-boy. The Israelis, says Mr. S., are horrid. They should have peacefully given up the hostages, and instead they resorted to force.

Saturday, October 7: I went early to the market. There too autumn advances. The asters are all but gone, chrysanthemums lord it over everything. It is the plain garden flowers that I can scarce resist buying armfuls of, the bachelor's buttons and zinnias and marigolds that one does not find in florists'. I bought some red zinnias and a gallon of cider – for do I not live in what the *New York Times* disparagingly calls "apple-cider country"? – and made my way up Huron Street to the Frieze Building. Behind the Methodist Church on Huron and State there is a somber old house with white wooden openwork along the eaves, pure nineteenth century. I had not noticed it before. It ought to be the parsonage; one can imagine Charlotte Brontë stepping forth to survey the flower beds. In front of the Frieze Building stands a large and gaudy billboard advertising BOM. BOM seems to signify two things: "Blacks Opposed to Miscegenation" and "Blacks on the March." How amusing that we should have black segregationists and black "anti-miscegenationists." The easy liberal solutions brought to their final resting places. I suspect it is the lady Negroes who are chiefly behind MOB, I mean BOM, in its first signification. One sees on the streets of Ann Arbor many Negro men with white girls, but one does not often see the reverse.

I worked through the morning and early afternoon on "Hotaru."[25] Yes, the treatment of Genji is distinctly ambiguous, ironical, one might wish to say; and there is an interesting foretaste of Niou. Genji pushes Tamakazura upon his brother, the firefly prince, or rather him upon her, and then tells her that she must be careful, for the prince has his little ways and is not to be trusted. Is he not like Niou? Having brought the second Uji princess to Kyoto, Niou sets about reducing her to utter confusion in her relations with Kaoru.

Many tedious details having to do with the iris festival. This business of showing off one's root, noted for its great length – rather suggestive, is it not, especially when the display is for the benefit of a coy mistress?

Tuesday, October 10: The Double Ten – not that anyone pays any attention to *that* sort of thing any more. Last night was our coldest night yet. The maple beneath my Frieze window is almost bare.

I did the usual thing through most of the day, worked on the *Genji*. I finished "Hotaru" and moved back to "Akashi."[13] As when I moved back from "Maboroshi" to "Yūgao," I had an immediate sense of moving into a younger world, not in that the characters are younger, but that the person who created them must have been younger. Everything simpler, clearer, more capable of solution – and the obfuscations with which Genji burdens Murasaki and Tamakazura in the later chapter are replaced by the easy remedies of a younger man on the make.

I like Tō no Chūjō, at the end of "Hotaru," describing Tamakazura as a valuable piece of property that has been mislaid. Now *there* is a refreshing sort of crassness – reminds one of a New York booking clerk.

I spent much of the afternoon on little research problems I have been collecting, such as whether Genji blackened his teeth. Probably not – men probably started blackening their teeth only a century or so later.

Thursday, October 12 : "Akashi" moves much more rapidly, and thus far is more fun, than "Suma." I saw Genji off to Akashi. So near Suma and yet so different – can one really believe that Murasaki saw either place? She needed a horrid place and a rather nicer place, and patterned the former upon the north country of her maidenhood, and borrowed the latter from – perhaps a Chinese treatise on the pleasures of country life? Already Akashi has a Taoist feel about it.

How very arbitrary and irrational is the behavior of the god of Sumiyoshi. If the god so wants Genji to move to Akashi, then he should just come out and say so, instead of sending these storms and portents and jet streams, and in general subjecting him to the most horrid uncertainty.

Yet a feeling of nearness to the dead and to the gods, whose chief requirement seems to be that one go to sleep from time to time, must have brought wonderful comfort to the troubled. Genji awakens from a dream of his father with feelings not of fear but of bliss, as of returning to childhood, and what he most wants is to go to sleep again (to approach the dead on their own terms). Might not the cheerful resignation that is among the more appealing of Japanese traits derive as much from Shinto (life with the gods) as from Buddhism?

Tuesday, October 17: We were supposed to have snow flurries this morning, but we didn't. It was a beautifully clear morning, the sort of bracing autumn day, thought Bob and Laura and Bill Sibley, for a drive along the back roads to Marshall. So in the afternoon we set out.

But before we did I had a good day's work on "Akashi." I got as far as Genji's first night with the poor, proud Akashi lady. She is almost as speechless as Ukifune, and yet she comes across with a strangely palpable reality, like the sudden fall of a breeze. Her dignity fairly rings through the silence, and pride and humility all at once seem very much akin.

Kokiden has come back into the story. I like her in spite of everything, and sort of wonder if I am not *supposed* to like her. She is a no-nonsense person, and very wise, in her hard, steely way. She would have made a good psychiatrist. She tells her son the emperor that on disturbed nights we are likely to dream of things that have been on our minds. Well, precisely.

All in all a nicely told story, is "Akashi" thus far. The alternation between the city and Akashi lends a certain elegant air of suspense. I find myself rooting for the Akashi lady, hoping she will get him before forces known to be at work in the city pull him back. So much is said about Murasaki the psychologist and Murasaki the social critic that a person tends to forget the most important Murasaki, the spinner of good yarns.

We drove to Marshall along the back roads, through Dexter and Chelsea and such places. The little towns, with their wide lawns and their autumn trees and their frame and brick and fieldstone houses, are very beautiful and unspoiled, and it gives a fine sense of repose to be on a road that is a part of the country rather than a cruel cut slashed through it. An organic sort of road, I suppose current jargon would have it. Down among the cornfields and red barns, Michigan continues to look richly rural, a land of sweet hills.

Tuesday, October 24: The marigolds on the street corners have all been done in by the frost, but they have these last two days or so been sending out a remarkably strong odor. I find it a fine, clean odor, but there are those who are repelled by it; and it *is*, of course, the smell of death. I am reminded of Narihira – was it not Narihira who was for Tsurayuki like a faded flower the fragrance of which remains?

Despite the wanness of the light, the view from my Frieze windows has been gorgeous. I must have three kinds of oak: the one on the left is yellow to gold to brown, the one in the middle has scarcely turned at all, small flecks of yellow and brown breaking the green, and the one on the right is a glowing mass of saffron. To the left of all three, the Norwegian maple is still a dark glossy green, with only the beginnings of an autumn tan. The burning bushes (an' that be what they are) over by Rackham back up the array with patches of brilliant red. And how nice my greensward should be when the snows begin.

In midmorning I went over to State Street to keep an appointment with Dr. Jingly Jones, my dentist, and learn that my teeth are in good repair. For the rest, I worked on "Miotsukushi."[14] Genji is generously bestowing his attentions here and there, after the fashion of Narihira, and his regrets at having been unfaithful to Murasaki have quite left him. Is Murasaki Shikibu idealizing him as a latter-day Narihira, or is she making fun of him? The old old question, and even if there is no answer, I know what I would prefer the answer to be. Comes the next question: if there is sardonic humor, how am I to convey it in English, without being less than faithful to my original? Waley had few qualms about infidelity, and yet very little of this humor, if he was aware of it, comes across in his translation.

Genji is at the summit of power, or very near it, and still only in his middling-late twenties; and he has no thoughts at all of seeking the throne for himself. The fortune-tellers and the god of

Sumiyoshi have told him where he is to be, and there he is. All cannot have been quiet resignation, of course, but such a view of oneself must have tempered the sense of personal achievement or failure, and made life less of a battleground. That the sense of failure should have been blunted seems somehow less important than that the sense of achievement should have been. The most admired of persons still did not think of themselves as gods. That view was reserved for our own godless age, with its poet-gods and psychoanalyst-gods and the rest. One might say that the struggle and the achievement and failure were forwarded to a higher echelon.

A gentleman of Japan who is a teacher of English somewhere has given me an article of his in which, by counting sentences and by counting the number of words within sentences, he seeks to establish the degree of fidelity of some thirty translations from Japanese into English. Though his figures are somewhat mysterious, they seem to argue that Glenn Shaw's translation of "Rashōmon" is the nearest to ideal fidelity. Of my own translations, four in number, *The Makioka Sisters* and Yokomitsu Riichi's "Machines" are taken to task because the first fifty sentences of the original become a hundred thirty-four in the former translation, a hundred four in the latter. In Donald Keene's Yokomitsu and Howard Hibbett's *Shunkin* the comparable figures are a hundred forty-nine and ninety; and these are the only four of the thirty, by a dozen authors, in which the disparity is sufficient to provoke a tut-tut. My translations of Shiga Naoya's "At Kinosaki" and Kawabata's *Snow Country* are, by the gentleman's standards, better: fifty becomes fifty-two and fifty-nine, respectively. I find this interesting not because it says much about the translations but because it may say something about the original Japanese. I may not have great admiration for Shiga Naoya as a novelist, but as a stylist he is without doubt the most straightforward and clean of my four, the one most lacking in mannerisms.

Thursday, November 30: I have pretty well decided to move, and the problem now is of finding someone who will take over my lease here on Maynard Street. It has its little complications. Today the manager's wife came around with a handsome Negro couple in extravagantly "mod" dress. But soon it became apparent that the wife was also a man. That didn't matter a great deal, said the manager's wife afterwards. What did matter was race. She could not turn them away without being accused of segregationist practices, and on the other hand she must somehow steer them to a "liberal" floor. They want to be on the tenth, but if she were to put them there everyone else would move away. This fourth floor, on the other hand, is liberal, and so she wants desperately to steer them despite their proclivities into my apartment. We may get angry with our managers from time to time, but their lot cannot be an easy one.

Today, it was on "Miotsukushi" that I worked again. The Rokujō lady has fallen ill and become a nun; and what a sad case she is, wishing everyone well with the upper part of her mind, and cursed, lower down, with evil impulses quite beyond her control. There is something Calvinist about it all – she is among the damned, and can do nothing but sink to lower circles. The juxtaposition with the Akashi lady is very effective, the one among the blessed for no very good reason, the other among the damned for no better reason. Their sort of Buddhism, taken seriously, could have been every bit as terrifying as brimstone Christianity; but of course it is one of the stronger traits of the Japanese that such considerations seldom get in the way of important things.

Saturday, December 2: It has been a rather nice day, fairly sunny, and the snow still not encrusted with grime; but somehow I have been feeling very grouchy and not at all alert.

I managed to settle down with the *Genji* late in the morning, however, and by the late afternoon had five more pages or so of "Miotsukushi" out of the way – as much as I have done on any day this last month and more. Tomorrow I should finish it and move on to – well, I don't know exactly what. There is great irony, towards the end of "Miotsukushi," in the treatment of Genji and his parental solicitude for Akikonomu. Obviously the author did not consider him the paragon, the ideal embodiment of *mono no aware*,* that she has been at such pains to tell us he is. It is as if she had her public image and her private image of him. Again one feels that there must have been a specific model, and that her audience knew who he was.

I still have no idea how to assign names. I have not yet really brought myself to call Murasaki Murasaki, and poor Yūgao lived and died as "the lady of the evening faces," and Hanachirusato continues to be "the lady of the orange blossoms," which somehow suggests a bad translation, in the exotic manner, from the Chinese; and now I have Akikonomu on my hands, still nameless, still designated "the former high priestess" – scarcely the most graceful designation one can think of. Perhaps the best thing would be to pretend from the start that they all have names.** But who is to announce them? An omniscient narrator? Or must I resort to some eighteenth-century formula? "We shall call her Murasaki." The scarcity of important characters in the Uji chapters made that particular problem a relatively easy one.

Lunch at the Town Club with Choo Won. She is taking American citizenship; and her chief reason, she says, is to make things easier for her family should they ever have to seek sanctuary. Poor old Korea, poor Koreans.

Thursday, December 7: In the morning and early afternoon I turned out a full day's portion of the *Genji*. It was "Yomogiu,"[15] "Where the Mugworts Grow," that I worked on. The description of the lady's mansion, with cows wandering in and out and creepers bolting the gates against intruders, is a wonderful blend of the sad and the comical. I got reeducated in a certain matter, perhaps trivial, perhaps important. I used to think that a sense of the past and a taste for things antiquarian came only late in the Heian period, and

* Pathos, *lacrimae rerum*.
** In the original, only persons of the lower classes have what can properly be called names.

that in mid-Heian what was old was dreary and dull and fusty; but we learn that there are people who have their eyes on the poor red-nosed lady's things precisely because they are old and by well-known craftsmen. And what a curious thing it is to be old-fashioned and unworldly and yet reluctant to shows signs of a religious bent. To be manifestly religious was obviously to be stylish and a part of the grand world. A sensible sort of religion.

After a faculty meeting, Marjorie Petring and I went over to my new apartment and measured all the doors and windows for curtains. It was rather fun, and I begin to look forward to the move. Nothing like having a woman in the house, to make you feel all eager.

Saturday, December 9: At the office all by myself through much of the day, I pressed on with "Yomogiu" and wrote more Christmas letters. Sometimes, as when the red-nosed lady digs up a few presents to give to her unfaithful Jijū, the pathos is so intense as to make one want to weep. A very skilled writer, and a mature writer – and yet the style is plain and straightforward, almost as much so as that of "Wakamurasaki," which it has been my inclination to think of as from a young and immature hand.

I have begun carrying my Korean pots over to the office as a sort of way station to 619 East University. It is a dangerous business over these icy sidewalks, but so far I have not smashed anything. "Not smashed, maybe," said Brower cheerfully in the evening when I spoke of this accomplishment, "but very likely to be trashed if you have them in that building." The social-work types who wander the halls even on days when the building is supposed to be locked *do* make me uneasy.

On my way back to Maynard Street I stopped by the friendly Ann Arbor Bank to get some money from a machine that feeds you money any time of the day or night. It flashed and snarled at me, and refused to feed me money. A nice man came out and told me why. When a person wants fifty dollars he must say five thousand to the machine. The wonders of technology.

1973

Thursday, January 18: Pleasant, balmy weather continues. The skies have been relatively clear, the temperature has gone up into the high fifties, and there have been gentle winds from the south.

I glanced through the *New York Times*, which dislikes Mr. Nixon more than ever these days, and was about to settle down with "Eawase"[17] when Marjorie came in and said, the air being soft and the breezes gentle, and there being a sale on at the Handicraft Furniture Store, that we must go out and spend some of my money. We must buy me a bedroom rug. So we had a bit of lunch and then went exploring for rugs. At Handicraft we found exactly what I wanted, an off-shade white rug, of American provenance, with a sort of knotted finish in large checks. Getting the apartment in order has indeed entered the fun stage.

With what remained of the afternoon, I did some "Eawase." It is a bright, lively, rather humorous chapter, to offer a change of mood and air after "Suma" and "Akashi," and the gloom of Genji's separation from his only daughter – and to give us a moment of rest before Fujitsubo's death and the domestic crisis presented by the summoning of the daughter to the city.

I do not know whether or not Murasaki is being ironical as she gives us the views of the highborn ladies on the array of paintings before them, but it certainly is art criticism of a very strange order, having to do much more with subjects than with execution. If the story is good and noble and edifying and original (not too old and familiar), why, then, it would seem, so too must the painting be. Such a position has something in common with a kind of modern literary criticism. If a good and noble and "moral" person (Shiga Naoya, Mushakōji Saneatsu) writes a book, why then it must be a good book, must it not? It is reminiscent too of proletarian criticism: what matters is a correct point of departure.

Monday, January 22: So Lyndon Johnson is dead. I felt almost none of the affection for him that I felt for Harry Truman, and yet I am sadder for him than for Harry. He was a very unfortunate man, our Neville Chamberlain. He would have been a fine leader if only foreign affairs had left him alone. He even got the wrong time for dying.

I worked, really worked, on the *Genji*, for the first time since before Christmas. It was "Matsukaze,"[18] and at this rate I should have it out of the way by midweek.

It is a lovely chapter. It would have been in any case, but the sudden and wholly appropriate change of moods and shadings makes it doubly so. We have had a little interlude, a little divertissement, in "Eawase," and now we get down to business again. Our author is a person who entertains ambitions and is quietly confident that she can realize them. We are at Akashi, the lady must go; and with wonderful control she does go. There is not a word that rings false, not a tear that seems excessive. There is even a bit of earthy repartee that informs us of the approach of the Middle Ages. This person from Saga has moved in and taken over land that by rights belongs to the wife of the Akashi monk, and is not prepared to be dislodged that the convenience of the legal owners may be served. So they began, the Middle Ages. (And the relevance to my Colorado affairs makes me squirm – the more uncomfortably for the fact that I ain't no aristocrat.)

In the evening I had more fun with my apartment. The fun is almost over – one of these days I must begin scrubbing toilets.

Tuesday, January 23: And so now, just a day after Lyndon Johnson's death, comes what ought to be a day of something or other – maybe jubilation.* Along towards evening the carillon began ringing, but I did not otherwise note signs of much other than weariness and boredom. The ones who ought to be jubilant are probably resentful, because the delicious things they had to complain about have been taken away from them, the supply of peace-loving brickbats has been severely reduced. And I myself? Well, I suppose I just feel tired too, and not really interested enough to stir up the sort of apprehension that I know is called for. Vaguely I fret about

* The pseudo-peace that Lyndon Johnson did not live quite long enough to see.

Korea – but not as if I were prepared to ask anyone to *do* anything about it.

> Sing dismalloo, sing dismallay,
> Joy is hardly the thing of the day.

The weather continues to favor us withal. I continue to move rather rapidly ahead with "Matsukaze," and to find it a delightful chapter, quietly pathetic, quietly happy, without thus far a misstep in the direction of wooing either emotion too openly. Even Genji manages to enter but not intrude – and so perhaps for the first time in the whole long narrative one feels really comfortable with him. The poise and confidence with which Murasaki keeps him in his by no means easily assigned place suggests that she is now far enough ahead of her audience not to fret about it a great deal – and so suggests that she has been at her business for rather a long time, and that the order of the chapters as we have it may not, after all, be too far from what it originally was.

In the lovely springlike afternoon – it should have set the lilac buds to swelling – I took a walk downtown and did some shopping. Then I came back to East University and breathed a sigh for Lyndon – I do feel very sad for that unlucky man – as I arranged and rearranged furniture and crockery. In the evening Sibley and Brower and I had much sadistic fun as, at the house of the last, we put together a comprehensive pre-doctoral examination.

Monday, January 29: It has been a savage of a day, with snow in the morning and a harsh north wind on through the afternoon. And at the same time it has been a little dear of a day, rolling along smoothly. Very largely the high quality of the day was due to the fact that I slept beautifully last night, and quite without the assistance of drugs. I had nice dreams. Benign, whimsical figures kept moving in and out of them. The one I remember best was a white-bearded little gherkin of a man who introduced himself as "Bacillus the First, King of the Picts."

I spent most of the day with "Usugumo."[19] Fujitsubo is dead.

She dies very quietly and inconspicuously and almost casually, but rather a lot of fairly heavy rhetoric follows upon her death. Maybe one thing that makes me like "Usugumo" a little less than "Matsukaze" has to do with that mystic, elusive element – "sincerity." Murasaki is not being herself, not allowing her honest feelings to have their way. Which is to say, in this case, that she is being Chinese. The heavy rhetoric is as from a Chinese history.

Bob Brower brought, from the *New Yorker* of January 27, a review by George Steiner of *The Master of Go*. Mr. Steiner is puzzled by the book, and says that my introduction is uninformative. As for my translation, he calls himself incompetent to judge, but says that "it does exude a condign strangeness and ceremonious deportment." Are those not nice things to exude? Bob told me that when Laura first saw it she said, "Oh my, we mustn't show Ed"; and he replied, "Oh, go ahead and show him, but don't rub it in."

Tuesday, January 30: I do not much wish to talk about the *Genji*. I must talk, sadly, sadly, of having to leave it. I approach the end of "Usugumo," and when I am there I must turn to Mishima. It seems such a pity, when things are going so well.

I do not think that "Usugumo" rises to the perfection of "Matsukaze." It is by comparison diffuse, badly focused. Genji himself was kept under control in "Matsukaze," but now, especially in the self-pitying dialogue with Akikonomu, he comes to seem distasteful again. So does Buddhism. When the old bishop tells the emperor about his paternity, it seems a religion less of acceptance and resignation than of sadism. "There is something I must tell you, painful though it is, for your own good."

The sorrow and the terror of the confrontation are so powerful, however, as to overcome one's doubts about the motivation. As the bolts come down from heaven, it is like the darkness gathering over Calvary. How similar it is to the scene in which Kaoru learns of his birth. The later scene has in it more of pity than of horror, but as an echo of the earlier one it takes on horror too, way out there in the wilds of Uji, with the river sounding its threnody.

I had a strange and wonderful dream early this morning, just as I was about to awaken – it must have been then, because that is when I have my remembered dreams. I was taking a class somewhere. I set off for school, and waited to be instructed. Nothing was happening. A person was shooting at a target here, clusters of people were playing pointless and ruleless games there – but no one would indicate what was expected of us. So I went away and came back to have another try the next day. Next day, more of the same thing. And likewise on the following days. So I began working out ways of parceling and occupying my time, doing unnecessary errands and going on unnecessary inspection trips. But as the time for the completion of the course approached, I began to get nervous. It seemed necessary to get involved in something. Back at the school, very much the same thing as always was happening, only people were getting together for commemorative pictures, and electing one another to this and that, and handing out prizes. And that was the end of the dream.

What was it all? Something altogether too real, in any case. I awoke feeling rather frightened, rather threatened.

Thursday, February 1: Today I forced myself, and the process was like pulling a tooth, and the person who first thought of that simile belongs among the immortals, to begin the Mishima novel, *The Five Spots on the Angel*. I was sullen and resentful, and these inclinations I must get over, for my speed must rise. I am determined to allow no more than a working month on a first draft. I managed to get a couple of chapters done all the same.

The process is a very different one from translating the *Genji*. I am completely immersed in the words of the *Genji* and almost never have to break the trance to look into a dictionary. With Mishima I know pretty well from the outset what he is trying to say – as likely as not he is merely trying to create an impression of saying something – but must constantly be taking up a dictionary in search of eccentric, pretentious words. There is a considerable difference between working with jewels and working with tinsel. I suppose the essential problem is the old one of sincerity. When Murasaki does something wrong she generally does it with honesty. Mishima is always covering and feigning.

Friday, February 2: I wasn't as angry with Mishima today as yesterday, yet translating him I still find to be a very different process from translating Murasaki Shikibu – or, for that matter, from translating Kawabata. I said in the course of my remarks at the New York Hilton that Kawabata seemed to me to have a visual sensibility, Mishima a verbal one. I think I might add that Kawabata had a *Genji* sense of beauty, Mishima a *Heike*. In Kawabata you lose yourself in a warm bath of bland words, in Mishima you are held off by a hard surface of shining words. Unlike Kawabata, Mishima announces himself too early and too openly. We learn too early that Tōru is the incarnation of coldness and cruelty, and so it seems unlikely that we will ever believe in him. In Kawabata we are rarely told anything of the sort – Kawabata is perhaps unique among recent Japanese novelists in not taking a "view" of his characters – and have we not here again a contrast between the poised, courtly *Genji* and the somewhat simplistic, medieval *Heike*?

I went out in the rain to do some shopping. I bought myself a couple of suits and picked up some Kelly-green blinds for my kitchen. I finished off the afternoon with more Mishima, and in the evening scrubbed my parlor floor.

Tokyo Sunday, March 18: There is growing through the Iwasaki stone wall, down the Slope of the Unremembered Dead, a bush which last autumn had lavender berries. I broke off a branch when I was here for the autumn PEN conference, and it has been on my desk ever since. It has kept its leaves, and the berries, though much darker, are still purple. The other day Fukuda came upon the shrub in the garden section of a department store. It is called Murasaki Shikibu. Is that not nice?

I have been reading the Enchi *Genji*. Most recently I have been reading her "Wakana."[34,35] What makes the difference between dullness and stately elegance? With its endless speeches, its endless ceremony, its increasing flow of tears, the first "Wakana" chapter could easily be a bore; but it has all the fascination of a grand lady in full court dress, it hypnotizes with its slow, sealike rhythms. I think of Mishima's Count Ayakura, disgraced at autumn and back at the New Year, quite as if nothing had happened, reading His Feeble-minded Majesty's poem. He knows that the *kemari* ball will come down if he but waits.*

Another couple of things that strike me as I read Mrs. Enchi's "Wakana": the concreteness, and the utter want of intellectual content. These are the things I take Mishima to be talking about when he refers to the Japanese spirit and the Japanese tradition. Viglielmo once told me that I was too much worried, in my *Genji*, about specific details, and not enough about the flow of the thought. However matters may be with other tales, flow of thought is about as alien to the *Genji* as anything could possibly be. And even in works with ambitions in the direction of abstractable ideas, the concern of the translator, I suspect, should be with concrete details. The ideas, such as they are, can be expected to follow obediently after.

I have thought recently that my handwriting resembles my father's. That is odd, for it never used to.

Friday, April 13: My tax problems still hang over me this Friday the thirteenth, and I had to write a letter or two first thing in the morning. But there is nothing to do but wait for some money to come in; and so I composed myself and turned to the *Genji*. With some resolution, after a lapse of some ten weeks, I moved on to "Asagao,"[20] and by midafternoon had my norm out of the way.

"Asagao" thus far is a rather uneventful chapter, though it does have its good things. The Murasaki of the tale seems very exactly herself, as of course a fictional character ought to, when we learn that she complains to Genji of unimportant derelictions on his part,

* Count Ayakura, in *Spring Rain*, is an authority on *kemari*, the Heian football game.

but not of important ones. This second major figure in Genji's life is so much better realized than the first. One feels, quite simply, that Murasaki Shikibu had a better idea of what she was up to.

And she saw how difficult it was. One could if one wished be put off by the way she stops and seems to apologize for allowing Genji to be so interested in a most (so we are told) uninteresting letter. But what she says is quite true: to set down in writing the whole of even a minor happening is a next to impossible task.

Monday, April 16: So tax-paying day has come, and here I am not paying my taxes.

I got in a good four or five hours' work on the *Genji*, and am within a hop of the end of "Asagao." How like the oldest Uji princess is Asagao, both of them brought up in seclusion by a father without the educational presence of brothers. Was the type, terrified of men, so common at court? Both ladies, it might be added, are the daughters of younger brothers of emperors. Did Murasaki have a model, or did her instinct for the workings of the human spirit tell her that such circumstances would produce a sort of suicidal frigidity, a wish to see oneself extinguished before doing anything about the perpetuation of the line? I suspect that the absence of brothers would be crucial. Their presence would tell a lady something of the world beyond her curtains, even though she did not see a great deal of them.

Today being the anniversary of Mr. Kawabata's death, there was a gathering in the evening to commemorate it. Mr. Serisawa made some interesting and amusing remarks to the assembly – that they should have been amusing seemed entirely just and proper. In a conversation at about the time the international PEN came to Tokyo, Mr. Kawabata told him how out of place he felt among Western writers, for it is their practice, he said, but not that of Orientals, to write of human beings. But is not Komako (in *Snow Country*) a human being, asked Mr. Serisawa. No, said Mr. Kawabata. An *obake* – a wraith – nothing more. I see, of course, what he meant. And are the characters in my *Genji*, so fleetingly present, so quick to fade back into the natural setting, also *obake*? Mr. Serisawa also said that Mr. Kawabata thought of a good dirty old-fashioned Asakusa show as one of the things foreign visitors to the congress might enjoy.

The Prime Minister, Tanaka Kakuei, was there. I was able to observe him at close quarters for rather a long time. He handles himself well, giving an impression of youthful vigor. We were spared the unpleasantness of listening to his gravel voice, at least so long as I was present.

Passover dinner at Ted Cohen's once more. What a sense of ancient, ancient lineage, traceable all the way back to Moses and the passage through the Red Sea ("our fathers") the Jews do give on such an occasion. Our true aristocrats.

Wednesday, April 18: I should be in Kyoto at about this time. Mrs. Tanizaki was going to take me viewing cherries. But I have not heard from her, and so here I still am, at work on "Otome."[21] It is just as well. I do not really like Kyoto, though I feel it my duty to go there from time to time, and I am happy here with "Otome." Of course I *am* a little curious about Mrs. T.'s silence; but no doubt one of these days an explanation will come.

Asagao's state of mind makes me feel that the popular Buddhism of the day was a bit of a muddle. If she is so intent on making her peace with it, then surely this hideous concern for what people think runs against her purposes? And if she were to take the opposite position, tell them all to go to hell, and seek to sever all bonds with the world, then she would be up against another contradiction. If all bonds are equally reprehensible, then how does one discriminate between the good and the bad? Shinran's radical answer came later. Not that I can be sure that my understanding of Shinran is very solid. We are hearing a great deal about him these days – it is his eighth centennial. One may wonder whether, making so much of a religious anniversary, the Japanese are really as indifferent to religion as we are always told they are.

The scene in which Yūgiri's grandmother thinks he should get a promotion and Genji thinks he should go to the university is rather wonderful. I think that for the first time, and we are already a third or so of the way through the story, I really like Genji. The use of the expression *Yamato damashii** is very interesting. It seems to mean almost the opposite of what it came to mean in later centuries, suggesting common sense and moderation and flexibility. This moderation and later extremism had in common, however, a tendency to put little emphasis on the intellectual.

Saturday, April 21: I wonder if the Japanese who took the Jewish pseudonym and wrote the great best-seller about the Japanese and the Jews had anything to say about the Japanese mama.** She is eternal, and Princess Omiya is perhaps the earliest evocation of her. Smothering her brood with affection while she seeks to run their lives for them, she could be the matriarch in any tenement or any farmhouse (if all the young ones have not yet deserted her) today. How much more convincing she is, too, than the tempestuously sobbing Kabuki mother or her heir in the "mother-thing" movies,† or the silent mother of the Nō. Yes, Murasaki was essentially a moderate and a pragmatist and a realist, avoiding stylization and extremes. And she did far more with her matron than did her predecessors in the tenth century.

In the late afternoon (it was a gray afternoon), my former student Sakaguchi took me to see a well-known garden, possession of an obstetrician, on the rise east of the Kōrakuen. The district was not bombed, and where it has not been laid waste by the apartment-house builders it still has some old-style student dormitories with brown lattice fronts, and some fine trees, including a camphor under the protection of the government (will the government be able to protect it from the builders?). It was a Kyoto moss garden, of a sort I had not known existed in Tokyo, utterly soft and green and

* "The Japanese spirit."
** I. Ben-Dasan, *The Japanese and the Jews* (Tokyo, 1972).
† There is a category of sentimental motion pictures called *hahamono*, "mother thing." See Donald Richie, *Japanese Cinema* (London, 1971).

quiet, complete with tea cottages; even the traffic noises outside seemed to withdraw. Very beautiful, and yet somehow oppressive and tomblike. I thought again, as I have often thought while viewing a Samurai movie, that the Tokugawa period for which people feel so nostalgic – the period that for practical purposes built Kyoto and all that quiet beauty at almost the speed of sound – was a dark and gloomy time. The house is Taishō, with deep eaves and wide verandas and time-darkened wood. It made me think of the house I occupied in Maruyama-chō in the early fifties, and the memory too was somewhat oppressive. I may have been entranced with shadows and mildew when I was young, but now I prefer sunniness and openness.

Tuesday, April 24: It threatened rain through much of the day, and in the evening it did rain – and so, as we shall see, added to the excitement of a very exciting conclusion to a day.

I moved briskly ahead with "Otome," on the whole a rather happy and uncomplicated chapter, despite Yūgiri's unhappiness – one rather smiles at it. He seems to be almost as resolutely ignored by his father as Kaoru by his reputed father, and yet how different the results. Part of the difference may have come from the fact that Kaoru did not have much by way of a mother either, whereas Yūgiri had that massive mama, Princess Omiya. One may imagine that Japanese men were over-mothered then as now.

A couple of hours with the Kanda bookstores, and then on to a reception for the Shermans, soon to leave. I returned by subway, and had a look around Ueno station. Everything seemed quiet, though disturbances up the line had stopped some trains.* I went to the Suehiro for a bedtime beer, and there learned from the telly that there were disturbances at Ueno as well. So I hastened to the station to observe. It was by then raining fairly briskly. When I got to the station the riot police, some four busloads of them, were going up the stairs to the Yamate and Keihin tracks. Then they came back and went instead to the main south entrance.

* There is always a rail strike at about this time of the year.

I followed close behind them. The rank and file seemed like perfectly nice boys, but the leaders were not at all pleasant to look at.

Things were going on in the main concourse. As the riot police approached they were met with a rain of bottles and rocks. The metal doors were half lowered and the lines were drawn just outside, the police neither advancing nor retreating, the mob demanding that they go home and screaming abuse at them. I was at first on the side of the police, who as in 1960 were most wonderfully silent and in control of their tempers; but at least some members of the mob were genuinely angry, and had every right to be, for by then no trains were running and it was raining very hard. Numbers of them had fists and pockets full of tickets and stamps and seals. I ran in and got a few myself. The newspaper reporters seemed as unpopular as the police. The *Asahi* man, rather young and too vociferous for his own good, seemed particularly unpopular.

Presently the police did withdraw, and the doors were closed all the way. Gangs of thugs, obviously too late for the real fun, sought without success to kick them down. A pleasant man named Arai, deprived of his ride back home, invited me to go for a beer at a place run by his sister-in-law. He too had a pocketful of tickets (the floor of the station was ankle-deep in such things) – lovely souvenirs of a most exciting time. No doubt the papers will tell us of popular rage at the wicked system. There was rage, to be sure, but I suspect that a good part of the mob was enjoying the excitement as much as I was.

The riot-squad buses were departing, sirens wide open, as I came back around the lake. There must have been disturbances at other stations, and it seems most unlikely that Shinjuku would have allowed itself to be left out of such events. The night continues to be filled with sirens. It is like the night of the assumption into heaven of Kamba Michiko.* The chief difference is that I felt threatened then, and I do not now. Nor do I feel in the least bit responsible, and I suppose I did, in a confused way, then.

* At the grand climax of the rioting of 1960.

Friday, April 27: The first chapter of "Wakana"[34] moves ahead, so rapidly as to make me a bit uneasy, for a highly specialized reason. We are concerned with the future of His Retired Majesty's own beloved daughter, and so the honorifics in the original are something to behold. The result is that relatively larger amounts of the original can be encompassed in fewer words of English. If I am right in thinking that rhythm and tempo should be matters of prime concern in a translation, then there is cause here for very considerable concern indeed. I am of course always transferring Genji and his cohorts into a world that moves at a different pace from their own; but here the change is more radical than usual. Should I seek ways to slow down the pace of the translation? If so, what should they be? Blessed if I know. I could be merely wordy – but that would not be right, since the original is not wordy but elaborate and ceremonious.

Perhaps more so than in any other section I have done, I was aware, when I began reading Mrs. Enchi's "Wakana," of a certain solemn elegance in the slowness of the pace, the endlessness of the speeches; but since it was the first passage of her translation I had read, I was not aware how much, in this respect, "Wakana" might stand out from other chapters.

To the bank in the afternoon, for to get me some cash. My, how the money rolls out – seems only yesterday that I was last in the bank getting me some cash. I have had no extraordinary expenses, and so maybe seventy thousand a week, or at the current exchange rate well over two hundred dollars, has gone into quite ordinary expenses. Exclusive of rent and utilities, which would not be included in this either, I doubt that I spend fifty dollars a week in Ann Arbor. Even if I were to go out every night in Ann Arbor, as I do here, I doubt that I would spend more than a hundred a week.

Late in the afternoon I went with Fukuda to look at the azaleas in the Nezu Shrine. They certainly are in noisy bloom, magentas and reds screaming at one another. It is not a good idea to plant several varieties of azalea side by side – they do not get along. The grounds of the Nezu Shrine are wide and well wooded, however, and we came upon things of great beauty in this and that corner: a wisteria trailing a mist of the most delicate lavender down over an oak; a *karatachi** coming into its trefoil leafing with the most wonderful geometric precision; a tangle of lush Musashi grasses, spared thus far by the automobile and the developers.

Then we wandered through Nezu and back to Ueno. It is an interesting district, a place from another day, a place of cluttered little secondhand shops, verandas lined with potted plants, ferns at eaves.

In the evening, off to Asakusa, where I looked in on one of the pornographic movie houses. The cruelty was perhaps more striking than the lubricity. The sadism was of an extreme sort that I was literally unable to watch. No one else seemed to suffer from this disability; everyone seemed enthralled.

It was an all-night movie, and I went to sleep; and when I awoke and came out at about two, it was to find that Asakusa takes on strange new life in the small hours. Nocturnal creatures roam its streets, offering themselves for sale, wares to suit every taste. It seemed a great pity that I was not more wakeful and energetic.

Sunday, April 29: A warm, summery sort of Sunday. 'Tis the emp's birthday, and the beginning of the Golden Week holiday. I am no part of "Goruden Wiiku," but I observed the day all the same by spending a good part of it going around and admiring our metropolis.

But before I did that I got through my quota of "Wakana." Good stuff, full of most admirable things, chief among them the stateliness of the language, which of course I despair of putting into English. How nice it is of these courtiers to defer absolutely to the wishes of an emperor whom they have at their mercy. Tō no Chūjō has Suzaku begging for little favors, but he grants them all, including the silly business of tying the apron strings, without a murmur of protest. It is what is known as civility, the highest of civilized virtues, and it is no accident that "civility" and "civilization" should share a common root. It is what young people will not understand. The young Australian at the Rabinowitzes' the other night was very

* *Citrus trifoliata.*

nice, but he displeased me there for a minute. He said that the British royal family was for the Australians an empty symbol which should be done away with. I said to myself: it is when symbols are objects of respect and deference demanding nothing but these things of you that they should be the most treasured. But I did not say it aloud.

In midafternoon I set out to call upon the wisteria at Kameido, neglected for maybe a decade or two. I first walked around Shinobazu Pond. If you stand a bit back from it, so that the reflection of the sky hides the dark green of the water, it is beautiful on a sunny April day. The first lotus pads have come to the surface, and to the north, over by the defunct restaurant (wherein seems to lie a scandal the details of which I have not thus far succeeded in apprehending), the new growth of reeds is rising; and in both cases, last year's growth still stands above, so there is a mist of old gold over the mist of new green.

Kameido was crowded with people and wisteria, the latter maybe just a little past their prime, a translucent awning of white and lavender spread all over the grounds of the shrine. Alas, there are azaleas too, quarrelsome creatures, which one must try to pay no attention to. An azalea is like a blue jay, handsome enough by itself, but noisily at odds with everything else in sight.

Monday, April 30: Another splendid day, to bring an end to April. I moved briskly ahead with "Wakana," in spite of interruptions and forebodings. The forebodings come from the knowledge that the report on the celebration surrounding Genji's entry into his fortieth year lies just ahead.

What exactly has Murasaki's view of her own position been? By no means as clear, one would imagine, as Waley would have it. She should certainly have confidence in her lineage, and the indications are that until the advent of the Third Princess she has thought herself the head of Genji's household.

In the late afternoon, to take advantage of the long, sunny spring day, I went for a long and on the whole interesting and rewarding walk: through Sanya and on to the river at Hashiba, and thence across Whitebeard Bridge and here and there through what used to be Terajima, and back to Ueno by bus.

It would seem that Sanya is quietly being left behind by the times. It may no longer even deserve to call itself the most interesting and turbulent slum in the city. The old denizens are growing older, and a new generation does not seem to be coming along to keep it vital and noisy. Most definitely it has a tired, aging look about it. The economic miracle seems to be taking care of its slums in a most sensible way, by outgrowing them.

Hashiba continues to be one of the better-preserved relics of the old city. It is a place of narrow lanes, meant for the rickshaw. Tiny houses with brown lattice fronts still line many of them – so superior, at least from the outside, to the stucco matchboxes that pass for plebeian housing in our own day. The street that once fronted on the river but does no more must have been very handsome indeed. There is still an imposing mansion, bearing the name Otani Yonejirō, and some of the shops still have mellow wood and heavy tile roofs.

And on the other side of the river, delight of delights, I found what I failed to find on earlier expeditions, the old Hatonomachi red-light district. It is no wonder I failed because the riverfront, from which I used to approach, has become a concrete jungle. As I turned right from Whitebeard Bridge, however, I found myself at the Whitebeard Shrine, and knew exactly where I was, on the street that once followed the embankment. It does no more, for the river is way over there behind factories and the expressway. The old main street of the quarter, miraculously, has been preserved almost intact. The gaudy tile fronts are as always, and here and there a stenciled "off limits" sign remains from a quarter of a century ago. It ought to be designated an important cultural property, though I doubt that any of our righteous newspapers could be persuaded to join a crusade to designate it so. I wandered nostalgically up and down for a time, and then stepped into one of the old tile-fronted bars, hoping to learn things from the bartender; but he proved to be young and recently in from the country, and did not know a great deal, save that the area is rather short on prostitutes these days.

Friday, May 4: I am to address a discussion group on my important work with and my profound insights into the *Genji*, and think my point of reference will be the intersection of the *Genji* and the *Heike*, the former representative of the common sense that keeps fanaticism from finally having its destructive way in Japan, and the latter representative of the medieval and modern romantic fanaticism which would as soon destroy everything to prove that it is right. One sees the contrast in the treatment of women: the *Heike* woman enjoys being knocked down and trampled on, sheds happy tears, and will do almost anything to keep pure the image of patient suffering; while Murasaki Shikibu takes the more realistic view that a helpless woman is in a pretty sad position and cannot be expected to enjoy it.

I am at the halfway mark in the first "Wakana" chapter. Murasaki was a great master, and her ability to see into human beings and report upon what she has seen is uncanny. We have admitted it, and praised her for it, often enough. Yet she lived in a society that in a way made things easy for writers of fiction. People who were really worth writing about saw each other only in pairs, and so dialogue need be no more than just that, converse between two. She did not have to try pulling off the difficult thing that Compton-Burnett achieved so triumphantly, keeping individuals separated as individuals even when the conversation is five- or six-sided. When more than two are together in the *Genji*, they are usually of different rank, and so one of them dominates the conversation and the others need be little more than sounding boards.

Perhaps it is the persistence of the limitations which served Murasaki Shikibu so well that makes the modern Japanese novel seem, sometimes, so thin. Kawabata rarely has more than two characters together at one time (and that is why the New Year's breakfast in *The Sound of the Mountain* is so memorable). When Mishima tells us that Tōru, for instance, has school friends, the fact that he does not introduce them emphasizes the essential isolation in which he preferred to keep his characters. When three characters are met together it is as in the *Genji*, one of them is of a higher rank and does all the talking. Prince Tōin lectures to Isao and the lieutenant in *Runaway Horses*, and when Isao does venture to speak he sounds utterly fatuous. (And remember how fatuous they *all* seem when, as in *Kyōko's House*, there are attempts at many-sided conversation among equals.)

I have compared the essential loneliness of the archetypal American fictional hero with that of the modern Japanese fictional hero. In the one case it is because society has not yet come into being, in the other because an old tradition and old conventions still weigh heavily. In the one case geography keeps people apart, in the other the pigeonholes into which people are thrust by tradition.

Sunday, May 13: A lovely old Mother's Day, though there was rain towards the end of it. The afternoon sky, with distant thunderheads, had very much the look of summer about it.

Yesterday I proceeded effortlessly through the climactic scene at the bottom of the first part of "Wakana," the pussycat scene. I kept thinking of Kawabata and Mishima. Kashiwagi's only *real* reason for wanting the Third Princess so desperately is that he cannot have her. Mishima said that for Kawabata the cult of the unblemished maiden was the pursuit of the unattainable, and Mishima's efforts to make himself over as a muscle man and a man of action were very much the same thing.

What a pretty series of tableaus the scene is: the handsome young men with their caps all askew under the cherry blossoms, the little princess and her silly women all agog over the kitten. That tragedy should arise from such idyllic innocence makes the tragedy seem not blacker, perhaps, but, well, more unfair, crueler, harder on the innocent.

Along the way I learned, and was happy to learn, that *kemari* was not just an idiotic kicking away at a ball. It was supposed to get more difficult as the ball went the rounds. I was also happy to learn that the Heian nobility did not, apparently, take *kemari* as seriously as in later centuries Mishima's Ayakura family was to take it.

And today I finished the first part of "Wakana." There is no reason at all to have the break between the two chapters come where it does, save that it is at about the halfway point. One has no feeling at all that Murasaki Shikibu thought herself at the end of a chapter. Indeed with the episode of the cat, which is broken in two, she seems to be finding her stride, and so taken with what she is doing that the concept "chapter" has left her. It is interesting (perhaps) to note that Waley includes the whole of the cat episode in his first chapter, and then, skipping over the Makibashira episode (perhaps because he does not have a name for the girl whom the Japanese call Makibashira), begins the second with Reizei's (Ryōzen's, says Waley) abdication.

Part of the morning I spent listening to Mrs. Nakajima, who came in to clean. I learned that she was born just down the hill from my old Koishikawa house and lived there until the war. She allowed as how her family may have belonged to the radical printers' union. She remembers nothing of it, however, and has all her grown years been an extremely conservative person. In more ways than one. She rarely ventures down the hill to the lake, and asked me if it is true that they built an aquarium there a few years ago (in fact it has been there for years and years).

In the afternoon I set out to pay my carpenter. His bill for my new shelves came to about ¥125,000. Of this less than a third was for materials, in which fact should be a small whisper of an answer to all the screams in the newspapers about hoarding and cornering the market as causes of our inflation. Anyway, I found his house and shop over in a fine old-fashioned part of Negishi, just the sort of place one likes to have one's artisans come from. He was not at home, and his wife greeted me with as much hostility and suspicion as if she had been a member of a remote hill tribe and I an inquiring anthropologist, but she smiled prettily when I identified myself as the alien person from the "mansion," and I was allowed to pay my bill.

Then I wandered in and out of graveyards – what a serene and inviting place a Japanese graveyard is. It occurred to me that I have a certain affinity with them.

On to Roppongi, to attend a reception for the Royal Shakespeareans, who are playing somewhere in town. There was a demonstration all along the street from Roppongi to Akasaka. It was mostly teachers who were demonstrating, and their aim was announced as the destruction of the Tanaka government, and their strident shouts and red banners under a lowering sky seemed very ominous, as though a long day might be giving way to a longer night. The female shouts – screams would be a better word – were especially awful. I thought of what Lee Chia said last night at the Press Club. He thinks of leaving Japan and moving on to Southeast Asia, because the Japanese game is up. The fiasco of election reform means the beginning of the end for the conservatives. In four or five years, he thinks, we will have a coalition government which will be transitional to a Communist government.

The party itself was delightful. Half the Shakespeareans were elegantly British, and the other half were in blue jeans and beads. I shall not try to begin naming all the charming and interesting people I saw. Perhaps the most charming and interesting of all was a shaven-headed lady named Rokujō, who is abbess of the Daimyōji in Osaka. Her real profession, she says, is housecleaning. She considers it her calling as a nun to keep the temple clean, which seems a most pleasant mating of Shinto and Buddhism.

Tuesday, May 22: I moved easily ahead with the bottom half of "Wakana."[35] One is sometimes made aware of something important about a novel by all of a sudden seeing what is missing. To be told that Tōru has friends and to have no glimpse of them made me see what a non-social sort of novelist Mishima was; and now to be told all of a sudden that the men of the Rokujō house are off at Nijō makes me see how completely feminine is Murasaki Shikibu's world. Where have all the men been keeping themselves? They must have been somewhere on the premises all the time, but we have had not a glimpse of them.

Professor Anzai said the other day that it is with Murasaki Shikibu as with Shakespeare, there is a growing abstraction, a doing without concrete details, towards the end of the career. I see what he means, and think he is right as I compare the Third Princess with Ukifune. The Third Princess is now having her moment of agony, but she does not seem as completely alone, faced with a terrifying destiny, as Ukifune. She has particular attributes, her girlishness, her talent as a musician, to make her seem like one of us. Ukifune has only her calligraphy, the most remote and esoteric of the arts, calculated rather more, at least as we have it from the hands of the Japanese, to interfere with than to promote communication. And the Third Princess has protectors, and the moment passes without doing her really grievous injury.

The evening with Tsuruta Kinya, soon to be of the University of British Columbia. We had *sushi* at the Kiraku (sixty-eight hundred yen, more than twenty-five dollars, as things go these days), and then rich ice-cream concoctions elsewhere. As we were about to leave the Kiraku, which was closing, a man came in and asked to be fed. A Korean, said Tsuruta. How did he know, said I. By the insistence, said he.

Saturday, June 2: Today I came to the end of "Wakana," and was much relieved to see, despite what memory had told me from as recently as my reading of the Enchi *Genji*, that I did not have to make my way through Suzaku's jubilee; only the rehearsals. I like the jubileeless ending. It leaves the destruction of Kashiwagi in the foreground. We move sadly into the last chapters, knowing that he has nothing to do but die.

And now, because of the accident that it is the earliest untouched chapter for which I have a library of commentaries assembled, I move back a few chapters, to "Miyuki."[29] A lot more things in "Miyuki" than in the bottom half of "Wakana" seem to impel the commentators to speak. Is it that the crisis in "Wakana" means a certain stripping away of decorations, and so there is less that even the most verbose of commentators finds an excuse for commenting upon? I have never much liked the Tamakazura sequence, centering upon a dry career-maker, the sort of woman who in our day would be earning lots of money leading a movement; and I doubt that I am going to like it this time around either.

Monday, June 4: Yesterday's languorous irritation went away, and I worked hard on "Miyuki." Genji's revelation of the Tamakazura matter to her grandmother is so very circumspect that one wonders how she ever managed to guess. Translate it literally into English or modern Japanese, and there would be scarcely a clue. Verbal communication is an exceedingly marvelous and mysterious business, and there is no reason to hold that one sort need be the only one; and so perhaps they were able to make themselves understood by evasive little clues such as fail to have an effect upon our more emphatic minds. Perhaps not all men over the ages have been brothers. They were different from us, not to the extent that a cat taking its clues through the eyes is different from a dog taking its clues through the nose, but different all the same.

Monday, June 11: I appeared not once but twice this morning in the nation's press, in both of its languages, Japanese in the *Tokyo Shimbun*, English in the *Nippy Times*. Mrs. Kenrick's interview in the latter is pleasant and friendly and accurate, but my passport picture looks horrible up there at the top of the page, all growling and snarly. The picture in the *Tokyo Shimbun* is good, and that interview too is friendly enough, but not in sum very pleasing. I am treated as a cute, amusing, eccentric alien from across the sea, and my attitude towards the Kagiya, our main subject, is made to seem condescending. The description of the drinking place in question is downright inaccurate, and yet the reporter must have gone for a look at it, for he took a picture of it. Seeing how the newspapers seem not to think twice about distorting fact, one wonders about their claim to special grace.

I moved ahead with "Fujibakama."[30] To my considerable surprise, for she has always been my least favorite she-character, I find that I am beginning to like Tamakazura. I like the solidity and efficiency with which she arranges her life. I suppose the truth is that as I grow older I like the sane, businesslike ones more and more, and more and more distrust the romantics. The latter may be all right in a novel, but they are not the sort one would wish one's sister to marry; and it is pleasing to have in a novel sometimes a character one would not at all mind seeing one's sister married to: Yūgiri or, if one's sister happened to be a man, Tamakazura.

Tuesday, June 12: The flowers of high summer are with us. Both my hibiscus, which makes me impatient for Honolulu, and my *kikyō*, my *Platycodon grandiflorum*, which makes me think of Bon, are coming into bloom.

I moved vigorously into "Makibashira."[31] Twice in succession, now, things of considerable moment have been made to happen on blank pages between chapters: the death of Princess Omiya between "Miyuki" and "Fujibakama," and the successful conclusion to Higekuro's suit between "Fujibakama" and "Makibashira." The former is easier to accept than the latter, and the way in which Murasaki Shikibu keeps us wondering for a time who the successful suitor might have been does not really seem worthy of the grand lady. On the whole she resists such trickery, however. Think of what someone like Bakin, interested chiefly in narrative gimmickry, would have made of the twist of events in which Tamakazura finds herself with a new set of brothers. Murasaki Shikibu makes very little of it. She is interested chiefly in human beings. I suppose it is as well that we do not learn precisely how Higekuro managed to have his way, for now the canny Tamakazura can pretend before us her readership as before everyone else that *she* had nothing to do with the matter, it was all the fault of that awful woman.

In the evening, to the National Theater to witness the opening night of Fukuda Tsuneari's *Tempest*. He had his actors talk at a fearful rate, I presume so that he can keep up with the original (he has complained of how sluggishly his Shakespeare productions go), and

I soon gave up trying to follow the words and instead watched abstractly, as I might watch a pantomime, or listen to music; and it came to seem that the play belonged to Caliban, and that Prospero and the others were mere adjuncts. I found myself saying somewhat grumpily to myself: he is *my* Shakespeare and not theirs. Rather an inappropriate thought, I know, for a person who is seeking to make their Murasaki Shikibu his.

Thursday, June 14: The last interview, in "Makibashira," between Higekuro and his insane wife is marvelously done. The woman's quiet bitterness moves effortlessly into English. Higekuro really is a bit of an ass, and Murasaki Shikibu does not need to tell us so, and for the most part is wise enough to let us have his words and acts without comment. He is, like Yūgiri, a good politician, a man of affairs, and not so very much concerned with polite accomplishments; but a subtle touch here, a delicate stroke there, and Yūgiri emerges as altogether the more likeable of the two – perhaps because, with a canny eye always turned on others, he seems so much the less self-centered.

Yes, I am enjoying the Tamakazura sequence more than I expected to.

In the late afternoon I went walking east of the river. The canal up which Kafū sent his couple in search of peonies* has a freeway running over it, and, though there are still pretty little gardens in secluded corners, I found the walk depressing. I took a bus to Asakusa, where I could think of nothing better to do, so unexciting is Asakusa these days, than have myself a sauna.

Friday, June 22: The heavy days of summer have come. The skies have been gray, the air still and sticky.

The morning and early afternoon went into reading the chapters of the *Genji* I have done since my arrival in Tokyo. There certainly are a lot of heavy dull pages, and I may congratulate myself, and ab-

* In "The Peony Garden."

stinence, on what a prolific three months it has been. And not really as heavy and dull as I might have feared. The conversational passages have a certain amount of spirit in them, and some of the natural description is rather nice too. The trouble is with the description of persons and of emotions. I do not know what can be done about the former, except to give it as few words as possible – and some of the latter will, I think, simply go, especially when it is obvious or bathetic. If anyone notices, I can perhaps justify both sorts of deletion on the grounds that the proper equivalent for some Heian words is tasteful modern-English silence.

In midafternoon I went on an expedition with Fukuda, a walk up the Edo River and from Shibamata to Kanamachi. The river was roiled by a south wind, far enough from the bay not to be noxious and near enough to be briny, and larks were trilling madly overhead and making their mad ascents and descents, and one could have romantic thoughts about the green far shore, where dwelt those eight dogs of Bakin's.*

From Kanamachi we took a bus back to Asakusa. Kanamachi is already decorating itself for Tanabata,** and when one's stay is drawing to a close one does not like having the seasons so rudely forced.

Monday, June 25: Six months till Christmas.

I got back to the old work of producing a first draft, commencing with "Umegae."[32] Had I remembered the sort of chapter it is, full of hyperrefined doings, I think I might have chosen not to interrupt myself but to charge through it before I read over those other chapters. I did not do too badly, however, perhaps because all the perfume-sniffing seemed rather comical. Can any pursuit be less fruitful, so to speak, than the development of a fine nose?

Speaking of scents: in the new instructions on how we should comport ourselves in this our Shūwa Residence is an admonition that we refrain from farting in the elevator.

Down to the spicy lotus breezes to await Bill Sibley. He arrived

* In his *Hakkenden*, a very long romance of the nineteenth century.
** The Star Festival, on July 7.

just as I was about to be propositioned by a tart. We (Bill and I, not the tart) went and had a beer nearby.

Tuesday, June 26: I worked on "Umegae" again, and did not find all the sniffing and scribbling as maddening as I might have expected. The descriptions of actual specimens of calligraphy, from the hands of old emperors, are fascinating, for one feels sure that Murasaki Shikibu saw them, off in someone's apartments. Probably they were lost when someone's apartments burned down. In view of the clutter which Heian living quarters must have been, the mind quite boggles at the thought of the sheer mass of things lost.

In an abstract way, I think I can see the point to the calligraphic theories. What is wanted is discipline with sufficient deviation from the prototype to establish the individual. It is what we wish in literature too, no doubt. I have been reading Kawabata's Asakusa stories, and finding them not on the whole pleasing and indeed rather annoying, because Kawabata sounds less like Kawabata than Saikaku or Higuchi Ichiyō or maybe a writer of Edo *sharebon*. With *Snow Country* he starts sounding like Kawabata.

Returning home from a dinner with Ted Cohen, by way of the lake, I was accosted by what the warning signs characterize as an *ikagawashii mono* – a "shady character." He wished money. I dragged him to the police box below the park, and we were escorted thence in luxury, a police car for him and one for me, to the Ueno police station. The police gentlemen were as sweet as they could be. They said they thought the provocation insufficient for taking him to court, but they would certainly reprimand him, and see that his employer, a dealer in electronic devices, was informed of his misconduct and enjoined to guard against repetition.

Saturday, June 30: Yesterday I lost a tooth. The incisor which Dr. Clouser, who later killed himself with drink, killed for me some forty years ago, and which has caused endless trouble, and endless discussions with this and that dentist as to whether it should be removed or root-channeled or something, quietly fell out, leaving no scars and drawing no blood and causing no pain. I said to myself, well, that is that and I am glad, and why all the fuss over the years. I wonder if one might not feel rather the same upon dying and seeing not a small blackened tooth but one's whole ugly fetid body go.

Then I worked on "Fuji no uraba."[33] Happy happenings, chief among them, of course, Yūgiri's receipt into Tō no Chūjō's family and delivery into the arms of Wild Goose up in the Clouds, all done with great elegance and circumspection, abstruse poetic references flying like mad, and no one failing to field a single one of them other than expertly. We have lost, in our own day, the ability to write of a happy scene. All must be black with despair or sniffy with derision – the legacy of the romantic movement, which led us to take our imperfectibility too seriously.

Funny thing this morning. As I read over the pages of "Fuji no uraba" that I proposed to do a rough draft of, I found myself getting terribly irritated, so full did they seem of unnecessary poetic allusions. Then as I did the draft itself I found myself charmed. They did not seem unnecessary at all, but wonderfully civilized, rather, making of a deflowering something very elegant in its adherence to forms; and even the hyperbolic terms seemed charming. I love the image of Yūgiri wringing his sleeves until his arms go numb. Maybe it is just that I like everything about Yūgiri, who turns hyperbole into sunny common sense. A big difference between my *Genji* and Waley's will have to do with his Yūgiri, a stuffed shirt largely of his creating, and mine, the incarnation of sunny common sense. Mine is surely the nearer to Murasaki Shikibu's.

To Asakusa in the evening, to see the second installment of the garden fair. There were hydrangeas everywhere last month; this month the things of high summer, *kikyō* and *tsukimisō** (always making me think of silvery June nights in Korea), are predominant. I bought my summer's supply of morning glories.

Thursday, July 5: I move swimmingly ahead with "Tamakazura"[22] –

* *Oenothera tetraptera.*

I pursue her across the waters, even as does that awful person from Kumamoto. I had always thought, in retrospect, that it was from Fukuoka that she fled, but no, it was from that loveliest of ports, Karatsu. Murasaki Shikibu seems to have had but a rough notion of the geography of Kyushu. The Kumamoto person goes back to Kumamoto and then, on a moment's notice, appears in Karatsu to take up the pursuit. Way off down there in Kyushu, one province is very much like another.

It was I, let the fact be recorded for history, who occupied Karatsu, back in 1945. I wonder whatever became of the sad Englishman whose Japanese wife lay dying and who could not tell her how sorry he was, because he did not speak her language. My occupation of Karatsu took place a very long time ago.

Down to the Imperial in the afternoon to have a cup of coffee with Sol Sanders, who has given up the Chinese University of Hong Kong and is going back to the United States to be of service to some consulting organization in Washington. He is saying good-bye to half a lifetime of work in this part of the world, and he has no notion what it has done for him or he for it. Of Hong Kong, he says that it is insane: the Communists have become the most ardent imperialists, wishing to keep it exactly as it is, and the British administration is "the dregs of empire" – which he wishes to make the title of a book some day.

Having an evening to myself, I spent it wandering around Ueno. The lotuses, most powerful symbol of high summer, are coming into bloom. In a month I will be gone. I sometimes seem to tire of Tokyo and its frantic stir; but I regret the passing of each Tokyo day, the dwindling supply of Tokyo days, all the same.

Saturday, July 7: I rushed ahead through "Tamakazura," and, with the help of Kannon, arranged a meeting between Tamakazura and her mother's lady Ukon. It is very fine that people can be so grateful to Kannon, or whoever, and have no feelings of anger, as we post-Christians might, that there had to be a separation in the first place. To look upon suffering as the results of one's own wrongdoing, and be grateful for alleviation: that is what civilization is grounded upon. To blame even the wrongdoing upon some other power, maybe a god, maybe society, maybe one's parents: that is the beginning of the end.

In any event, I worked with much efficiency upon "Tamakazura." Fukuda says that my energy is due to the prunes and apricots I feed myself each morning.

To a bookfair in Asakusa in the afternoon. On the theory that prices are going to rise and rise, since they have never gone the other way, I bought several hundred dollars' worth of Meiji things. Fukuda was with me, very disapproving. He thinks I should give the money to worthy and needy persons, such as Fukuda.

In the evening I had a brush with Tokyo high society: a concert and a showing of a movie about Zeami. There was a party between the two. The Japanese on such occasions certainly are not very helpful. They talk to one another, and cold-shoulder the blue-eyed outsider. It is hard, in such circumstances, to wish them well – indeed one begins wishing one had a few more things like soybeans to deprive them of. I nodded my greetings to the actress Tsukasa Yōko and Prince Mikasa. And comforted myself afterwards at this and that friendly place in Ueno.

Saturday, July 14: The news in the papers is good. The Tokyo electorate had the great good sense to vote against the Socialists, and our grinning governor says that it is a time for sincere self-reflection.

In the morning and on into the afternoon I pushed my way ahead to very nearly the end of "Hatsune."[23] I do not have the feeling I sometimes have elsewhere in the *Genji* that Murasaki Shikibu does not know where she is going. There is an almost unbearable amount of happiness, of course, an amount such as to put us of the twentieth century on our guard; but what it amounts to is preserving the moment. Hot days and dark days lie ahead, and when they come it will be important to have stored up in memory a gentle spring day or two.

To the Kōrakuen in the evening to observe the kick boxing. The

Japanese are clearly better at it than the Thais, but one feels somehow that they are missing the point, and perhaps discarding something good in their own tradition, in their determination to win. To the Thais the manner of administering the blow would seem to be as important as whether it is a telling one or not; and so of course it has in the past been with the Japanese when they have lifted a longbow or slapped down a Go stone. It is a pretty savage business, in any case. There were several knockouts, but none by Thais.

Afterwards several of us, Herb Passin and others, went to a Korean restaurant and a club in Shinjuku, guests of a very pleasant gentleman named Hirota, who owns a kick-boxing gym. There were some foreign hostesses in the club, one of them a sweet little girl from North Dakota, who wanted only to discuss her Siamese pussycats. The Japanese hostesses kept asking what it was she was talking about, and it seemed best to be enigmatic.

Monday, July 16: I sometimes think that my Colorado relatives would be a little less unhappy if they paid some attention to the first call of the meadowlark, or the first Indian paintbrush to come into bloom. I wonder whether the Indians noticed. I doubt that the first European settlers did, and that may be among the things that are wrong with us. Here in our Tokyo, the summer days are dreadful, but they have their little delights. Each evening when I come home there are cool little *tsukimisō* moonflowers to greet me, and I know that they will be there all through the night, and the knowledge somehow makes me sleep better. And when I awake there are my bell bugs, just a-singing away and a-singing away.

I am enjoying "Kochō"[24] more than I remember having enjoyed it under Waley's auspices, Genji going over Tamakazura's letters and offering paternal advice and generally having a great time over the ridiculous situation he has created. But why does he not express himself more clearly? It is really very difficult to believe that Ukon understands all these instructions so deviously given, and amounting in the end to something like an order to do nothing at all. One suspects that Ukon, and Murasaki's original audience as well, merely caught the general drift, and really did not wish things to be too explicit. So too with the poems. It was enough to know that this was a poem of frustration, that a cry of longing, the other a twitting for an insensitive failure to catch the signals.

In the morning a gentleman who writes a column for the *Asahi* called with an interesting question: why have the Japanese always been so little interested in the stars? I could not answer, save to say that I had been aware of the fact, and that it has very long been the case that the things which seem to the Japanese most Japanese have been foggy, inchoate things and not clear, sparkling things.

In the evening I went for a leisurely walk with Fukuda from Dangozaka through Yanaka to Nippori. He was wearing *yukata* and looked very handsome, but he complained a great deal, that he was hot, that he was itchy, that his feet hurt, that he felt as if he were coming to pieces. We looked in upon several temples, heavy with summer grasses and the shrilling of cicadas, and thought how good it would be to live in a quiet cemetery off in Yanaka, away from the growl of the city. In one temple an assembly, mostly of middle-aged men, was sitting in solemn meditation. What did he think they were meditating upon, I asked Fukuda. How many times they were going to do it tonight, he replied. Over near Nippori station, just outside the big cemetery, there is a fine ruinous old building that may once have been an inn, and is now dark and uninhabited. I tried to get Fukuda to make inquiry as to whether it might be for rent, but he demurred, saying he did not wish to attract the attention of the police. That seemed a curiously old-fashioned excuse.

Wednesday, July 25: I read through the remainder of the chapters I have in first draft, a couple from early and a couple from late in the Tamakazura sequence, as well as the last two chapters in which Genji is still alive. No surprises, really – I felt things steadily improving. One of the messages of the whole huge story might be that sorrow ennobles. Genji, after he has had a few knocks, is vastly superior to Genji as he is sitting on top of the world and making things unpleasant for the helpless Tamakazura. And on the other hand Murasaki Shikibu is not actively distrustful of unhappiness, as are so many writers of our day. Happiness and its opposite are among the realities of this ephemeral world, though the opposite is perhaps the profounder, the more deeply real, of the two realities.

Tuesday, July 31: My moonflowers are outdoing themselves, killing themselves, I almost fear, to be of service. My solitary tomato has been cut and stuck into my favorite Korean vase, Yi blue and white, and it is as beautiful a piece of *ikebana* as I have ever produced, utterly sere and autumnal.

Genji is very fine indeed as he criticizes Tō no Chūjō's treatment of the Omi lady in that single brief sketch which is "Kagaribi."[27] We have often enough been asked to believe that he is a man of charity and sympathy, but now perhaps for the first time we actually see him as such. Perhaps we are at a great turning point: "Wakana" is a half dozen not very long chapters away, and it may be that we here begin to have foreshadowings.

It was only when I began working on Heian literature that I became aware that the moon sets early at the beginning of the cycle, and gradually later. In Colorado we scarcely noticed the moon. Indeed we scarcely noticed nature, save when it was being cruel, as when it hailed on us. We built our houses as if we hated it and wanted to keep it out of sight. I rather think that my mother, at least, did indeed hate her surroundings; hence our almost window-less living room, with its one prominent window behind the sofa. Had I been she I think I would have lost myself in gardening, using nature as a refuge from nature. She seems to have hated even that, and it was only upon my own insistence that a fence was put up to protect the lilacs from the sheep.

Honolulu Tuesday, August 7: The spell of Honolulu is such that already I am beginning to ask myself why I should ever go anywhere else. Why not just stay here, and hope that money will continue to mean a little something? And what a great effort it is, in these charmed surroundings, to sit down at a desk and stay there, and keep one's eye from wandering out to the terrace. I did this morning get a little done of what I have appointed to be my Hawaiian task, comparing such chapters of my first draft as I have with me against Waley. My chief impression of Waley, after having been away from him for so long, is that he is very wordy. He embroiders, of course, that we all know, but he embroiders with such a heavy stitch, reminding me of my maternal grandfather as he made us little ones fidget and look out the window from the lunch table. We have always excused Waley his liberties because, we have always said, he wrote such beautiful English, but I am not sure that it is all that beautiful.

Bill Malm and two of his girls came around in the afternoon, looking somewhat melancholy, for Joyce and the middle girl are in California, where, as Bill put it, Joyce's mother is dying of something terminal.

Dinner at Juanita Vitousek's, down on a moonlit beach beyond Diamond Head. No talk whatever of politics. Its absence made it a palpable presence. So I had my politics on TV when I had come back up the heights. Watergate once more. I am struck at how gentlemanly, how gentle, almost, the proceedings are compared to the McCarthy caper of my youth. The senators seem almost reluctant to touch upon painful truths.

Wednesday, August 8: This morning, after seeing to the needs of the botanical gardens that are mine, indoors and out, and meditating again for a few moments on what a magical thing is the tropical, I finally got down to work, comparing my first draft with Waley's last, beginning with "Asagao."[20] The time does not seem wasted, and this for a number of reasons: for one thing, Waley does catch me in occasional error, though he has not yet caught me in what I would describe as a real howler. But, most important, the boost to my morale is considerable. Though I mean to refrain from "improving" upon Murasaki, it should not be hard to improve upon Waley, in the direction of quietness and unobtrusiveness. Waley once said to Ivan

Morris, I think it was, that the translator, having taken so much away from his original, must add something by way of compensation. The principle is a dubious and dangerous one, and when what is added seems in dubious taste, why then things are dubious twice over. I take much courage from the thought that, though I am translating many things that Waley did not, there is a good possibility of ending up with fewer words than he.

There is a half-moon coming through the monkeypods. Save for the soughing – the right word, perhaps, though I have never been quite sure what it conveys – all is quiet. We seem to have no nocturnal birds, at least no vocal ones.

Saturday, August 18: Each little detail adds to my satisfaction with my Makiki pad. I noted how still the air was at Violet's last night, and how plentiful were the mosquitoes in her garden. I thought it must be a still, mosquito-filled night. But no – I was told that the few paces from here to there make a great difference. There is not as much wind, to keep away mosquitoes, on her side of the street.

I pushed ahead with the business of comparing Art Waley and me. I have elsewhere seen him creating a character of his own, and here he is doing it again, in the Tamakazura sequence, making of Kumo-inokari's nurse a "featherheaded" young thing. She is nothing of the sort in the original, but rather, as we get a brief glimpse of her, a strict and rather acerbic person – we do not, I think, even have evidence that she is young, and nurses tended to be at least as old as the mothers of their charges. Then there is the escape from Tsukushi: Waley makes it rather exciting, and leaves us in little doubt that the Higo person is in the smaller boat. In the original we have no more than a disquieting suspicion on the part of Tamakazura's party.

Waley does some wonderful things, all the same. His caricature of the Omi lady is much more amusing than Murasaki's. She but tells us that the lady talks too fast, and has her use a curious word or two, and Waley has her being garrulous and uncouth all over the place. He has her actually doing what Murasaki Shikibu only avers that she does, and so is, in this instance at least, the better writer of fiction. And what will I do? Be faithful to Murasaki even as she is performing inadequately?

Victoria Judd's wedding in the evening, at Punahou, that beautiful place whence comes – or at least used before statehood to come – everyone who is anyone in these islands. There is no doubt about it, Honolulu is something special. The flowers made a great difference. Victoria had a garland of little white native flowers called *pikake* or something like that, and some of the men had about their necks strands of a fragrant connubial vine called *maili*. It would be nice if in Colorado we had similar little vestiges of the aboriginal past, maybe a scalp hanging from the groom's neck.

Tuesday, August 21: I have taken to working on what the natives call my *lanai* – my porch, or terrace – from morning until, in mid-afternoon, the western sun, going down towards the Waianae Mountains, becomes too warm. I spend too much time watching the birds up in the monkeypods. Though I cannot distinguish individuals within species, as I could among my Tokyo pigeons, each species, plumage and size and shape quite aside, has its own traits. The Java sparrows are curious and seem to want to be friendly, the cardinals are hostile and cluck angrily from branches at a safe distance. The doves are like Tokyo pigeons, brash and importunate. That most amusing of birds, the mynah, used to frequent my tropical dell, but seems to no more.

Today I did most of "Fujibakama,"[30] comparing Waley and me. Of the chapters I have gone over since my arrival in Honolulu, it is the one in which Waley departs most radically from the original. He rewrites liberally, and he deletes the whole rather lengthy interview between Tamakazura and Yūgiri, and so, naturally, the poem whence comes the title, which he uses for the whole sequence down to Genji's final appearance. No one seems to have asked whence it came (and where, by the way, did he get "The Lady of the Boat"?). It sort of fills a person with chagrin, that he should have got by with so much.

Dinner at the Wiswells', on the beach at Waikiki. I had thought that few things could be lovelier than my sunset here on Makiki, but a thing is at least as lovely, a good sunset over Waikiki. Tonight's was especially radiant. The masts of the little boats danced and frolicked about in it, and Diamond Head turned rosy.

Wednesday, August 22: I had another very bad night, pains shooting, or rather creeping, all around my chest. I give them one more night, and then, most reluctantly, go to see a doctor – reluctantly because I foresee an endless series of tests, which will eat up the rest of my stay in, as they say, paradise.

Waley is said to have refused drugs as he lay dying of cancer. Pain, he said, is a small price to pay for being oneself. The minor amount of pain I have had these last days makes me sure that I would be capable of no such courage. If I knew it was something that would not go away, I would immediately be whimpering for drugs.

Whatever it is is much worse when I am reclining than when I am rampant. I got through the day with considerable uneasiness but not a fearsome amount of pain, and managed to get a good amount of "Makibashira"[31] done. The most interesting discrepancy today between Waley and Murasaki Shikibu comes when Murasaki's (the other Murasaki's) stepmother speaks her mind. Murasaki Shikibu has her railing at her husband about Genji, and Waley has her railing both at and about her husband. Is it that he made a mistake, or that Western wives tend to blame their husbands for everything, and he wished to make her more Western, a more approachable and familiar sort of termagant?

And then on to "Umegae."[32] Waley makes a most sensational cut, almost a third of a chapter, in which we are preparing for the advent of the Akashi girl into court, and do a lot of talking about calligraphy. I can see, I think, why he did it. The talk is complicated, and there is not a great deal one can say about calligraphy save that this piece is good and that bad. Yet it is interesting in its way, too, for we see the pride that is attendant upon the emergence of a distinctly Japanese way of writing. In most regards the old days were better than the new, but here, in the perfection of a calligraphy in which the Japanese sense of the passing moment has precedence over the Chinese concern with unchanging forms, the new day has the better of it.

To the Goyas' for dinner. They have moved to an apartment down near the beach and Fort De Russy. It is the fashion to lament the way the highrises have destroyed old Honolulu; but the view of all of them from high in one of them is very grand. They are clean and for the most part in good taste, and give one a sense of being in a far grander metropolis than Honolulu in fact is. Even the roar of the traffic contributes to the sense of vitality and metropolitanism.

Then we went to Kapiolani Park to watch some young people from Yaeyama in the outer Ryūkyūs perform Yaeyama dances. It was very fresh and good-natured and winning, and of course one is always pleased to see young people interested in preserving something of an old tradition. They were from all over, even such remote outposts as Hateruma and Yonaguni, where they used to make a practice of murdering the magistrates sent out from Shuri. Alas, however, the leaders of the group live in Tokyo, and one doubts that many of them will ever go back to Yaeyama.

Monday, August 27: I moved ahead with a draft of "Nowaki,"[28] and should have it finished before I move on across the Pacific. And then I will have the dark chapters to look forward to during the dark months.

Agnes Conrad, the state archivist, led us on a tour of the Iolani Palace, which is mostly closed for renovation. It is all stripped down, and one wonders how the gimcrackery can ever be reassembled again. I was a little disappointed to see that it is brick with stucco decorations – for some reason I had thought it to be wood. Miss Conrad told a very sweet story. On a recent anniversary of King Kalakaua's birthday a barefooted person succeeded in making his way past all the burglar alarms, and put leis on the king's portrait and on the bed of the one bedroom that has been restored, and made his way out again, taking nothing.

After lunch she took us through the archives, which are fascinating – a repository for anything that might have to do with the Hawaiian monarchy, much of it charming junk, medals and tureens and the like, for there is no museum competent to house such things. Unique among the states, Hawaii has in its archives a treaty section, in a trunk. We saw an 1871 treaty with Japan signed by Emperor Meiji himself, and the X that is the only known specimen of Kamehameha's "signature," and the instrument of Liliuokalani's abdication, and the original of "Aloha Oe," and all manner of other things.

Ann Arbor   Tuesday, September 11: It has been a bright, sunny day with a touch of autumn in it, and in the evening we had a beautiful full moon. Verily, the nicest sort of Ann Arbor day, and I am sort of happy to be back.

I was almost completely undisturbed in my work on the *Genji*, and made it through to the end of "Nioumiya."[42] It certainly is a strange chapter, telling us numbers of things we do not need to know, leading us absolutely nowhere, introducing with some fanfare a character, the daughter of the emperor Reizei, who is to amount to absolutely nothing. Yet it is hard, in the last analysis, not to believe that Murasaki Shikibu wrote it. If someone other than she, then common sense argues that it was someone who came after her; but would anyone who had read the Uji chapters have written a chapter like this one? It may be argued that the Uji chapters too are by someone else, but my common sense, at least, holds that to be unthinkable.

So now only two remain; and inane though they are, I look forward to seeing how, upon close examination, I will feel about *their* authenticity.

Saturday, September 15: I worked hard through the morning and half the afternoon on "Kōbai,"[43] and so short a chapter is it, hurrah, hurrah, I am almost halfway through already. It is, like

"Nioumiya," a very strange chapter, leading nowhere. It is badly written, and appears to mark something of a reversion to a far more primitive form of narrative than the best of the *Genji*, a form in which we are confronted with sudden and not very believable postures and appearances, and motives and states of mind are quite ignored. Yet I cannot help thinking all the same that Murasaki Shikibu wrote it. The most important question is why anyone else would have written it; and a later person, trying to fill in the gap between "Maboroshi" and "Hashihime," would surely not have turned to characters for that purpose irrelevant. Dare one venture a wild suggestion: that an old and failing Murasaki Shikibu herself returned to the filling of the gap, in the vein and mood of the Uji chapters, and found herself not up to the task? Has anyone made the suggestion before in the millennium of speculating on the *Genji*?

In the evening I went down to Main Street to see what the Ann Arbor "ethnic" fair might be like. Though there were Chinese selling horrid Maoist propaganda and art, on the whole it was fun. As I watched the folk dancing, I said to myself: really, Edward, you were young at the wrong time. I have reference not to the Depression but to the awful ballroom dancing we were required to enjoy. Had we had folk dancing or rock I would have been much more of a participant. I tried to buy some Mexican food, but the lazy Mexicans were closing shop, so I bought a Greek pastry and turned to go home. A most cheering discovery: the president's house has been repainted, white or yellow, I could not tell which – an enormous improvement over that battleship gray.

Thursday, September 20: Each night the insects sing and sing. Some of them chirp, some of them tinkle, and some of them sort of thump and click. In Colorado forty years ago, we had bird and beast sounds in the night, but I can remember only one insect sound, the sad, monotonous one of the cricket.

I had appointments. In the morning I had to go to the hospital, St. Joe's. All I had to do was have some blood taken for a test or two, but the few moments required quite ruined the morning. The girl who took the blood was very amusing. She said yes, she knew what a bore it must be to have people constantly joking about one's name. People are constantly joking about her calling. Hearing that it is bloodletting, people always screech, "Oh, a vampire!"

Nevertheless, working on my electric typewriter, which is so jumpy (just brush a finger against it and it jumps straight into the air) that it makes me jumpy too, I got a super-duper day's work done on "Takekawa,"[44] and tomorrow or so I should be halfway through it. The arguments are much stronger for thinking it spurious than for thinking the two preceding chapters so, because in their case the fundamental question, "Why would anyone except Murasaki Shiki-bu have done it?" seems next to unanswerable. In the case of "Take-kawa" it is very easy to answer: some hack thought of having a try at something vaguely related to, tangential to, the great lady's work. The subject matter is vaguely *Genji*-like, but the tone is not. It is a very flabby chapter, with a great deal of mooning, and poems that serve no purpose but to use up ink and paper, and meetings that lead to nothing but partings. Even when Ukifune writes a poem to herself it serves a purpose, to emphasize the silence and the lone-liness, and even when Kaoru and the Uji ladies meet only to part the sense of meeting is palpable. Here everything is loose, limp, feckless – and the presence of such large numbers of young men (Murasaki Shikibu never brought together more than two or three plus extras) only makes their essential anonymity the more striking. It is the mood and tone of late-Heian fiction. Do I really want to translate some late-Heian fiction when I have finished the *Genji*?

In the evening I went with Choo Won to a rug auction. The auc-tion was of Middle Eastern rugs and was presided over by a Levan-tine type. He made us, or at least me, feel guilty that the bidding was not more daring and energetic; and finally, for a hundred twenty-five dollars, I found myself the owner of a little Bokhara. Now that I have it at home I don't much like it. Pink is what it is, and I hate pink, because it makes me think of the intellies.

Saturday, September 29: A gray, rainy day in an unheated office.

I told myself that we must save fuel, and tried to feel virtuous.

I did not go to the market, my usual thing on Saturday, but rather got to the office early, and pushed on towards the end of "Takekawa," not with the feelings of eagerness that ought to accompany the approach of such a consummation, but with feelings of sleepy boredom, rather, and of vague dread at what is to come next. For all this, I liked the pages I did today better than anything else thus far in the chapter. The exchange between Tamakazura and Kaoru, in which she is complaining and he is evasive and she is her old ironical hardheaded self again, is nicely done. But for all the fact that she seems her old self again, the dialogue does not, somehow, feel like Murasaki Shikibu. It is more clipped and staccato, and lacks the solemn sonority.

Over to the library in the afternoon to fight my way through all the encrustations of Japanese students for a look at the *Asahi* and the magazines. I was seeking material for possible use in an article about the intellies, and I was chiefly impressed with how empty the *Asahi* and the magazines are. They even *look* empty, all shot through with empty *katakana* jargon, "outsider" and "establishment" and "Gesellschaft" and "Gemeinschaft" and the like. There is a lot of talk about pollution, utterly useless, all of it. Nothing in the world is more uninteresting than general agreement in a matter that does not call for action.

Sunday, September 30: I don't know how it has been for all you others out there, but for me this last Sabbath of September, 1973, has been a memorable day. I FINISHED MY FIRST DRAFT OF THE *GENJI*. "Takekawa" came to a listless, wholly unmemorable close, and there I was, at the end of the first draft. So now the more difficult work of rewriting lies ahead.

Wes Johnson was also in the office. When I announced that I had finished, he said we must celebrate with a glass of bubbly and opened a bottle of Seven-Up. I liked that.

Marjorie Petring came for me at noon, and we went to her house in the western suburbs. Feeling athletic, we decided to go for a walk. We – she and I and her Afghan, name of Genji – went first to pick up a gentleman friend of hers, and then headed out across the hills and meadows, generally in the direction of the Huron River. It was sad to see all the abandoned fields, for they were in cultivation such a short time, the hopes and the fields exhausted so quickly; and the brambles were rather dreadful, especially for one used to open Colorado walking; and Genji was uncooperative, from time to time quite refusing to move, though I must say that he was very good-natured when we pummeled him in an effort at persuasion. But despite these shortcomings, it was a nice walk: the autumn sun was warm, and the wild asters were very beautiful in among the goldenrod, and the gentians were sweet and fresh, and already the sumacs are red.

I feel tired but happy, as at the end of a camping trip.

Thursday, October 4: I sorted out my *Genji* manuscript, all forty-four unrevised chapters of it, and made sure that everything was accounted for, and then began the work of reading over, from the very first chapter, the chapters yet to be sent off for the meditative gaze of Miss Odagiri. Though I got only three of them done, the work was very encouraging. After the flabbiness and insubstantiality of "Takekawa," the forty-fourth of the forty-four, I found myself unmistakably in the hands of a master once again, even through the uncertain filter of my first draft. I found myself unmistakably, that is to say, in a world of people and not of wraiths. I wonder if Waley had read "Takekawa" when he said what he did of "Kiritsubo."[1]* I doubt it – for "Kiritsubo" is far the firmer and more assured of the two, not at all the work, as the other might well be, of a hesitant beginner. "Hahakigi,"[2] with its caricatures, is a little more that way, a little more tyroesque, so to speak.

Dinner at the Johnsons', over across the river where the hickories fall. We listened to beautiful vocal music after dinner, the poems of Yeats, recitative.

* In a famous footnote at the end of the chapter, Waley describes it as an early and immature chapter which should be read with forebearance.

Sunday, October 7: I spent the day in solitude in church and office. I read through the last of the chapters to be sent off to Miss Odagiri – a total of only twenty-odd, but covering the whole span from "Kiritsubo" through "Takekawa." Reading rapidly through them has been extremely interesting. The only surprises have been, I suppose, that "Suma"[12] and "Akashi,"[13] in which almost nothing happens, seem so exciting, and that they are followed by a series of somewhat tepid chapters, including "Usugumo,"[19] which, containing the death of Fujitsubo, ought to be memorable. The chapters dominated by Yūgiri are splendid. He is without doubt the finest specimen of healthy sturdy manhood in the whole long tale. It seems wrong that Genji should have even one son, but quite just and proper that Yūgiri should have a half dozen or so. As always, I had special thoughts about "Suzumushi."[38] I wonder if Waley ever read it. I can imagine that he was put off by the elaborate ceremonials with which it begins, and went no further. Did he then never take the trouble to associate those lovely scenes in the scrolls* with his text, and see that the chapter whence they came is equally lovely? Maybe, unthinkable thought, he never looked at the scrolls.

Tuesday, October 9: In the morning I started comparing my very first chapter – "Kiritsubo" – with Waley's. I wonder at what point I told myself that I was not going to look at Waley while in the process of setting down my first draft. It is clear that in this first chapter, done, a bookmark tells me, back in 1965, when I was still at Stanford, I both looked at him and was influenced by him. The influence is apparent in word usage and in richness of embroidery, and the chief result, other than that in some places it sounds rather like Waley, is that it is a good bit longer than it needs to be. There is explanation and there is inference that we could very well do without.

At noon I went over to the post office to put a bushel or so of paper into the mail for Miss Odagiri. It took me a half hour. The lines were as at the height of the season to be jolly. Thence to have

* The "Takayoshi Scrolls" of the twelfth century.

my teeth cleaned and inspected. It continues to be cause for wonderment that there should be people willing to spend their lives cleaning teeth. I have always thought the task of the girl who cleans the old man's false teeth in the little Kafū story about the bill collector the most disgusting in the world; but this is just about as bad, and it is, moreover, a full-time occupation.

In the early afternoon I went downtown and bought myself a bedspread. Love it. It is orange and green, the colors of autumn, in broad stripes, and reminds me a little of the curtain at the end of the passage to the Nō stage. Just before class someone came breathlessly in with news of Agnew's resignation. I was reminded of the Palo Alto November morning, almost exactly a decade ago, when I was about to hold forth on the *Pillow Book* and someone came in with news of the Kennedy shooting.

I am mentioned in a book about the Japanese language, by a Mr. Toyama Shigehiko. He says that in that embarrassing incident, still, says he, fresh in the public memory, in which, in Stockholm, I botched Mr. Kawabata's reply to the question about how he meant to spend the prize money, the fault was Mr. Kawabata's and not mine, for Mr. Kawabata did not know how to address an audience of redheads.[*] At first I was somewhat discomfited to learn that it is still fresh in the public memory, but then I said to myself it is nice of the public to remember me, whatever the context. Who knows, it may be the context in which I am longest remembered.

Saturday, November 10: Earlier in the week I took several deep breaths and began A New Phase in the *Genji*. I commenced typing out a final version of "Kiritsubo" to be sent, with some slight last revision, to the typist, which office Choo Won has most kindly volunteered to fill. It may be a bit stiff and ceremonious, but I do not think, as Waley did, that it is merely juvenile. That charge might better be leveled at the two following chapters.

[*] It was reported in the Swedish press, because of a misleading rendition into English of a clear enough Japanese statement, that he wished to make some sort of commemorative donation.

Today I worked on "Hahakigi."[2] It really is not very interesting. I remember having been bored with it – the story of the governor's wife is what I have reference to – when first I read it, some thirty years ago. I still am. It does not signify anything, tagged on as it is to the discussion of middle-class ladies by way of bringing one of them into Genji's own life. It may be that the article itself is seldom as interesting as the advance publicity; but a surer and more mature Murasaki would have succeeded in making the disappointment interesting. Of course it is not for Genji, really, a disappointment, despite his frustration. The disappointed one is the reader. Now if *I* were to improve on the *Genji* as Waley is always said to have done, I might begin by deleting the governor's wife.

Tuesday, December 18: The nervous days are here. Suddenly I am aware of how few days there are till Christmas, which means that there are yet fewer till my departure from these frozen regions. I ought to be used to semi-annual departures and to know that things will somehow arrange themselves, and I do know that in years past they have arranged themselves with very little help from drunken me. Yet I go on getting nervous. But I think there is something wrong with the season too. What ought to be a time of repose has become the jumpiest of them all, with the material sprawled over everything, and the spiritual not allowed a place to hang its coat.

I did not do very well with the *Genji*, though I did finish comparing my "Wakamurasaki"[5] with Waley's and Murasaki's, and started upon the same service to my "Suetsumuhana."[6] I made a rather charming discovery: that Waley's "saffron" has *purple* flowers, and so his translation is in error. I had assumed that the correct translation was "safflower," which has orange-red flowers. Anyway, I am delighted to say that that is what *my* translation will be.

"Suetsumuhana" is a good chapter, and certainly all the surface indications are that it follows immediately after the evening faces. The gourds, the gromwell, the safflower – what a sequence! Even the names suggest that the middle one does not belong there. But as to the safflower in isolation: the climax is brilliantly managed. Some of the comedy, alas, does not come across. It is too much concerned with vogues and fads. (It is interesting that Murasaki Shikibu is not consistent in giving her tale a retrospective aspect. The garments and the color combinations that are good are those of her own day. So it is too with the calligraphy; and the tale is therefore not to be described as a carefully contrived and controlled historical novel. Just something with retrospective details.)

The Malms came over in the evening, and presently we went out for dinner, to a Chinese restaurant over on the west side, not at all good, name of Lim's. We had one fine time – "a cheap thrill," Bill called it – getting back over the skating rink our city has become. I managed to fall flat on my face several times.

Thursday, December 20: It went on snowing through most of the afternoon, and we ended up with a foot of snow; and so it is but an inch short of being the snowiest December on record.

In the time before examinations, I finished my three-sided comparison of "Suetsumuhana." How charmingly it ends, with the plums about to break into bloom, and Murasaki into adolescence – that last moment of innocence so beautifully caught and, horrid word, packaged. There are no other such moments in Japanese literature, and there must be perilously few in the literature of the world.

As I waited for my little ones to compose their examination papers, I looked out at the snow, and listened to but did nothing about raucous music in other rooms and strident snores in our own, and wrote end-of-term reports.

After lunch I read over the papers. They were better than I would have expected from the mediocrity of the term papers, and some were rather spirited. The statement I liked best, I think, averred that Genji's women all got "the short end of the stick." Several people hotly denied that Japanese literature is depressing, and their remarks much accorded with my feelings about the conclusion to the safflower chapter; and so I think that on the morrow I shall tender an uncommonly high list of grades.

San Francisco–Honolulu Sunday, December 30: Eight decades ago, in the city of Chicago, my mother was born. I got up early and went to mass. The sermon was about the pursuit of ideals, which was held to be a good thing.

The afternoon finds me aboard United Airlines, bound for Honolulu. Maribel and Al drove me to the airport by the high road. Even now in the dark time of the year the hills look radiantly vernal. There were a few unseasonal poppies along the embankments, and the hills of the East Bay seemed impossibly, smoglessly near. I have been glad to be in California these forty hours, and much of the gladness comes from the sense of not being a part of it.

I don't suppose I am quite as displeased with United vulgarity as I was on my last Hawaiian flight, but it is pretty hard to take all the same. One sees too clearly the difference between good manners and Madison Avenue manners – between household manners of the better sort, acquired at the hearth and the dinner table, and charm-school manners. And the line United Airlines gives you over its public-address devices is such as to make you think it was maybe a bad idea to head for the islands in the first place. All sorts of highly romanticized and not very accurate stuff about their history, and cute lessons in the Hawaiian language, and that sort of thing. I got so annoyed, as it went on and on, that I took to hating my fellow passengers, who seemed to love it.

So here I am in Honolulu. I found awaiting me in the mail a demoralizing thing – a demoralizing thing is generally awaiting me each time I take up residence in one of my several apartments. This one is Charles Hamilton's appraisal of my first three chapters. They are, he says, in a "throwaway" style, and, with a very low specific gravity, tend to get away from the reader unless he keeps a close watch. I do not know exactly what this might mean, but am un-settled, so much so that I consider telling Choo Won to desist from typing a final copy, that I may have another look at my work after I have been away from it for a time, and after I have learned a bit more specifically from Charles, who proposes to come out next month, what he might mean. Though upset, I am grateful. It is far better to have such an appraisal from him than from a reviewer.

1974

Friday, January 4: I got in my first really good day's work since before Christmas, rewriting about half of "Wakamurasaki," which I am probably going to call "The Lavender." It is a slight chapter. Too much is said about Genji and his charms, and not a great deal of anything at all is said about anyone else. I found myself thinking how nice it would be if Murasaki Shikibu, like Miss Austen, had written several novels, each to be taken by itself – or if we could separate her big work into several smaller ones, each to be taken so. *Sense and Sensibility* is by no means as good as *Emma*, and, off by itself, it does not detract from the latter. "Wakamurasaki" might be deemed a part of Murasaki's *Sense and Sensibility*, but it does take something away, for one may not tell it to stand off by itself.

Perhaps I can say in my introduction: "Dear reader, do as Zeami said the Nō actor should do, proceed through the greater and the greatest and then return to the lesser. Begin with the Tamakazura chapters and come back to the beginning after you have read the Oojy chapters." I complain; but each time I am reminded of the *Tales of Ise* I see how superior even "Wakamurasaki" is.

Val and Frances Viglielmo came around in the evening, and we went to a place called the Osakaya for dinner, and afterwards to their house out towards Koko Head – Ainahaina, affectionately referred to as "Ainahaina Nachtmusik," is their suburb. Their house has doubled in value since they bought it, and so I suppose I must wait for the market to collapse before I buy anything. Frances thinks of suing the island school system for racist bias. All the teachers are Japanese-Americans.

Monday, January 7: Charles Hamilton arrived in the afternoon, to be my guest for perhaps a week, perhaps a fortnight. I learned a little of what he means by "throwaway." He means a style which seeks to be colorless and unassertive – the antithesis of the Waley style. It is true, I suppose, that I have so sought. How very difficult it is. The very effort to be unmannered produces mannerism.

In the late afternoon we drove out to the Blow Hole. At the sound and smell of warm seas breaking on lava spits I felt happy to be in

Hawaii again, as I have seldom this time felt. We had dinner at a Chinese restaurant, and then went for a look at North Hotel Street. Bits of old Honolulu remain, Oriental markets with green battened walls, whores sitting outside their chintzed cribs.

Friday, January 18: An extraordinarily clear day, like California in the summer, but not really Honolulu. There should be visible happenings in the sky, clouds pursued by other clouds. Today the clouds went away, and nothing at all happened.

Yesterday I finished my final version of "Suetsumuhana" and went over the first half of it yet another time. I think I have managed to convey the ineptitude of the princess's poetic style, but the reviewers will no doubt, if they detect it at all, set it down as my own ineptitude. It is a very dangerous business, seeking to imitate ineptitude, and translators are probably well advised not to try.

Then Charles and I went up to the university and looked in on the Japanese literature people, or some of them. Jim Araki showed us a translation he has been working on of a prose rhapsody having to do with the tea ceremony. One sentence bothered both Charles and me. Three men are waiting in an anteroom for the ceremony to begin. They look into one another's eyes and break into smiles. "I would expect them next to form a daisy chain," said I. "Couldn't you have them exchange glances?" said Charles. "Good idea," said Jim. "They exchanged glances," he wrote down.

Today I worked on "Momiji no ga."[7] I did well, accomplishing the rewriting of about half of it, despite the fact that it is a rather hairbrained chapter. Things somehow do not hold together, characters, even a former emperor and an emperor's son, are mentioned, not to be mentioned again. The single reference, all through the long tale, to a surviving emperor who reigned before Kiritsubo is so remarkable as to make one suspect that an adolescent Murasaki Shikibu might have been having giddy spells when she did the chapter, perhaps suffering from an infatuation with whoever was the model for Genji. She reminds me a bit of Isabella Thorpe – or maybe the chapter is a good candidate for the title "spurious."

Charles has been making me nervous by going over my final versions in my presence. I wish he would take our rented car and go down to the beach for the purpose, but that is not his style. He says – I have not gone over his notes – that he finds much more to criticize in my "Suetsumuhana" than in my "Wakamurasaki," and that is interesting, in a disquieting way, flying in the face of one of my favorite theories, that a person is more likely to produce a good translation of something he admires than of something he does not. Readers of these pages will know that I like "Suetsumuhana" very much, and think "Wakamurasaki" in some ways childish.

Thursday, January 24: How much better is the air, how much more happily one works, when the trade winds bring the clouds in over the mountains. There is now in the evening from up the hill that extraordinarily strong flower scent. I have not been able to determine from what flower it comes. It is the scent of the tropics.

I have finished typing out my final version of "Hana no en."[8] I liked the chapter, on reading it over, and think it not really the triviality I thought it yesterday. Better by several degrees, indeed, than "Momiji no ga." It is a happy episode. The meeting with the lady of the misty moon is deftly and expeditiously handled, and the evidences of Murasaki's entering upon puberty are presented with great delicacy and yet with much purposefulness. One cannot imagine, as with "Momiji no ga," that Murasaki Shikibu does not know where to go. She marches firmly ahead to the deflowering of the other Murasaki.

In the afternoon I was domestic. I cleaned my feelthy kitchen, or part of it. I sort of enjoy housecleaning – sometimes at least I do. I wonder if the pleasure I take in making neat an apartment or a garden might not be an atavistic reversion to my peasant ancestors making neat their fields in the English midlands or South Germany.

Friday, January 25: The fine trade-wind weather continues.

I began rewriting "Aoi."[9] It went well. There are other good chapters preceding it, but the first fine *scene*, surely, is the lustration and the disagreement over the carriages – the oxcarts. The gaiety is so beautifully conveyed – and then the sudden black bitterness. Perhaps the death scene in "Yūgao"[4] might qualify as "fine," but that is in the realm of Gothic night, this in broad cheerful daylight; and of course there is always a possibility that "Yūgao" was written later – next to a certainty, indeed, some of us might say.

And then the defloration: one may consider Genji a complete bounder for his behavior towards Murasaki, but one cannot accuse Murasaki Shikibu of gaucheness in her management of it. She gives us subtle, delicate little hints of what is approaching, and when it finally happens, the exchange in which Genji gives Koremitsu proper intelligence is delicious. And maybe it was not such a curious thing, in days of yore, for a gentleman to wait for a lady to grow up. I think of Knightley waiting for Emma, and my grandfather, out there on Plum Creek, waiting for my grandmother. I wonder if my grandmother ever had feelings of outrage similar to Murasaki's.

The two things that gave me the most pause were a name for the chapter and one for Genji's wife.* Because of the pun, I thought of either leaving the title in the original or abandoning the original and, by some such device as "The Kamo Festival," arbitrarily switching to one of its several significations. And of course if Aoi is going to be called Aoi, it had better be no later than this chapter, for, poor girl, she is henceforth but a memory. So at the moment the title is "The Aoi." But that is sort of Waleyesque, and besides it makes me think of a nasty giaour. I think I will change it back to either "Vine of Meeting" or "The Kamo Festival." As for calling Aoi Aoi, I finally decided to do it all of a sudden and explain in a footnote. It is not a very slick device, and I feel doubly clumsy for having used it twice, here and for the little gromwell.

Thursday, January 31: I think maybe in my declining years I am

---

* *Aoi*, the vine that was one of the symbols of the Kamo Festival, also means "day of meeting." Genji's first wife has traditionally been known as Aoi, because she dies in the chapter.

becoming a cracker-barrel weather prophet, one of those who feel rain in their bones. I felt listless and wanting in energy yesterday, and the rains came, and today I continued to feel listless, and the rains endured.

I managed to get to work on a new chapter, "Sakaki,"[10] of course, and did not at all dislike what I was doing. Indeed the knowledge that a favorite scene was approaching was one of the forces which compelled me to sit down and make a beginning. It is the scene in which Genji travels out over wasted autumn moors to visit the Rokujō lady, and catches strains of he knows not what music as he comes near the shrine. The loneliness and the austerity of the autumn night and of the shrine are beautifully done, as is the lonely indecision of the lady herself.

In the afternoon, Jack and I went down to the Bishop Museum to look at an exhibit of early photographs said to be of Honolulu Chinese. Some were Japanese, but that is all right. My favorite scene captured a moment, five to two one afternoon in the Aala Saloon, with fifty cents rung up on the cash register, and two Oriental bartenders behind the bar, and two Oriental drinkers before it. A pity there was no calendar to show the year.

Then I wandered around looking dreamily at Hawaiian artifacts and paintings of Hawaiian villages and old photographs of Honolulu. My fascination with Hawaiian culture has to do with the fact that it is so utterly gone. I have no great wish to go and look at cultures that still survive elsewhere in Polynesia. The photographs of Kalakaua's coronation seemed very silly in view of the fact that he reigned over a nation of fifty thousand people. Maybe, after all, the Hawaiian monarchy was too silly to survive.

Saturday, February 2: Such a beautiful day, despite the fact that the clouds continued to come in from the south. I decided I must go out somewhere in the afternoon, and therefore worked with uncommon intensity on "Sakaki" through the morning. I was rather more successful at viewing the forest and not the trees; and it is, I think, a grand sort of forest, with Fujitsubo quietly taking her vows as the crowd turns to depart from the majestic show that is a reading of the Lotus Sutra. So great is the difference, one imagines, between the elegant garden of a Heian retreat and an American nunnery that the word "religious" does not seem broad enough to cover both.

So, having done my day's bit, I got aboard a bus and went down to the end of the line, at Kapiolani and Hotel. Then I walked back down Kapiolani and Ward, and through Ala Moana Park all the way out to the end of Magic Island. It is a horrid name for a beautiful expanse of green, dotted with those regents of the tropics, coconut palms, and at the end is a charming little cove encircled by young coconuts, to demonstrate that reclaimed land can if there is a will be put to pleasing use. The view back from the cove is magnificent, the whole sweep from the Waianae Mountains past the central valley and the Koolau Mountains to Diamond Head.

Jack came to pick me up at about five, and after some shopping we went for another grand view, from another very beautiful park, on top of Roundtop. On Roundtoptop? There, while the thrushes sang and pleasantly bouncy young Japanese, guests to these islands, took pictures of one another, we watched the sunset. The corals, magnificent trees, are coming into bloom.

Monday, February 4: With the early half of the day I finished rewriting "Sakaki" and did the whole of the rewriting of "Hanachirusato."[11] The final scenes of "Sakaki," in which Genji is caught in the act and the Minister of the Right and then Kokiden have their say about it, are splendid, giving us voices from the early eleventh century that still sound like voices, and where else are we to find such? I obviously enjoyed doing the two long speeches when first I did them, because my first draft has a vitriolic tone that I did not feel I must do a great deal about.

But my mind, for some reason, was more on small technical problems than on grand literary matters. What is one to do, for instance, when Genji suddenly comes into Fujitsubo's parlor and catches at the hem of her kimono? Somehow to have him do literally that is to have him groveling on the floor. May one properly have him catch at her sleeve, or will one presently be pilloried by a Joyce Ackroyd for doing so? The crown prince's decayed teeth are another little problem. They don't sound very pretty, really, in English. As for "Hanachirusato," it is a triviality, and there is not much one *can* do about it.

In the evening I went down to Mrs. Doubleday's in Kahala for tea. I had not really had time to appreciate her house before, but it is very beautiful. I sat in a corner of her enormous parlor looking out over a dozen or so sofas and overstuffed chairs at the garden, framed in French doors, like a florist's window. The Allisons were there.* The ambassador told of riding to Haneda airport with Nixon, then vice-president, and the foreign minister. Nixon turned to him and said: "Put on a hat. Only I go hatless."

Honolulu–Tokyo Friday–Saturday, February 15–16: The day of the dateline once more. On Pan American's number-one flight, I must be just about smack over it. Pan American, the world's most experienced airline, used its very great experience to confuse things most ingeniously at the airport. All of a sudden, while I was walking over to the inter-island terminal, the gate assignment for this number-one flight was changed, and so I had to make my way twice through the throngs being investigated for potential hijacking. The crowds were more than half made up of young Japanese, neat and pleasant and well behaved. It is hard to see, if these are the sort doing things abroad these days, whence arises the image of the ugly Japanese, in the islands among other places.

I am whiling away the time in two ways: remembering the things I forgot in Honolulu, chiefly tribute with which to ingratiate myself with the Japanese; and reading through "Yomogiu"[15] in my version and Waley's and Murasaki's. Very touching indeed, and very much alive – I am at the worst of the red-nosed lady's tribulations, and her nose gets redder and redder.

The skies below are looking wintrier. On the screen John Dil-

* John M. Allison was the second postwar American ambassador to Japan.

linger is about to meet his end on Clark Street – or was it Wells Street?

We are now a couple of hours out of Tokyo. I have just finished "Yomogiu," and so it has been, for me, a remarkable day, a day of travel in the course of which I have finished as much *Genji* work as I might have expected to on a day at home – nay, even a little more. Asked to name a half dozen chapters that remain vivid in the memory, I doubt that I would have thought of "Yomogiu"; and yet it is a telling combination of the pathetic and the humorous, with sardonic little touches along the way (Genji's less than sincere speeches, the cynicism of the red-nosed lady's ladies) almost worthy of Jane.

And now I have finished "Sekiya,"[16] and we are an hour or so out of Tokyo, and the sea is clear, and not in the least wintry looking. Very balmy looking, friendly looking. "Sekiya" is by no means as distinguished as its predecessor. It has rather the look of having been tacked on later. An afterthoughtly look.

Fukuda was at the airport, having come two days running. I think of myself as well organized now that I have stopped drinking, but I doubt that I appear so to other people. I forgot about the dateline, and reported to him the day of my departure from Honolulu and not that of my arrival in Tokyo.

Our aircraft came into Tokyo by a new, for me, route. Instead of cutting directly across the bay from Chiba, we skirted it, so that the whole expanse of Tokyo lay off to the right. I had a window seat on the right. A bleak expanse it is, too, ashen and gray, with not even Ueno Park capable of doing much to break the bleakness. I thought of the description of the red-nosed lady's house in "Yomogiu," desolation from the outside, but preserving an old-fashioned elegance within. One knows that there are delightful holes and retreats in Tokyo, but from the air it is as if God had sent his angels last week to destroy some godless religion.

Vaguely depressed by the approaches, I was further depressed by the drive into the city. In earlier years I have been put off by the senseless building that has seemed to be going on all about, but this time the lack of it gave a feeling of desuetude. It was intensified by a walk through Ueno, which seemed somehow subdued. The lights in front of the dubious cabarets burn as brightly as ever, but the crowds seemed thin and listless. What a horrible thing stagnation, if it comes, will be for this country. Growth has been its whole reason for being; and when growth comes to an end? Yet it has mysterious depths, and maybe, as with Mr. Kawabata, that most Japanese of Japanese, a kind of sweet acceptance will take over.

On my way back up from Ueno I passed the Yushima Tenjin, where the plums seem to be retarded. It has been a balmy day, but thus far, I am told, the Winter of the Arabs has been a very harsh one. The plum trees were utterly quiet in the beginning of spring, and the ground below seemed utterly quiet in the farewell to winter, and a gray pussycat made its way across the scene, tickling its nose against the lower branches. I thought again of the red-nosed lady's mansion.

Monday, March 4: I went out again, in midafternoon, to inspect the plum trees at the shrine. They are very beautiful, some in full bloom, some laden with buds, some, the most beautiful of all, with a few white dots deep among their dark branches, and pinkish dots on the tips of all their twigs. The first plum blossoms make me think of Kafū, and the fact that they are so much more beautiful backed by shrine buildings than by new highrises makes me think of him again. They are losing their proper element, a harmony is being destroyed, with all this new building.

Some more of the routine through the morning and early afternoon. I got upwards of half of "Akashi"[13] typed out in a final version. I suppose the chief thing to remark upon is that a secondary figure, the old man, is so lively and energetic, and the chief figure, his daughter, is so faceless, a sort of abstraction. I think of Fujitsubo, and how faceless and abstract she too is. The main point to Genji's career, perhaps, is that he is not a successful lover, or that his life is dominated by a sort of disembodied love. The mothers of two of his children are cold in the sense of never being infused with life, and

Aoi is more literally cold, frigid might be the better word. And the more enduring loves are barren. When Genji looks about, among what should have been an abundance of ladies, for ladies to bring to the new mansion at Rokujō, three of them are barren, and one of them is a sort of quasi-stepdaughter; and the fourth, off in the winter quarter, has been separated from her child. It is not a very domestic sort of arrangement. Domesticity is granted to Tō no Chūjō, although no woman seems to mean a great deal to him, and to Yūgiri, but not to Genji.

And I worked on "Miotsukushi."[14] The thing that gave me pause, a half hour or so of it, was the title. I finally hit upon "The Channel Buoys," which, if it does not perfectly match the image, comes much closer to it than does Waley's "The Flood Gauge," which has always sounded to me as if the dam had burst.

A cup or two at the Rika, where a surly old man kept telling me that I did not understand the "dirtiness" of Japan. He was very unpleasant, but I think he made an interesting point. Japan as we write about it emerges all femininely, exquisitely pretty, and we do miss the dirtiness that is so important a part of the fascination. That is why I like Ueno, and have in years past liked Asakusa and the regions east of the river. In fact I still do like these last, but they do not seem to return my affection quite as they once did.

Thursday, March 7: I finished rewriting "Miotsukushi." I have said that Genji's career is a tale of unsuccessful love. Sterile, unproductive love; but genuine love all the same. I think of Jane Austen, and how her characters go through elaborate nuptial dances, but one cannot believe that the nuptial bed really exists. I think of Dickens, who so sentimentalizes his women that one would as soon go to bed with soft taffy. And I think of Murasaki Shikibu, and how genuine Genji's espousals of love are, even when mixed with cruelty.

A ball or two of rice with Fukuda, at the Monta, over beyond Okachimachi station. Such a lovely shop, so, well, traditional – one feels that it grows there. Afterwards we went to look again at the Tenjin plums, which are at their loveliest, about a third open, little white disks floating upon little white balls, blossoms against buds, like tiny birds in gentle, wet snow, all in the soft lights which the Tenjin sets out for our pleasure. As beautiful, surely, as any of the famous spots of Kyoto – and it is not famous in their commercial fashion. How I would love to have a house below it, looking up at the plums upon the cliff.

Saturday, March 9: Much on my mind as I banged out my final version of "Yomogiu"[15] was the problem of coincidence. Murasaki Shikibu has people come calling upon the poor red-nosed lady at the worst possible times, when her life has managed to outdo itself in new lows. This is impossible, for we know that it is the way of extraordinary things to happen at ordinary times. I used to be bothered enormously by coincidences in Kafū, but I have not been bothered much at all by the most unashamed coincidences in Dickens; and it is the same in "Yomogiu." I don't think the point is that I have changed, become more tolerant in these matters. It is that Dickens and Murasaki Shikibu invest their works with such life that the coincidences seem minor. Kafū does not. That is the first question – is there life? – and if the answer is negative, there is no point in asking any of the others.

The evening in Shinjuku with Donald Richie. We had pork chops, or rather *tonkatsu* – pork chops à la japonaise – at a very nice place called the Tonton, which I take to mean the Pigpig; and then went inspecting low places. The most remarkable was a shop which specializes in sadistic appliances, mysterious objects that look like wisdom teeth and germ cultures and bolts of lightning and oh, many other striking and emphatic things. Its most interesting feature, perhaps, is its – what would you call it? – guest log. Customers there describe their predilections and endowments and leave telephone numbers for fellow spirits.

Thursday, March 14: Yesterday I finished the tripartite comparison of "Usugumo,"[19] and did the same thing for "Hotaru."[25] The management of Fujitsubo's death is, I suppose, the most interesting thing in "Usugumo." It is preceded by portents from the heavens of a most alarming nature, and then itself takes place in an altogether disembodied manner, and so is of a piece with the whole strangely abstract Fujitsubo affair. I suppose that after all it must have been planned that way, and artistry has more and incompetence less to do than I thought with the strange absentmindedness of its origins. As for "Hotaru," Waley's handling of the principal matter, the dissertation on the art of fiction, seems rather gauche. In her laconic way, Murasaki Shikibu seems more modern than he.

Today I rewrote most of "Eawase."[17] After "Hotaru," I am compelled to conclude that the author was a better critic of literature than of art. Indeed the trouble with her remarks upon painting is that they are over-literary – though that failing brings her close to the mainstream of Japanese criticism, in which a mixing and confusing of forms prevails. Among her remarks on painting, however, is the most telling of all her remarks, that a person can be trained to be almost anything else, but cannot be trained to be a painter or a player of Go. In those pursuits innate abilities are everything. The word she uses for "painting" is ambiguous, and can cover calligraphy too, most aptly. Just as I am suspicious of a poet who cannot write decent prose, so am I suspicious of a painter who does not write a decent hand.

In midafternoon, I finished translating Kawabata's "The Camellia" for Howard Hibbett's anthology and then started on one of my favorites, "The Red Plum," a deft little exercise upon those favorite themes of the postwar Kawabata, senility and forgetfulness.

Wandering around Ueno in the evening, I came upon a shop that even outdid the one to which Donald Richie introduced me in Shinjuku. Such a variety of tresses and fetters and dildoes, some of them with batteries to make them swell and squirm. Even more charming were the customers. One handsome young couple was solemnly deliberating the relative merits of a variety of enema syringes. Who, I wanted to ask, was going to do what to whom? The name of the place is Atene, which I take to be Athens. I wanted to ask about that too. But I was timid both times.

The town has been full of red armbands and headbands, for there has been a big rally supporting the Spring Struggle. To see them all in their blue jeans as if going out to climb a mountain or barbecue something, it is hard to think that the movement is very militant.

Wednesday, March 27: We have had a rather persistent, if not heavy, snow in this time of the cherry blossoms. Below my window, it turned the Sumitomo, I mean Iwasaki – can't keep my wealthy acquaintances separate one from another – roof, usually an unpleasant mottled green, a glistening white. And indoors, while my pigeons tapped on the pane asking to be let in, the gardens at Nijō were being turned a glistening white in that lovely, lovely scene at the end of "Asagao,"[20] which I have now finished rewriting and have given a smoothing over. To have the seasons in the *Genji* and the seasons before one suddenly merge as they have today makes one aware of the extraordinary lyrical power and the extraordinary way in which it is maintained through the whole great span. Yet it all fills me with a certain disquiet, for the seasons are so completely those of Japan. As the Japanese are fond of saying, will foreigners really understand? The glistening of a Colorado winter's night is something much wilder and starker. One would not send little girls out to make snowmen in it.

Last night Mr. Iwasaki told me a sad thing about the row of zelkovas beyond his house. I remarked on my pleasure in the way they do not simultaneously come into leaf, but have a spread in their time of leafing, and are therefore, on well into the summer, a variety of greens. It is because some of them are enfeebled, he said, and fall behind. They were planted by his grandmother, and it is the concrete buildings of the legal gentlemen nearby, depriving them of water and impinging upon their roots, that have enfeebled them.

The evening down in Ueno with Homma, the Nō actor. There is certainly not much of Zeami spirituality in him. He questions me so persistently about my sex life that I find myself making up more and more elaborate lies. I suppose the day will come when I will have to seek to support some of them.

Monday, April 1 : It has been a lovely April Fools' Day, the weather so warm and May-like that one would not have been at all surprised had a voice said "April Fool" and jerked it away.

I almost but not quite finished "Otome."[21] Yes, most definitely one has a sense of coming to the end of things, a stronger such sense than I at least had when I came to the last chapters. So I suppose I am now about two-thirds of the way through the rewriting, and the end of the whole enormous undertaking for the first time seems in sight. I ought to feel either joy or fear, I suppose, but I do not feel much of anything save a mild interest in seeing what the next chapter will feel like, once the big acme is past.

"Otome" is a good chapter, a happy one, with a lot to keep a person occupied. But if it were mine to do with as I wished – as Waley was so ready to do – I think I would have Yūgiri flunk his examinations and be put on probation. But maybe that would really be too bourgeois, and we should not complain, when things are on the whole moving so nicely in the direction of sensible realism.

It was such a lovely afternoon that I went for a walk around the lake. After admiring the forsythia and the willows, which had in them all the freshness of early spring, I went on to look at that old favorite, the magnolia in the Gojōten.* It too was very beautiful, like a flight of egrets across a remarkably blue sky. The Gojōten being open to worshipers, I had a good look inside for the first time. Indeed I do not think that I have ever before had a good look inside a shrine of the Kasuga sort. It is very ingeniously contrived and completely unlike a Buddhist temple. The function of its two buildings, the porch, so to speak, and the sanctuary, is to create a long passage at the end of which is nothing – empty, austere mystery. In a temple the heavy decoration and the massing of images press down upon you. Here the empty distance draws you quietly forward. It is rather marvelous that Shinto, embodiment of the *Yamato damashii*, the "Japanese spirit," should have kept to its own simple essence through all the buffetings from outside, and a pity

* A Shinto shrine in Ueno Park, Tokyo. The great Kasuga Shrine in Nara has given its name to the style of Shinto architecture represented by the Gojōten.

that its purity should sometimes go insane, as in the writings of Mishima and the deeds of Lieutenant Onoda.*

Saturday, April 6: The warm, pleasant weather continues. The cherries are in full bloom, and all day there have been drums in the distance, and voices raised in a cross between shouting and singing.

I worked on "Tamakazura,"[22] and came near finishing it. Be suspicious, I kept saying to myself, of chapters that go too smoothly. I had very little trouble with the rewriting, which I completed yesterday, and now, in the setting down in final form, nothing seems quite right. Things seem indefinably graceless and awkward, and there is very little of the "poetic" to hide the awkwardness. But there is another factor: my original too seems somehow inadequate. The story moves swiftly ahead, not as breathlessly as in the Waley version, perhaps, but swiftly all the same, through the return from Kyushu and the miraculously arranged meeting and the depositing of the treasured object at Rokujō; and there is a sense of missed opportunities. Little glimpses of Murasaki Shikibu the sociologist, in for instance the matter of the tradesmen's wives – one can see them then as now picking up all the backstairs gossip, and imagine how important they were in the various intelligence systems – make one wish that it had all been told more as it might actually have happened, and we had learned how the local gentry behaved when ill served, and how a lesser member of the bureaucracy made his presence and the nature of his treasure known to Genji or Tō no Chūjō.

Out flower-viewing in the afternoon and evening. I first did the ones nearest at hand, the delicate cascade of pink that is the weeping cherry over on Muenzaka, and the two Yoshino specimens in full bloom down at the foot of the hill, a strange and wonderful color, rather weird, not white or pink, a very pale mauve. Then over to Mukōjima, where I had the cherries, not quite in full bloom, virtually to myself, and back to Ueno, where I had hundreds of thousands

---

* The army intelligence officer whose alleged sense of duty kept him in the jungles of the Philippines until almost thirty years after the war.

of fellow viewers. I met Fukuda, and we had dinner together, and then wandered around the park. The mountains of rubbish were perhaps more marvelous than the cherries, and the general good humor perhaps even more so. For all the drunkenness, the bodies scattered here and there, rare were the notes of ugliness, and the policemen making their way through it all seemed wonderfully tactful and permissive. One of the bodies proved to be dead, and an ambulance came for it, and even that was somehow good-natured and tactful. And over the enormous clutter and commotion, a full moon.

Monday, April 8: A day of chilly rains. No doubt, though I have not been out to look at them, the blossoms are at, for this year, an end.

I finished typing out my final version of "Tamakazura" – it will be "The Jeweled Chaplet" – and so, with Tamakazura in somewhat ambiguous residence at Rokujō, we are ready to begin the review of the Rokujō seasons. Dostoievsky broods over the meaning of life, and Tolstoy over the meaning of history, and Dickens over pretense and social injustice; and each of these is a liberty which we permit only to the novelist who has done the important thing first, filled his pages with life. Now we are to permit Murasaki her thing, for she too has done her work well. Hers is yet another thing again, and something else, too, perhaps, from the transcendental generalizations which the learned commentators have her making. No doubt she is concerned with Buddhist truths, but she is more concerned to crystallize the moment in the flow of nature, make it be still. In this Bashō is like her, and Kawabata. In most of the latter's little stories I am translating, it seems clear that his concern, and mine as translator, is more with the setting than with the players.

The evening with Muramatsu Takeshi and Saeki Shōichi.* We had dinner at a tiny little restaurant, one of those beautiful nooks in the ugliness of the Ginza highrises, run by a friend of Mr. Kawabata's and bearing the friend's name. My, such numbers of books as these gentlemen have read! The most interesting talk was of the late

* Professors and literary critics.

Tokugawa period and of the black irrational strainings beneath the sinified rationalism of such persons as Bakin and Akinari. It is the Mishima paradox, and I sensed it in these gentlemen too: all the book-learning only takes them farther away from the subterranean flows which they feel most strongly to be most strongly theirs.

Wednesday, April 10: The restlessness of the weather makes one wonder whether it might not some day just pick up and leave.

I continued to have trouble with "Hatsune."[23] I very laboriously laid out a revised version, agonizing over every sentence, and then, going over it and giving it a smoothing out, I decided it was not too bad after all. In a strange way, even after a millennium, the characters do come across through the mediation of their clothes, Tamakazura all regal in her gold, the orange-blossom lady calm and unassuming in her blue – and the safflower princess protruding, like an Evelyn Waugh character, from a badly wrapped package.

Having finished retyping the last of the Kawabata stories, and somehow afraid to go back and read them over lest they seem too much of a stuck whistle, with a ruined affiancing or marriage and a sad lady in almost every one of them, I went for a walk. The cherries are being remarkably tenacious. I would have expected the rains to finish them, but they are only very slightly past their prime. Then I stepped into a movie to see how the pornographers might be doing. They have made no advances at all. It is still very much a matter of gasping and writhing under a blanket.

Friday, April 12: A day of rail strikes. It has made me aware of the unusual sort of life I live, unusually lonely and isolated if you wish to call it that, unusually self-sufficient if you wish to call it *that*. I sat at my desk working on "Kochō,"[24] and nothing in the world seemed different save the piping of little pigeons on someone's balcony somewhere, and the deeper green of the zelkovas over beyond the Iwasaki house; and then I went out in the evening and saw the largest city in the world virtually closed down. It was very weird, very dark and ominous; and I hope that these ritualistic strikes are coming to an end, and that it is being made apparent to the unions that they risk losing something.

Having finished rewriting "Kochō," I moved on to "Hotaru."[25] The most famous passage – the discourse on the art of fiction – is of course so familiar that, repeating it each autumn in the course of my weighty lectures on the *Genji*, I almost have it memorized; but I was struck, through the whole chapter, by the frequency of Murasaki Shikibu's editorial comments, so frequent that they almost come to seem mannered. I wonder why. It is almost as if she were having doubts about the worthiness of what she has been up to all these years – in which case the discourse becomes a big joke, and should not be taken as seriously as we have all been taking it (in part, perhaps, because Waley ignores Genji's less-than-serious manner).

In midafternoon I went for a leisurely walk of some three hours' duration up through Mukōjima almost as far as Whitebeard Bridge and back down to Asakusa. Just north of the Chōmeiji temple is probably the most gorgeous display of camellias I have ever seen, like huge tree peonies, red and pink; and there was no one admiring them but myself. How hard the lady who did the arrangements for the Kawabata *chanoyu** had to hunt, I thought, to find camellias with that perfect look of half-opened innocence. The Chōmeiji is full of memorial stones, rather sad, really, because no one pays much attention any more. I munched upon an ear of roast corn at just about the point where old Ragetsu** must have boarded his ferry, slightly drunk, and I thought how strange that when I first came to Mukōjima by myself, when the New Year kites were flying in 1949, I felt insecure and apprehensive, lest someone come up and molest me. Now it is among the places where I feel most serene and secure.

Monday, April 29: The beginning of Golden Week. I have done it again, failed to provide myself with enough money.

* An actual tea ceremony, attended some days previously.
** In Nagai Kafū's "The River Sumida."

While the populace was out grimly seeking pastoral pleasures, and of course finding urban crowds everywhere, I stayed with my *Genji* and finished the task of reading over the early chapters, preparatory to sending them off to Choo Won. It has been extremely hard work, and the nervous strain has been ridiculous, for no piece of frivolous narrative literature should be allowed to become so important; but now that it is finished I have great feelings of accomplishment. I think it can be stated as a matter of objective fact that they are much improved, and I doubt that Charles would be as inclined to use the word "throwaway" as he was four months ago.

Then I finished rewriting "Nowaki"[28] and got most of it set down in a final version. I suppose that, though there *are* less-favored chapters, I tend to like best the part of the *Genji* I am in at any moment – in that respect it is like Mozart's music – but I think a good argument could be made that in the light seriousness of these little Tamakazura chapters, coming before the heavy seriousness of "Wakana,"[34,35] Murasaki Shikibu has her best moment. The quiet before the storm – though "Nowaki" is the charming chapter it is because the better part of it is the quiet *after* the storm, the round of the ladies at Rokujō, and Yūgiri's eagerness to be off relieving himself. How beautifully Murasaki Shikibu does capture the freshness of the morning after the typhoon, with the first touch of autumn in the air.

The afternoon being a lovely one, I went for a walk. I did the temples at the foot of the hill, in the nicest of which the wisteria is just coming into bloom, utter elegance – it seems quite proper that wisteria should have been the flower of the Fujiwara and of Murasaki Shikibu. Even lovelier, however, are the little weed patches among the paving stones, each little weed and bit of moss a perfect marvel. I always think at such times that I do not really believe in evolution. The hand that shaped these wonders cannot have used such coarse methods.

Tuesday, May 7: I have been trying to do my duty as a citizen and have an opinion about the Nixon papers, but God, what a job it is!

Must we make our way through upwards of a thousand illiterate pages before we are entitled to have an opinion? That would seem to be what the son of a bitch has in mind, to overwhelm us with a huge mass of illiteracy. But it all makes me feel somewhat comforted about the sophisticated electronic devices which can, if they choose, learn all our secrets. To learn everything must be to be utterly confused. What sensitive filtering and organizing devices we are, that we should live in such a welter of words and somehow derive meaning from it.

Beginning somewhat earlier than usual, I managed to finish rewriting "Fujibakama"[30] and to begin "Makibashira."[31] Yet I had strong and persistent feelings that something was wrong, and that I would not be able to work tomorrow. I suppose the chief trouble is that I have set myself too fast a pace. When I start out badly and it becomes apparent that I am not going to get a norm turned out in the course of a day, I panic and get nothing at all done – for I seem convinced that faltering means stopping completely, and the conviction leads to the actual fact. So it is a kind of insanity – grim dedication to an unreality.

The fact is that I grow weary. It was along about here, perhaps, that Waley too grew weariest, cutting away large chunks of "Fujibakama" and its successors, and presently doing away with a whole chapter; and I wonder if he might not have considered quite giving up. Thank goodness the Uji chapters are finished – my morale would be frightful at this point if they were left to do. Mrs. Enchi has told us that with the death of Genji she felt such a falling of spirits as to make her think that she may have been in love with him. That is a nice romantic way to put the matter, but I wonder if she wasn't just plain tired.

I can see why Waley might (if in fact that is what happened) have become exasperated with the interview between Tamakazura and Yūgiri, the best thing that can be said for which is that Murasaki perhaps wished to show Yūgiri in less than complete control of himself. But I do not see why he then cut the interview between Yūgiri and Genji, which is superlatively good. It is true that the second interview grows out of the first, but Waley is seldom without devices for covering the liberties he takes. Here, for instance, he could have had Yūgiri deliver a message from Tamakazura to the effect that she would not at all mind going to court (we do not in any event have anything very clear from her), and then proceeded with the serious business at hand, Genji's own intentions. So it all remains very mysterious.

Saturday, May 25: This morning I started reading through "Wakana"[34, 35] in the three versions, Murasaki's and Waley's and mine; and I was happy. The pleasure must be rather like that derived from a complex manual skill. It is fun to do something the mastering of which required very great effort, with little effort. Had I found my translation notably inaccurate, why then I suppose I might have had a nervous breakdown; but I did not. I found just enough mistakes or dubious points to make the work seem worthwhile.

In the warm, sunny afternoon I went over to see how the Tenjin festival was doing. Learning that the *mikoshi** were out, and making inquiry as to where they might be, I picked up their trail way over by Ochanomizu. I thought I would watch for a few minutes and then go to Asakusa, but I was soon so completely enthralled that I spent the next several hours following them, down towards Akihabara, back up (wonderful name) Tsumagoizaka, "Spouse-yearning Slope," and along the heights to just short of the shrine. It really was marvelous, the sense of subdued power and open communion absolutely hypnotic. Fukuda joined me for the last stages, and said that last year's festival, which he saw but I did not, was by no means as crowded and tumultuous. Bands of young people had come considerable distances to wear the skin off their shoulders (there was much proud comparing of wounds), and it would seem to be the case that, after all these years of the modern and enlightened, superstition has come back into vogue once more. I only hope that the vogue lasts: the sense of community and common purpose that comes from milling about under a *mikoshi* somehow seems very important. If it has its xenophobic side – well, maybe

* Portable shrines.

that cannot be helped. The foreigners upon the scene, myself included no doubt, did rather seem like excrescences.

Monday, May 27: I have been thinking a good deal, as I have gone about my business, or rather sat here at my desk, sometimes tending to business, sometimes gazing ruminatively at the Iwasaki magnolia or my own hibiscus, which today for the first time came into bloom – I have been thinking about the weekend festival, and the power of that monotonous chanting and prancing to keep me entranced for all those hours. No theatrical performance would have been so capable of holding my attention and fending off boredom – not even a Tora-san movie.* I think I am beginning to understand Kobayashi Hideo's admiration for Shiga Naoya and the undeliberated act – for that is what a Shinto festival is, all act and no deliberation, participation without cerebration.

I continued reading through "Wakana," comparing the three versions. The Waley version caused me no small astonishment. He cuts a very large part of the jubilee celebrations (a little technical problem there, for the natural thing in English is "celebrations honoring Genji's fortieth birthday," or something of the sort, only of course it is by the Oriental count, which falls short of a full forty). That is understandable enough, because he has a well-known aversion for ceremonial fuss, and they are troublesome, and I would like to cut part of them too. But then he cuts a passage that has always been among my favorites, that in which the old Akashi monk, having learned of the birth of his grandson, retires to the mountains. I found it as touching this time as all the other times. Did Waley perhaps find it sentimental? – for sentimentality is a subtle and delicate matter, and we are skirting its fringes when we treat of the emotions at all. Or did he just get impatient, or was he in the sort of slump in which I have been these last weeks? It is in any event not a very conscientious sort of treatment to accord what is generally recognized as the grand climax.

* A popular series by the director Yamada Yōji, who has been honored by a festival in New York.

In the afternoon I had a cup of coffee with Tom Harper, who has been here for some weeks enjoying a case of shingles. He reminded me of his favorite expression in the old Kenkyūsha dictionary, which, he says, survives in the new – the translation of the earthy Japanism about the rising and sinking testicles: "My heart is in my throat."

And on to Shinjuku in the evening, for a tea ceremony. Only there was none. We had dinner, and then everyone got up and left. I have fallen into the deplorable habit of not listening very carefully when a proclamation is made in Japanese, and so I suppose I will never know exactly what happened. Maybe the charcoal went out.

So now we go into June, and high summer. The signs of it are present. The buds of oleander swell, there are already hydrangeas coming into bloom by the lake, a pomegranate is in bloom over near the shrine, and yesterday someone gave me a spray of *unohana*,* which I have here on my desk in a saké jug. It is a sensuous flower, all rich and fruity, and one is hard put to understand the sensuousness, since it is plain white and odorless. I wonder why so much was made of it in ancient times, and so little is today. I am always sad when the summer flowers start coming into bloom, for it means that my departure for the far shore approaches. I like Ann Arbor well enough, and can look forward to walks among the autumn leaves and Saturday mornings at the market; but it is quite clear, as the end to either approaches, which half of my year exercises the stronger pull.

Tuesday, June 11: I finished rewriting the first "Wakana" chapter and, in fairly high spirits, began typing out a final version; but the signs of fatigue are insistent. I am aware of them particularly in the fact that, though I fret a great deal about how I say things, I do not pay much attention to and am not much aware of what I am saying. That I suppose is the way things are with a flashy stylist – at least it is the sort of thing I am always accusing Mishima of, letting a flashy style blind him and all the rest of us to the vapidity and triviality of the contents. It might be the sort of thing that hap-

* *Deutzia crenata.*

pens to an aging and weary novelist, too. For Hemingway the sentences of *Across the River and into the Trees* must have seemed very much like the sentences of the *The Sun Also Rises* – and then came the awful shock of finding that the effect was utterly different.

Wednesday, June 19: My veranda looks like midsummer: little yellow and lavender and white cups among pale green leaves, and the heavier sensuousness of oleander off to the left, and the shimmering of *hagi*,* and morning glories leaping up an inch or two every night. So beautiful that my attention is always wandering from my valuable work.

Which was today to give "Akashi"[13] and "Miotsukushi"[14] yet another reading. I am in better form in the one than the other, and would be hard put to define the difference. I do not find much in "Miotsukushi" that obviously calls for change, but it sort of plods along while "Akashi" trips and dances and seems – I wonder if I exaggerate – about to take off. More interesting and unsettling than the problem of characterizing the difference, perhaps, is the question of whether people will notice. If they do it will of course be not to praise me for the superior chapter but to blame me for the inferior.

In the afternoon a walk down the hill and to the post office and around the lake, where midsummer holds sway. The dots of white and purple on the causeway are like an early French tapestry, magical and fairylike – one wants to see a unicorn sporting among them. The lotus breeze is fragrant.

A stroll through Ueno late in the evening. A man called me a *hen na gaijin*, a "queer foreigner," and I astonished myself by swinging on him, quite as in my old drunken days. Fortunately he thought I was being sportive, and was sportive in return.

Thursday, June 27: It was a morning to try one's patience, and I think mine held up rather well. I went over the new installment,

* *Lespedeza*, sometimes called bush clover.

thirteen single-spaced pages, of Charles's "Poisoned Dew."* I don't think I really mean "try one's patience" so much as "try one's morale," for fully nine-tenths of his points are extremely well taken, and leave a gnawing feeling that for all the time and energy that have gone into my *Genji* it is full of lapses and evidences of absentmindedness. It is always a painful business to have individual sentences lifted from context and held up for examination, because each one, so viewed, seems to have something wrong with it. Yet in this installment as in earlier ones the frequency of his challenges falls off very markedly as he moves ahead – which leads to at least the possible conclusion that the reader is lulled into acceptance of the flow, and no longer pays so very much attention to the isolated ripples.

In the afternoon, a gray, muggy one, I went to renew my acquaintance with Sanya, the best publicized of the Tokyo "slums." Its inhabitants are not a very lovely lot, really, and I felt again that they are not as young as in the early years after the war. I have always been struck with how much less dreary it seems than slums in the West, but it occurred to me that the fact that I always see it in the evening, when people are returning from the bathhouse and gathering for a drink, may have something to do with the matter. It probably looks pretty dreary early of a morning after a night too hot for sleep. I sat in the park and had a talk with a metal welder, younger than most of the inhabitants. He was very pleasant and very sensible. He said that he disapproved of imperialism. I replied that I did too, most especially of the Russian and Chinese varieties, the only ones that survive. He soberly agreed.

As I passed a range littered with golf balls, a thought came to me for a *waka* for our time: "Is it a fall of golf balls, or is it snow?"

Thursday, July 4: Mrs. Enchi's remarks on the difficulties she had with the Uji chapters make me wonder whether all of us translators of the *Genji* go through a time when we fear we cannot make it to the end. I do not remember that Tanizaki or Yosano Akiko and all those

* The title of Charles Hamilton's list of suggested amendments to my translation.

181

others had anything to say in the matter, but Mrs. Enchi's time of troubles and mine seemed to have roughly coincided, four-fifths or so of the way through. She said that the early Uji chapters were for her the worst, and for me the rest of "Wakana" loomed as an insurmountable, or so it felt, wall. I am not at all inclined to think the "Wakana" chapters inferior, however, and would not dream of suggesting that they might be by someone else.

"Wakana" went well today, in any event. I arose feeling very sleepy and grumpy and feared it would be one of those days when I can barely struggle through my allotted five hours. But things went swimmingly, and I am over half finished with the rewriting of the second "Wakana" chapter. There are even a few sentences that did not seem to require any rewriting at all, and such sentences are very considerable rarities; and so I must have been in good form when, just about a year ago, I did the first draft. This in turn suggests that the chapter itself, now that the blatting and twanging are over, is pretty good; and indeed it is. The timing of Murasaki's illness is especially affecting.

I have forgotten to announce that I went to Asakusa to pick up my Meiji prints, four of them for a hundred thousand yen. One of them, a triptych of Asakusa, is splendid, and I do not feel that I have been cheated. Decadence is certainly to be observed in the execution, but not in the conception, which is bold and clear. I also bought, for thirty thousand, a little wooden frog, and the pillbox that goes with it, mostly because I was so taken with the frog. I am thinking of buying an array of combs and bodkins for three hundred thousand. It will be seen that my sensitivity to inflation is dulling.

The evening in the Iwateya, visited for the first time this year. It is as friendly as ever, though the old man is in very bad health and is no more to be seen. The death in quick succession of two favorite customers seems to have ruined his morale. Two extremely pleasant and well-mannered boys have taken his place, and the poise with which they do it makes one marvel again at the tenacity of tradition.

The lake was very beautiful as I came home, the lotuses utterly still and delicately fragrant under the night sky, mists rising from the groves of Ueno. As I walked along, a man struck me with his umbrella. There can be no other way to describe it. He took aim and swung, and then marched on.

Friday, July 5: The streets are noisy with the last of the election campaign, candidates chasing each other around in stentorian vehicles. It reminds me of the battling oxcarts in "Aoi."

As they say, *isogaba maware*. Make haste slowly. By slowing down my pace even a little, I might have had a gay May, and been spared most of those pains. It seems a great pity that what should be the nicest month of all was such a nervous one. By doing just a little less every day, I move steadily ahead with the second "Wakana" chapter. The princess's misstep seems so real and pitiable by comparison with the great precedent which immediately leaps into Genji's mind. It is very well to say that the poor little thing brought it all on herself, that a word from her would have sufficed to send Kashiwagi on his way. She is very sad all the same, and Genji's conviction that what she and Kashiwagi did is worse than what he did is not borne out by the facts, and only adds to one's feeling that he is not a very nice guy.

In the evening, at a Chinese restaurant, there was a gathering of acquaintances from my days in Tokyo University. It was very pleasant and very friendly, and I couldn't help thinking, ungratefully, that it would have been nice if they had been friendly when it mattered more, in my early days at the university. All of them are now professors or instructors in this or that lesser university – they were not born at the right time to return to the great one. I learned for the first time that one of these acquaintances was a prisoner in Siberia for four years. I do not remember that so much as a word was ever said of it during our student days (I wonder how he felt about the sentimental fellow-traveling, so popular among our professors). It was he who had the most to say this evening about what interests me most, the *Genji*. He fears that a great deal of it is untranslatable. He is right, of course, but his notion of what specifically is untranslatable seems to me rather far from the mark. He offered as an instance the Akashi lady's reluctance to move to Nijō from Oi, lest

Genji be unkind to her. That is exactly the sort of universal feeling that seems to me most likely to jump boldly and easily across language barriers.

Monday, July 8 : The ease with which I moved ahead through "Wakana," to within a trice of the end, took me back to the best days of the winter and early spring. A great deal of what I did is very, very good, and the conversation between Genji and Kashiwagi when the latter arrives at Rokujō for the rehearsals is splendid. They talk exactly as well-bred Japanese would talk in similar circumstances today, and thereby demonstrate that the national polity is there, alive and thriving. Them Fascists, as they are commonly but inaccurately called, were very silly to talk about it. Reduced to words it too becomes silly, but there it is all the same, stubborn and undeniable.

In the afternoon I started for another walk through Yanaka, but I got no farther than the lake, which is beautiful if you pay no heed to the murky water, and which seemed worth a time of quiet and fragrant meditation. What a delicate, spicy smell it does emit. The lotuses are coming into bloom, though only around the edges, and I do not know why. They are quietly, coolly majestic, fit symbols of paradise, and the pads, some a foot across, wave grandly in the wind. But I almost think that as in a land garden it is the weeds that I like best. The *hishi* ("water caltrop," says Kenkyūsha) is so thick that it pushes itself up into the air like a folding crust, and there is a plant with tiny round leaves of a wonderfully fresh yellow-green which I cannot identify.

Tuesday, July 9 : It has been a blazing hot day. A typhoon over there somewhere seems to have filled the land with hot air.

I did not have my whole five hours in which to toil at the *Genji*, but I finished rewriting the last pages of the second "Wakana" chapter, in which Kashiwagi commences the long work of dying and Kaoru swells towards birth. *Umarete wa mita keredo* – that splendid

Ozu title would do nicely for a brief description of the life that is to follow. "I was born, but . . ." Then I began setting down my final version of the chapter.

To Asakusa in the afternoon to pick up a set of combs, antique, I hope, which I finally decided to buy from Mr. Sekine, the art dealer, for a quarter of a million yen. It was the first day of the *hōzuki** fair, so wonderfully cool with its oranges and greens and tinkles; but the prices were at least double last year's, perhaps even higher.

Tuesday, July 16: I moved rather jerkily ahead through the second "Wakana" chapter, and if tomorrow proves to be a good day I should be at the end of my final version. What is most striking about these pages, among the most famous in the whole long tale, is that they are what a novel should be, impartial. A feminine bias is present, of course, in the selection of the material, in the decision that the little princess is to be completely innocent and that Genji is to be a self-righteous prig; but the details selected for presentation are then presented in such a manner that we must accept them. They become facts, not interpretations or judgements. Fact: the little princess is speechless, and so Kashiwagi is led on. Fact: Genji thinks himself more sinned against than sinning. So it should be in a novel. We should have facts, and the judgements upon those facts should be for us the readers to make.

To the Palace Hotel late in the afternoon to have a drink with Roy Klavercamp. He had in his possession a real treasure, an ad in a Minneapolis newspaper which has incited Matsushita to sue the advertising agency for three-quarters of a million. On one of the television screens shown is a good American family scene, father and mother and soldier boy. Only trouble is, father's fly is open and his weapon is hanging out.

Down to Ueno in the evening. Ueno is, with Asakusa, the part of town I feel I must say good-bye to. It looked somewhat bedraggled, but I shall miss it: of all the major centers of the city it best combines prosperity with a distaste for the chic and pretentious. In a

* *Physalis alkekengi*, sometimes called Japanese lantern.

drinkery called Peaceful Radiance I found myself in conversation with an *Asahi* reporter who informed me that America will shortly expel the Jews, and that will be the end of American democracy, which has thus far been sustained by the Jews. I am glad he told me, so that I can be ready. Mists were rising from a quiet, fragrant lake, the winds having subsided, as I made my way home to sleep my last Tokyo sleep for this 1974.

Honolulu Monday, July 29: I worked hard on the typing of a final version of "Kashiwagi."[36] I continue to look for signs that Murasaki Shikibu was preparing the ground for the Uji chapters and signs that she was not. Kaoru's precocity seems to be looking ahead to something, and on the other hand there is no suggestion that anyone in Kashiwagi's household is in on the awful secret, and it is very important, for Uji purposes, that there be such a person. And so, in sum, one does not know. And never will, and the instinctive response is probably as valid as any, in my case the disconcerting one that the Uji chapters were not planned far in advance, but it was Murasaki Shikibu herself who planned and executed them.

Fukuda and I went driving and swimming in the afternoon. We drove through Waikiki and out to and beyond Makapuu Point, stopping from time to time to look at the near and far sea, both of them extraordinarily lovely, Maui and Molokai and Lanai dim but very visible, way out there. Blue Hawaii – it is a silly, trite expression, but a part of the spell is in the blue islands in the offing. Not very much about Hawaii is as it was two centuries ago, but that is.

We went swimming at Kailua, where I spent so many happy afternoons during the war, taking that breakneck bus over the Pali road, now deceased and discarded. The feel was as of then, thirty years ago. I have taken to swimming with my glasses on, like Harry Truman. How fine it is to lie motionless in tropical waters and look up at a trade wind making itself evident in a coconut palm.

Wednesday, July 31: I am feeling settled. I sit on my veranda, among the birds and the monkeypod branches, and work on my favorite sequence, and sometimes a cardinal comes up to express his indignation at my presence, or a little Java sparrow to indicate friendly curiosity as to what I might be up to. Today I finished smoothing out the final version of "Kashiwagi," and began rewriting my draft of "Yokobue."[37] These must have been among the earliest pre-Uji chapters that I did in first draft. My methods seem so quaintly old-fashioned, with the terminology all wrong, and slow, time-consuming inquiries into matters that do not matter. Whenever I see one of my working manuscripts from some years before I smile to think how I have improved. It is not necessarily true, of course – I have refined my techniques in, for instance, the sticky problem of what to call people, and I have compiled unwritten rules as to what is important, and that is all.

Jack has discovered that the pit in the garage is full of toads, some alive and some dead. They fall in and cannot get out again, and seem to survive on cockroaches. A pit of toads surviving on cockroaches is about as horrid a little zoo as you could hope to come upon.

He invited us down to dinner, and so naturally we went – I and my two house guests, Willie and Fukuda. Afterwards I gazed spellbound some more at the impeachment proceedings. Everyone on the committee seems earnest and well disposed save Sandman of New Jersey, who is a stereotype of the ranting, deceiving trial lawyer.

The moon is near full. In the moonlight the tree which the natives so imaginatively call gold is more regally tropical than the monkeypod. It speaks of jungle openings.

Thursday, August 1: I continue to think "Yokobue" splendid. One of the fine things about it is that Genji is so horrid, so lacking in sympathy, and there is no pretense that he is anything else. He will not let the little princess alone. He insists on being friendly when she would much prefer aloofness, and he goes on making insinuations about her past. And little Kaoru slobbers and slobbers, and another child screams and vomits. We need not fear, for all the Buddhist mooning and sighing, that the race is in danger of extinction.

I am struck with how often the things I spent all that time annotating in my first draft, three or four years ago, quietly fade away from the final version. Is it "we talked about the things we have not forgotten over the years," or "we talked over the years about the things we have not forgotten"? Well, in the end "over the years" just goes, and so goes the problem, something that does not matter. I get letters from Miss Odagiri telling me, in her Japanese sectarian way, that the Iwanami text is all wrong and I should not be using it. I could not change at this late date if I wished to, but when I decide I should worry about the matter and spend a little time looking into it, I find very much the same thing again, that most of the apparent problems simply go away. They have to do largely with honorifics, and there is not much you can do about honorifics in translation.

In any event, I moved on to "Suzumushi,"[38] and almost finished rewriting it. Not a very striking sort of chapter on the whole – but Waley did wrong to cut it even so, for something is needed, as we near the end of Genji's participation, to break the lightheartedness of the Yūgiri episodes.

The afternoon down in the Foster Garden, so filled with impossible things. The cannonball tree, with heavily scented flytraps presently becoming cannonballs all up and down the trunk, would very likely win a large vote as the most impossible thing, and the Mindanao gum tree would this afternoon have won my vote as the most beautiful. If there are such unthinkable variants upon essentially the same form of life, what other forms must there not be scattered through the universe?

Saturday, August 3: Another thing Miss Odagiri says is that some of the characters in Mrs. Enchi's translation sound like characters in Mrs. Enchi's novels. I have accused Waley of making some of the characters sound tartly British. That is the sort of thing that happens, I suppose – in the effort to make them seem "natural," which is to say, to make their speeches seem speakable, one ends up by making them talk like oneself. Probably, despite my sharp words for Waley,

I do the same thing, insofar as I succeed at all in this matter of naturalness.

Our cultural thing this afternoon was to drive down to Ala Moana and walk from there down to Waikiki and back again. Waikiki is an awful clutter and a high concentration of vulgarity, but I shall always love it for the happy hours it gave me during the war, when among hotels the Royal was dominant and the Moana still showed. And the water is a brighter color than most places, and the waves are straighter and cleaner. There was a Japanese with a large black panther tattooed on his back. I wonder if he knows the significance. I think it would be great fun to deport him – there are so few Black Panthers we *can* deport.

In the evening the three of us went to watch the moon rise over Kaneohe Bay. It was a cloudy moon, weird through the ironwoods, faintly silver upon the bay. Light from the sun to the moon to the sea to me – which seems like a great deal of trouble.

I read an article, sent for my opinion, on "Kawabata's Dilettante Heroes." Random musings on life, beauty, and death, such as the intellies go in for, and not very pertinent, really, to Kawabata and his heroes. Here is my favorite sentence: "Kikuji, annoyed by his entanglement in the swamp of desire and determined to free himself from his father's curse, decided to give up tea and to sell his house."

And that son of a bitch Nixon is finally being forced to admit that he lied to us. As I watch the Republican gentlemen on the Judiciary Committee making the best of the bad business of defending him, I think how vindictive *he* would have been in similar circumstances. The papers describe him sitting alone with his tapes and a tape recorder from which the erasing mechanism has been removed. There he sits, listening himself in deeper and deeper. Nightmarish.

Thursday, August 8: Once again I was determined not to let the heavy responsibilities of a host keep me from getting in a full day's work on the *Genji*, and once again I did let them do so. I wanted Fukuda and Willie to go off to the other side of the island together, but they debated and debated the possibility. Then a telephone call came summoning Fukuda down to Waikiki – a friend passing through – and so I had to figure out how to get him down there. Then, after more debating of several possibilities, Willie set out for the Polynesian Cultural Center. By that time the morning was nearly complete.

I rewrote a couple of pages of "Yūgiri,"[39] enough to make me suspect that the Second Princess, she of the fallen leaf, does not mean it when she tells Yūgiri please to go home (but why does Murasaki seem to insist so that she *does* mean it – a little private joke with her readers?). Then Jack and I headed out into the commercial wastes between the city and the airport to redeem my Magnavox, which was being repaired. We had a perfectly awful time finding our way out of them, the roads appearing to fall into an involuted spiral configuration; and that is why we did not get back to Makiki Heights in time to hear the great resignation speech.

Indeed we got little but commercials on our electronic equipment through the rest of the afternoon, and I for one had a strong sense of being far away from things, farther, indeed, than when I am in Tokyo. It was already late at night in Washington, and who could know what sinister things that man might be up to in the last hours of his despotic reign – and we got commercials and more commercials.

Just before we gathered for dinner, we had a rebroadcast of the resignation speech. I thought the spirit of our gathering somewhat vindictive. The speech on the whole seemed to me dignified, and even in a way persuasive, but Jack hooted derisively, and Willie laughed and laughed. There were matters of detail, however, which I too found it hard to accept. When he told us how near he has felt to all us Americans, it just seemed like old Dicky fibbing to us some more.

We have been through agony, all the local notables said when it was over. Somehow it hasn't felt that way to me at all. I have rather enjoyed it, and do not think I have seen the country so united since the end of "my" war.

Saturday, August 10: Yesterday, when the great republic smoothly changed presidents, the three of us, Willie and Fukuda and I, smoothly changed islands. As regards the former event, it was early in the morning that the new president was being sworn in, and our electronic devices again gave us commercials. There was no announcement, at the expected hour, that the change had taken place, and I felt distinctly uneasy, wondering whether our apparently fallen leader might have changed his mind, or be up to one of the countless diabolic schemes which the resources of the office make possible. Well, it all went smoothly, I was assured when we arrived at the airport early in the afternoon; and so it seems that he was not completely evil after all.

We are in Captain Cook. At first it seemed a stupid waste of time, justified only by my responsibilities as a host, that I should be back here, about to commence another review of all the old sights. But this evening we went down to look at Kealakekua Bay and the City of Refuge, and the witchery began to assert itself once more. The warm waters lapped and sighed, the rosy light went out, the palms, utterly still, were like silent ghosts in the gathering darkness. I wonder if I would have been frightened had the silence suddenly been broken by drums and chanting – something of the sort seemed called for, an amiable spirit or two to tell us how it really was, whether the gentlemen of the park service had done their reconstructing well.

I did not fare so well with the *Genji*, though, in the morning. Again the trouble was logistical, getting people mounted and pointed in the right direction, but finally I settled down and rewrote a few more pages of "Yūgiri."

Colorado Tuesday, September 3: A lovely day, cool and clear and windless, with snow on the high mountains, and all the crags and crevices of the near mountains marked in varying shades of blue.

In the morning I did something remarkable, something I very rarely manage to do when I am traveling: I worked a little. In Mary's kitchen, despite the distractions, the callers, a radio and an insistent pussycat, I gave "Tokonatsu"[26] and "Kagaribi"[27] another going over, preparatory to passing them on to Choo Won. Returning to the *Genji* after an absence, I was upset by what seemed a jerky, staccato quality. It may just possibly serve a purpose, to make the narrative seem more rapid than in Waley's version, but it is something not in the original, an unfaithful something, and I suppose the only solution, since the ornate verb forms must for the most part go, would be to do what Waley did and decorate elaborately. I was aware of a very similar matter in the case of the lady from Omi. Both of my readers objected to my management of her, detecting a kind of gum-chewing slanginess which is far from Heian, even second-class Heian. The only thing I can think of to overcome the difficulty and yet convey something of her risibility is to make of her a Miss Bates, someone who speaks in cultured enough patterns, but endlessly. And would that be faithful? Anyway, it is too late. I cannot go back and rewrite in the direction of prolixity.

In the afternoon, the weather continuing to be fine, we went for a drive, the Briscoes and Willie and I, in Willie's car. We drove over Wolfensburger Hill to West Plum Creek, stopping at the Castle Rock cemetery, and then to Sedalia, where, because Charles said they are the only good old-fashioned ones to be had any more, we had ice-cream sodas, and then back up West Plum Creek to Perry Park, and over the rise to Lake Gulch, where we inspected *my* property, and back to Castle Rock by the Ridge Road. The oldest graves in the cemetery have just passed their centenary, all unnoticed. And where are the graves of the people who died in the first fifteen years or so after the pioneering? Though somewhat freshened from the Labor Day rain, the countryside seemed dispirited. Vast stretches have been taken over by Russian knapweed, and it looks very arid and dusty, and the flowers, though of several colors, yellow and lavender and white, all look like variations upon the sunflower. Douglas County, however, is better to look at, greener and more forested, the farther you go from Denver; and *my* land is very beautiful, more beautiful than I had known it to be, on the divide between Cherry Creek and Plum Creek, very near the top of the grander divide, between the Arkansas and the Platte. It looks down over a couple of hundred miles of Colorado. Not of much interest to the farmer since someone named Selner starved to death thereabouts, it should be of enormous interest to the developer. Me, I only wanted to get away from it and the property-owning responsibilities suggested by the sight of it. I do not have property-owning instincts. I am like the Akashi lady's father, happy enough to have someone else grubbing in the dirt, and asking chiefly that he keep the fences up and not come to *me* with his problems.

To my sister's in the evening. An almost full moon was rising, very lonely, through the aspens. East has always, in our part of Colorado, been the lonely, unfriendly direction. Communications are north and south, and to the west of course are the mountains, with their festive, holiday connotations, and to the east is nothing at all. In our dislike of looking and going east was the mark of our isolation. The talk this evening was of the price of cattle, and how strange it is. Certainly it does seem very strange, falling while everything else in sight, including the price of meat, is rising. Strange, and ominous too. One is reminded of a half century or so ago, when a farm depression led the way into a general depression.

Ann Arbor   Saturday, September 21: The morning of the equinox dawned gloomily, but by eight o'clock the rain had stopped and the sky was clearing in the west, whence comes the weather. So off I went to the market. I bought some asters of all the colors asters come in and some orange zinnias, despite being half of the opinion that cut flowers are not worth the trouble. You pamper them with warm water and carefully strip their leaves away, and they wilt on the morrow all the same.

Very weary, though the day had scarcely begun, I had a nap when I arrived at the office, and awoke feeling astonishingly alert and vigorous, and got in a good five hours on "Maboroshi,"[41] rewriting about half of it. The long section from "Tamakazura"[22] through "Maboroshi" emerges as a unit of very great formal beauty. The joyous review of the seasons in the Tamakazura chapters has a sad echo, muted and abbreviated, in the review of the seasons in this "Maboroshi"; and the joy and the sorrow so massively brought together in "Wakana"[34,35] are echoed in alternation through the chapters that follow. The contrast is very affecting indeed, and we are made to feel at the end of things in "Maboroshi" as we are not, perhaps, in the last of the Uji chapters. I think the effect is rather blurred in the Waley version by the fact that he deletes a number of the ironically festive episodes, and so makes us less aware of the passage of the seasons. There is a conclusion in another sense: we seem to be coming home to tenth-century origins, and this too is obscured in the Waley version.

Somehow it would be wrong, after this sad recapitulation, to pursue Genji's career further – though the new departure in "Nioumiya"[42] is of course even wronger. Again I am pushed in the direction of thinking it spurious, an idea which I rejected when I was working on my first draft.

Tuesday, September 24: This is the top headline from *The Granite Tower*, fortnightly publication of Korea University, for March 15: "History Forged by Men Educated in Universities."

A very unsettling day. I kept my annual appointment with Dr. Waldron, and we went through the usual cheerful formalities, at the end of which I mentioned the itchy spot on the lobe of my right ear, a spot which has for some weeks, perhaps months, refused to go away. He took a look at it, and said I must see a dermatologist. When I pressed him for a view of his own, he said: "Well, it looks benign enough except for the history."* Then, of course, I started imagining the worst possible. I rushed back to the Frieze Building and sought an appointment with a dermatologist, but none is to be had for upwards of a fortnight. So through that time I will almost be able to hear myself being cancerously eaten up. And who knows, it may prove to be true that I am.

I had finished rewriting "Maboroshi" and was comparing my version of "Nioumiya" with Waley's and Murasaki's before I went to keep that darkling appointment. It was not a good day, once the appointment was over, for much of anything that required close

* A sore had stubbornly refused to heal.

attention, but I forced my way through to the end of the chapter. "Nioumiya" might be considered a reasonably competent introduction to the Uji chapters, but in itself it is nothing at all, and there is no compelling reason that we must have an introduction. Why not jump immediately into the Uji sequence? In a strange way, the very uselessness of the chapter seems to argue for Murasaki's authorship. Why would anyone else have taken the trouble? Why would she herself? Well, she was trying to get started again, after the letdown that is the other side of triumph, and it just didn't work. I think I may have ended up by making the matter of the body odors even sillier than it is in the original; but then, who knows – she may have thought it rather silly herself. Indeed it is difficult to imagine that so essentially hardheaded a lady took it seriously. I kept wondering why Waley translated the whole of this chapter when he so boldly abridged much better chapters. Probably there is no real explanation. Just caprice, and the matter of what came easily.

Tuesday, October 1: I kept waking up last night and finding that the moon was still there. A beautiful moon behind wispy clouds, very romantic. I kept wondering how many people all across the land were noticing it. The harvest moon used to be among our popular symbols, to judge from the barbershop quartet, but it is no more.

I had already made a considerable start on comparing my draft of "Kōbai"[43] with the original and with the Waley version, but I found that I had quite lost the thread and began all over again and read all the way through. It is a very incompetently written chapter, obscure in detail and in narrative line. I don't think I have felt on earlier readings as strongly that there is a considerable falling off from "Nioumiya." Kōbai is an utterly silly man, and the worst of it is that he seems silly to no purpose. There is sadness in the dwindling of substance from Genji to Niou and Kaoru because one feels it, somehow, as a truth; but here one feels nothing at all, for the characterization is of two wholly different and incongruous orders, and comparison is not possible. It is like trying to compare Shakespeare and Julia Moore, the Sweet Singer of Michigan. Anyway, I read the three versions through, and once again marveled that Waley cut so little of the chapter, when he cut so much of far superior chapters. What can he have been thinking of? And I embarked upon the rewriting, and got about half of it finished.

I alas had by accident an illustration of how the process of rewriting, the effort to produce English, can gradually lead one away from the original. At the beginning of "Kōbai," I have Kōbai a patron of the arts. In the original he is merely an interesting person, a person of substance; and I can see, step by step, how I was led into infidelity. It is a tricky, dangerous process, the process of rewriting; one cannot be, and yet one must be, forever looking back at the original, to make sure that this sort of departure has not taken place.

Dallas Finn called. I learned that Dick is thinking of resigning from the service. "There are about four people after every job that comes along, and then Shirley Temple gets it."

The Malms, all five of them, came around late in the evening bringing a present, an early Edward Gorey book. So the day concluded with an Exceedingly Nice Happening.

Saturday, October 5: The early morning, when I went to the market with Hanna Lerski, was cloudy. There was a glorious sunrise because it was so, all the way up to the zenith. Precisely up to it, indeed – half the universe was rose and half gray. Winter is coming much too soon this year: the leaves are falling, and of autumn flowers only the chrysanthemum remains. No other flower has a richer variety of colors, surely, than the chrysanthemum, white to the deepest of reds, and no other is capable of such subtle changes – and yet I do not like it. I think the reason perhaps twofold: that it stays around too long (though if that be the case I should loathe the petunia, which is everywhere always, and I do not), and it announces the coming of the dark time of the year.

Back in the Frieze Building, I worked on "Takekawa."[44] It is a lot of empty chatter, about and by people whom it is our high good fortune not to have to put up with in later chapters. The change from the last chapters in which Genji figures is a change of kind, not of degree. Here we have the work of someone who knows some of the tricks and has read what has gone before with a certain attention, but does not know or ignores the most important things. What would it take to transform this speciousness into something of value? Well, a flair for fiction writing, obviously.

The good Nagara stopped by late in the afternoon and inquired whether I would like to go picking apples. I said yes, and so we gathered his children and went to an apple orchard just south of Saline. I had not been to Saline before. It is a pleasantly green village, and it has at least one very grand mansion, in the General Grant style, with a couple of acres, I should guess, of park. The apple trees were splendid, heavy with fruit, but the orchard as a whole seemed ragged and badly kept. Japanese trees are much neater. It was an enjoyably Hoosier-schoolboyish couple of hours, better spent, perhaps, than on "Takekawa."

Thursday, October 10: When, at a few minutes past eight, the sun comes over the south slope of the Rackham roof and floods into my office, I find it hard not to be happy. I know that I am an alienated intellectual, and that Western civilization is going to pieces, and yet I find it hard not to be happy.

I was at the office early, and working briskly on "Takekawa," about half of which I got rewritten, when Choo Won called to say that she was catching up with me. So I reread an earlier chapter or two, which I turned over to her in the evening: "Yūgiri"[39] and "Minori."[40] The *Genji* at its very best, surely – I shall be surprised if I like the Uji chapters better. There is scarcely a thing wrong with "Yūgiri," though it might be a small improvement if we were given a little less of the princess's somewhat vapid view of things; and once again "Minori" brought me to tears. It actually did, for about the twenty-fifth time. It is brilliant of Murasaki Shikibu to say almost nothing of Murasaki's death but to let us rather see the effect upon Genji. Such a device is possible only after long and sustained preparation – sufficient answer, I should think, to those who say that the *Genji* is dull and too long.

There was a bag lunch at which Miss Kamachi told us what it is like to go back to Japan after an absence of a certain duration. She was both amusing and interesting. She described how the Japanese immigration office goes about keeping Japan homogeneous. Chiefly it is by not having any codified rules, so that no one knows what he must do to get Japanese citizenship, and everyone can be kept waiting forever. It is a venerable method, very cruel and no doubt very effective. I could not tell whether she approved or not, but think myself that it is a tenable sort of policy. The Japanese have enough examples of the multiracial society here and there to convince them that it is not the sort of thing they want.

The *Genji* class was even more amusing than usual. Our undergraduate, Rymer, offered a perfectly charming rendition of a sentence in the passage in which Genji's woman Ukon visits the Rokujō mansion after her return from Hatsuse: "You learn a lot from watching Genji and Murasaki be intimate with each other."

The after-office hours were somewhat frustrating. It being time to get some laundry done, I went down into the basement of this 619 East University and sought to use the machine. It was plain all busted up. So I went over to Forest Street and in the laundromat there was received, as if in a reception line, by a series of inoperable washers and driers, each of which happily gulped down coins and then refused to work. Finally I got the laundry done, but I understood a little of what it is that makes students angry. This is a place that caters to students, and it is, in their jargon, a "rip-off." South University and the streets that run into it are just one large conglomerate of rip-offs, or rips-off, and there is very little that one can do about them except write to the *Daily* and join the tenants' union.

Thursday, October 17: Winter now seems next door. The oaks below my office window are more somber than a few days ago, but they still glow in the morning and evening twilight. It is curious that they should glow more warmly from above than from below. When you look up at them from the ground they are merely brown, but from above they are russet and gold.

It certainly does seem that I have been at work on "Takekawa" for a very long time. I worked on it some more today, worked very hard indeed, and I still am not at the end of the rewriting. As I glance back over my "Takekawa" footnotes I become aware of how much makes it look like an oddball chapter, to say the least: the use of the word ōue, which I translate "dowager," twice in this chapter and nowhere else; the promotions that are forgotten in later chapters; the looking ahead to the Uji chapters even while there is a looking back to a time earlier than the preceding chapter. I cannot think of another chapter that has so many striking oddities in it; and added to the fact that it just does not feel very good, they push a person yet further in the direction of being a little suspicious about it.

A concert by the Polish Radio Orchestra at Hill in the evening, with Hanna Lerski. It was a very noisy concert, and heavily Slavic: a little Strauss, and then a lot of Dvořák and Shostakovich. The sort of concert which, since I am resigned from the outset to making little sense of it, sends me wool-gathering. There was a very pretty girl in the cello section, but she did not seem to be playing what the other cellos were playing. I was constrained to wonder whether there might not be some sort of extrinsic reason for her being there.

Friday, October 18: The most important happening of the day was that I finished rewriting "Takekawa," and now I have but to get it set down and smoothed out in a final version, and the last of the forty-four can be turned over to Choo Won for typing. It finishes in a singularly pointless fashion, with the statement that a young gentleman from whom we are not going to have another word is remarkably fluent and persuasive; but there is not much I can do about that.

To celebrate completion of the hardest work of all, the rewriting, I went over to Van Boven's on State Street and bought myself some neckties, the first since last summer, and then the impulse to be really extravagant came over me, and I bought myself a suede coat for a couple of hundred dollars. It was very extravagant indeed, in view of the fact that I spend only a couple of months a year in really cold weather, and will be spending none at all next year; but a fellow needs to buy himself a considerable present when a hard job is finished.

To St. Joseph's in midafternoon to have my ear looked at. The infection seems to have subsided, and so I guess I will go ahead and get myself operated upon. It was a very cold walk. Winter has arrived. It may have been this fact which persuaded me to be extravagant. I debated being *really* extravagant, both temporally and monetarily, and going up to Toronto with everyone – everyone is going this weekend, on a chartered flight or something, to see the China exhibit – but no, "Takekawa" must be finished, and besides I could not bear spending a weekend with all those China-lovers. If there is one thing I cannot abide it is a China-lover.

I have acquired a considerable talent for going to the wrong movie. I did it again. I went over to Architecture Auditorium thinking to see *Shanghai Express* and instead I saw *You Can't Take It with You*. A very silly movie. Movies should not point morals, and this one had a very silly, not to say immoral, moral. And why did we ever think Lionel Barrymore a good actor?

Saturday, October 19: Cold weather can be very nice, even invigorating, at the beginning of winter, when it is clear, and when a fellow has a new suede coat. I felt very snug indeed setting off for the market in mine. Hanna Lerski went with me, as usual. The market already has the stark, sparse look of winter about it. Of flowers there are only chrysanthemums and a few calendulas and snapdragons.

There is a transcript of one of the Nixon tapes in the *Times* this morning, a conversation between Nixon and Dean. It is next to imcomprehensible. Through the densest vapors one senses a vague intimation of meaning. And yet it was a matter very important to them, and they must have understood each other – through tone of voice, facial expression, gesture, it must have been. I kept thinking, as I forced my way through it: even such is the prose of *The Tale of Genji*, and perhaps it was through such extra-verbal devices that meaning was conveyed.

In the evening I succeeded in seeing what I failed to see yesterday: *Shanghai Express*. In addition to displaying Dietrich, who perhaps rolls her eyes a bit too much, it actually conveys a little of what it must have been like in China during the Great Confusion. Extraterritoriality seemed like rather a good thing.

I forgot to say yesterday that late in the afternoon I got in my weekly hours on the *Asahi*. Great good news: the Giants lost, and Nagashima has retired. He is to be manager, and maybe we can hope that he will be a flop. Of course we can – I remember how earnestly I hoped, back all those years ago when he was a student at Rikkyō University, that he would be a flop as a professional player.

Monday, October 21: To Choo Won's yesterday evening. It was great fun sloshing through the fallen leaves, green and brown and a hundred shades in between, and the dinner was as always Korean and very nice. At the end of the evening I proposed taking home the clean copy which she has so faithfully produced for me these last months, and my immediate reaction when I saw it was, "My God, what have I done!" It is perfectly gigantic, far more than I could have carried, and so she will deliver it by automobile in a day or two.

Today, nervously, I got ready for my two classes. Dread of having to call St. Joseph's this morning and hear about the testing of the skin of my earlobe quite dominated the weekend, and the apprehension grew and grew as the sun rose higher. I suppose it is not remarkable, and yet it seems remarkable, that the mere fact of there having been such a test should so have intruded itself upon my consciousness. I began to feel, as the time for the call approached, that it would have been altogether better just to let the sore have its way. And then I called, and was assured that everything was utterly benign, and that was that – the pleasure of the relief seemed almost adequate recompense for the apprehension.

In the afternoon the time had come to think what to do next with the *Genji*. Should I start going over the Uji chapters once more, or should I start trying to whip the notes into better order? I ended up by doing nothing at all – nothing of a *Genji* nature, that is.

Tuesday, October 22: I decided that I must next go over the Uji chapters again. Seated at my desk, watching the leaves fall from the Norwegian maple, I fretted and stalled, and at about nine took up the first of them, and worked on it for the rest of the morning. I found it awfully slow going. I can see that I have been moving back again in the direction of my youthful liberalism. Things which I would today be inclined to cut on the grounds that they are obvious and do not need stating and in many cases serve the purpose of punctuation marks and no more are most faithfully translated. So I cut many of them. But it may be that I am too tense and self-conscious – in such a state of mind that everything seems wrong. When I look at my translation of the *Kagerō Nikki* I do not usually find much in it that seems wrong, and it is hard to believe that this is a vastly worse translation. I shall have a try at relaxing – and I shall not hurry. It is sad to think how much further along I would be were it not for great binges over the years; but an awareness of the sad truth is, no doubt, fit punishment.

In the early afternoon I wrapped my illustrated *Genji* of early Edo and took it over to the post office and mailed it to New York. We have decided to make the illustrations ours. I am very pleased, having become very fond of the little dears, even though I am aware that they are perhaps too cheerfully Genroku, too mercantile, some might say, to quite catch the *Genji* spirit. I was sweating profusely as I made my way to the post office in my new suede coat. A wind was coming up from Ohio, and it was suddenly almost summery.

Wednesday, October 23: I won't say I slept badly last night, exactly – sleeping beautifully is one of the pleasantest things about the temperate life – but my sleep was disturbed. I had a very bad dream about a fire in which an important manuscript was lost, and when I awoke my *Genji* was on my mind, with such urgency that I had trouble getting back to sleep again. There it sits, the first thirty-seven chapters of it, in my office, waiting for someone to touch a match to it. So when I came home this evening I brought my own final version with me, and it and Choo Won's pretty typescript now rest on opposite sides of the campus. There are those who say that this sort of insurance only invites trouble, but I do not like having my sleep disturbed.

A letter from a friend, describing a conversation in which his informant, anonymous, said that my *Genji* has already become a celebrity of sorts. The whole world is taking sides, and wearing either an *S* or a *W*!

In between classes I worked on my first Uji chapter. Again it went very slowly, and all manner of things seemed to call for rewriting, and I only barely managed to get through the translation proper and the notes, and at this rate it will take a month or so to get through the Uji chapters, and that is far longer than I would wish. I rather enjoyed going through the notes, slashing murderously about me. One of the directions my development has taken is clearly that of briefer annotation. Many of them are unnecessary and many are rather pretentious and pedantic. Indeed I enjoyed going through the translation too, difficult though the task was. I have very forcefully the sense of being with the real thing once more, after that specious thing "Takekawa." Kaoru is thoroughly believable in his woodenness, and that he should be is an extraordinary achievement; and already doom seems to be approaching, in the evocation of the weird Gothic mists and waters of Uji. It is wonderful stuff, and I am very happy to say that my immediate and very strong reaction puts me at odds with Mrs. Enchi and her belief in dual or multiple authorship.

Thursday, October 24: Another two months and we will be at Christmas Eve.

I grow panicky. The Uji chapters move slowly. They are going to take a very long time. I worked hard, longer hours than usual, and I did not finish, quite, the second one. It is awfully difficult, indeed impossible, to know whether I am being merely fussy, finding so many things that seem to call for slow, painful revision. I wish that some power would inform me – but the only power at work in the matter informs me that I must stop every other sentence or so and do some more revising. And there is always the alarming possibility that I may be revising for the worse.

But the other side of the matter is pleasure that the Uji chapters seem so good. I think that I am right and Mrs. Enchi is wrong: they are not duller and less convincing than earlier chapters. They are more solemn, and awareness of a confrontation with fate hangs over them. And the story moves much more rapidly than I had remembered. Already the Uji prince is dead, and soon Niou will come attacking, and the oldest princess will be dead too.

Sunday, October 27: Another bright, sunny, warm day, and the earth seemed to lie all quietly awaiting the winter. It was the day when we went off daylight-saving time, which did not last out even its first year. Lots of mamas seem to have complained about how sad it is to see their darlings go off to school in the winter darkness. No doubt it is, but if that sort of consideration is to be decisive, then it is hard to feel that we are being very resolute in facing our problems, or are able to make even the first of the sacrifices the orators tell us we must make. And it does not seem to bother Norwegian mamas enormously that they must send their darlings off into the winter darkness.

I almost but not quite finished what must be done with "Agemaki."[47] I went on to the end thinking it less effective than its immediate predecessor, and a great deal less effective than "Minori."[40] Kaoru's grief is made too explicit, and somehow we have not seen enough of him, not been made to accept his presence in sufficient degree, to find it convincing. The artistry which compels us to accept Genji's grief without argument is missing. Argument is necessary, and it fails to persuade.

It was dark when I came back to East University, and a moon of melancholy beauty, fit background for tragic happenings, hung in the sky.

Wednesday, October 30: So here I am in St. Joseph's Hospital in dismal early evening. Well, that seemed the thing to say, although actually it is not so bad. The hospital is on the whole a cheerful place. The young ladies are friendly, and a priest has been in to comfort me, not that I have needed comforting. If there are nuns about they are not recognizable as such. I doubt that there are very many, and to one who occasionally visited a Catholic hospital in the course of a Catholic boyhood, that seems a pity, another sign of the way the world insists upon going to pieces. The room is on the seventh floor and looks out to the north, over a wintry expanse inhabited by such people as the Nagaras and the Malms. I have a roommate, an elderly man from Whitmore Lake who has been three months recovering from heart surgery. He is pleasant enough, though he finds life bleak, and in his circumstances I would myself find life very bleak indeed. He reads little, he says, and neither watches television nor listens to the radio, and lies sleepless through the long nights.

In the early afternoon, feeling more and more despondent, I brought myself, unescorted and unassisted, to room 747 (which is the *Kokinshū* number of Narihira's poem about the spring and moon of old, a fact which I judge to be propitious). I managed to read a few pages of "Yadorigi."[49] I did not understand the first page of my own translation, could not identify any of the characters, was not even sure in whose reign it might be taking place. With such utter fogginess, how can I expect to catch and hold anyone's attention? So I rewrote it very thoroughly, and hope that now it is less ineffable. More effable. There is a great and constant danger, in this sort of work, of talking too much to oneself; and I fell victim to it.

I have had callers since I composed the above, Bob and Laura and Choo Won, very good for the morale, three callers more than I would usually have of an Ann Arbor evening.

I forgot to mention that Choo Won took me by her apartment the other day to look at the furniture that recently arrived from Korea. The principal objects are two chests, one a charmingly rococo little thing aswarm with bats and butterflies, and the other solemn and grand, with panels of light cross-grained wood, perhaps pear, set in darker wood, and with plain metal trimmings; and the inside is lined with colored paper, like a Korean room. Indeed the whole feel of it is as of a massively secure Korean room transported across the water. It is very beautiful and very sad.

Tuesday, November 5: Though I stayed on my feet all day, figuratively speaking, I have been thinking that perhaps my convalescence is not as I had taken it to be. There have been no striking symptoms (as there never are in the *Genji* – impossible ever to know what anyone dies of), but I have felt sort of funny, sort of heavy and lethargic.

I got in my five hours on the *Genji*, and did other things too, a few of them. I finished going through "Azumaya,"[50] all but the notes. There are splendid things in this chapter, notably the flight to Uji – though I wonder whether, in my intentness upon stanching the flow of tears, I may not have done what I have charged Waley with doing, relied too heavily on comedy, indeed put in a bit more than Murasaki did. For the most part, however, I was too occupied with small technical problems to take much note of the grander sweep. Chief among them was how to avoid that very ugly word "substitute." I ended up by not avoiding it at all, but only wishing that poor sweet little Ukifune were not quite so insistently being offered up as a substitute for her sister.

In the afternoon I set out in the early winter chill to vote. I thought and thought what to do, for there are numbers of Democratic candidates for whom I have taken a considerable dislike; but finally I decided that the important thing this election is to be anti-Republican, after what they did to us; so I voted Democrat all the way, for all the bearded radicals and Lesbians (bearded Lesbians?!). In the evening I learned that it made no difference, my friendly Republican governor and friendly Republican congressman having been reelected.

Thursday, November 7: I went over to St. Joseph's early in the morning, for I had an appointment to have my ear looked at. I was kept waiting for an hour, and there was not a word of apology. How arrogant they are, these high priests of medicine. I had "Uki-fune"[51] with me and read over the first ten pages or so, and the time was therefore not wasted, but I was pretty angry all the same. I was informed that I am healing well and that my graft is still in place, but it will be some time before we can be sure that it will stay that way.

"Ukifune" appears to begin strongly – I seemed to find less that demanded rewriting. I am very glad now that Harold Strauss talked me out of publishing the Uji chapters first. The technical difficulty of bringing them in line with the earlier chapters would have argued strongly against ever publishing the earlier chapters at all. If I had not translated the earlier chapters I might never have come to have my high regard for Yūgiri and Tamakazura; and it would have been very unpleasant to have the regard and to find the Uji chapters impeding translation. These last would have been an albatross the whole way through.

Sunday, November 10: Another lovely, sunny day, with a crescent moon in the pre-sunrise sky as I made my way over to the Frieze Building. I stayed there the whole day save for a time in church, and made my way back to East University under a sunset sky.

I worked on "Ukifune," and did rather well with it, reading through to the end of the text proper and making a start on the notes. It is a marvelous chapter, such, surely, as only the great lady herself could have written. The sense of impending doom, of the approach of The Great Thing, is most splendidly maintained and intensified, and only an artist of the highest order could have blended it so successfully with humor, and by the blending made it purer, almost unbearable in its purity. I seem to remember that it was on "Ukifune" that I used to get hung up in my youthful readings of the *Genji*. I cannot imagine why. Maybe the fault was Waley's, and maybe it was merely typographical. The last chapters do, in the Waley version, have a black, unrelieved look about them. If he was trying to catch the feel of the contents in the look of the page, why, it was a most ingenious endeavor.

I have been going over the chapter of Charles Hamilton's "Poisoned Dew" pertaining to "Ukifune." It was more damaging to my morale than most chapters have been. The humor seemed of an almost contemptuous sort, and though the suggested changes (and I always accept most of his changes) are rather minor, the way in which they are proposed suggests that he has grown weary of me and Murasaki Shikibu. Indeed he once or twice comes out and says so. I have a puzzling way of getting Kaoru and Niou mixed up, giving the one the other's name, and what this says about the characterization I would prefer at this point not to go into; and once or twice Charles says that he has passed the point of caring which of the two is doing what with what and to whom. Then he brings Waley into his remarks from time to time, always to demonstrate superior verve and elegance.

Chinese opera in the afternoon. Enormously skillful acrobatics, great fun. As for the more serious parts, I marveled, as on earlier such occasions, at the sounds which people can be persuaded to think pleasant (call me a vicious ethnocentric if you will), and I could not help thinking it much less tightly controlled, more casual and offhand, than Kabuki.

Monday, November 11: Though the weather was grim again, and though once again I failed to provide myself adequately with sleep, I was in far better spirits than yesterday. These rises and falls of the spirit are even more mysterious than rises and falls in the stock market.

Between classes, I read over and did something about Charles's installments of "The Poisoned Dew" for "Yadorigi" and "Azumaya," which I had somehow overlooked earlier. I found his notes amusing and interesting once more, and not, as was the case with "Ukifune," destructive of morale. He caught me in an absolutely wonderful typographical error: fat, he found me saying, had not been good to the Uji princesses. "The common lot," he remarked. And he made the intriguing point that whereas the narrator in the Waley translation seems to be masculine, in mine it seems to be sometimes masculine and sometimes feminine. I suppose he is right about Waley. And about me? Well, even if he is, the matter is much too complicated to be tended to at this late date.

Tuesday, November 12: At the Frieze Building all day, looking down at stout laborers taking in leaves, and rather wishing they wouldn't. The carpet of oak leaves has been a lovely warm brown, and to have it there gives a pleasant, serene sense of being in harmony with a natural cycle.

The last installment of Charles's "Poisoned Dew" came in the mail this morning, down through "Takekawa,"[44] and I was made aware of how important it has been to me. I do not know that I had been even vaguely conscious of the fact, but now I can see that I have been in considerable fear of having him give up on me. To have an alert reader with a good nose for lapses in taste is essential.

As for "Kagerō"[52] – I seem to have neglected to mention that when I finished "Azumaya" I pushed ahead with the reworking of "Kagerō" – it is better than I had remembered it to be, not so thin and bloodless. Murasaki Shikibu seems to know more clearly what she is up to than I had given her credit for – and somehow I could not help feeling that she is quite aware, as she takes us through this chapter, that Ukifune is still alive – though she does have Kaoru rather unspeakably at loose ends.

A small happening, to stir very slightly the quiet waters of Ann Arbor – our quiet Midwestern backwaters. Bob encountered Joyce Malm in the bank. "When is Bill coming back?" said he. "I'll tell you in private," all mysteriously said she. So naturally we are wondering whether he has run off with another woman, and our curiosity is all the more deeply piqued by the fact that there has been no trace of the other-than-normal in recent telephone conversations I have had with her. And that is the sort of thing that from time to time brings a bit of excitement to Ann Arbor.

Thursday, November 14: Yes, the first days of winter are invigorating, almost exhilarating. It was splendid to look out this morning at the white lace that the walnut trees had become, to go squeaking over the snow to the Frieze Building, to have a west wind snapping at the nose and ears. But one wishes to say of Michigan winters what Koreans say of their governments: they go on too long.

In the afternoon class yesterday we made our way into the much-noticed treatise on the art of fiction, and we did it in great good spirits. Apropos of the poem about the *niodori*, the grebe, that immediately precedes it, Winslow told a charming story of standing on a lake shore one afternoon with a gentleman who knew how to imitate the call of the grebe. No one had suspected that there were grebes for miles around, but suddenly there it was, a grebe, rising from the water at their feet.

I had a relatively uninterrupted day on "Tenarai,"[53] and am not too far from the end, and of course that means that I am not too far from the end of the very last thing. My goal for finishing the Uji chapters was mid-November. I shall not miss it by a great deal. I thought my translation of "Tenarai" rather good, not impossibly far from the serene, flowerlike elegance of the original. It is very wonderful – quite enough to take away lingering doubts about the authorship of these last chapters, I think – the way in which the still spot at the center of things yet manages to seem exactly that, the center of things. With great delicacy, at a properly deliberate pace, it resumes its functions, and the shift in its apprehension as it moves from feeling to remembering is completely valid and acceptable. It somehow makes the chapter that precedes and the chapter that follows acceptable also, to make the one seem not quite the loose end I have long thought it to be, and the other a fitting conclusion to the whole grand tale, with revulsion in the matter of Niou and resignation in the matter of Kaoru demanding that Ukifune refuse to see even her own mother, and end her days at writing practice. (The art, as we all know, in which, more than any other art, we find ourselves poised on the edge of the unknown.)

Lunch with Joyce Malm. Bill is in Europe. The incident that so titillated us the other day, Bob's encounter with her in the bank, meant no more than that she does not like to announce in public that her husband is away and will not be back for many a day. Paranoia, if you wish – but life in these United States is pushing many of us in that direction.

Friday, November 15: Very wintry, all of a sudden. As I went to the office in the dawn, dry snow was blowing over a frozen campus in knife-sharp jets, as during a good high-plains blizzard. Late in the day the sun came out, but for the most part a hibernal pall hung over things.

I got through the translation proper of "Tenarai," and the notes, and a couple of small things remain to be done with it, and then there will be but one short chapter more. As I did the last pages of "Tenarai," Kawabata was much on my mind. It could so easily be bleak and desolate, the process of stripping everything away from the poor girl's life and leaving only her writing practice; but there is a serenity that comes very near being a Buddhist transformation of darkness into light, or rather, a denial of the difference between the two. The frozen waters seem to speak with their own voice – and somehow the girl seems to be embraced, and we too, in that most hostile of elements. Query: when we say, with Kawabata, that Oriental darkness is not mere bleakness, are we saying that bleakness is a state which the Japanese are not capable of knowing and communicating?

Lunch with Choo Won, at the League. She is off for Chicago this weekend, to seek to be a comfort to her sister-in-law, who is quite distraught, it seems, with loneliness. She sits in a dreary western suburb miles from the nearest Korean, and can neither speak English nor drive an automobile. Someone should have warned her that America is a mistake.

In the evening Maeda, who is working for Japan Express, arrived from New York to spend the weekend. I went to the Union to meet him, and he could not get over how I have aged in the two years since last we met. I am all stringy-haired and bloated, he said. How honest are the Japanese. He is the fifth house guest I have had in six months' time. An annual rate of ten. Ten times as high as usual.

Saturday, November 16: I left Maeda to catch up on his sleep and went over to the Frieze Building, there to read through the very last chapter and do some rewriting. I would have liked to make the last sentence seem memorable, but of course the most memorable thing about it is its utter casualness.* A glimmer of a suspicion crosses Kaoru's mind, and that is that. And it quite refuses to answer questions, does that last sentence – you can take it if you wish for exactly the quiet conclusion that is needed after everything has been denied Ukifune; and you can if you wish take it for an interruption that was not meant to be a conclusion at all. I was of a mood to view it as a conclusion – maybe only because I was wistfully wishing good luck to a sentence of mine that is certain to receive scrutiny.

Maeda came to the Frieze Building at noon, and we went to the Pretzel Bell for lunch. He wanted to go to the football game, but I persuaded him that it would be uninteresting, which indeed it was, fifty or so to nothing. During lunch a man came up and asked how many touchdowns he should give another man, who was prepared to bet on Purdue. Two, said I. He took my advice, and so it was no bet. Had he known where I live he would probably have come around and beaten me up.

Maeda cooked a Japanese meal, which was very good, and then we went to see *Frankenstein*. The film had been patched up all wrong, and the wedding scene was upside down; but that was the only good thing about it. Some very bad works of proto-art can become "classics." The original novel is perhaps an even more striking example. Boris Karloff is rather appealing as he grunts and moans, indeed the only vaguely likable creature around, and he would have been intolerable had he, as in the original, given us eloquent and polished discourses on human nature.

Sunday, November 17: The last of the snow is gone, and the lawns have seemed all fecund, as if spring might be coming. The return of

---

* In my translation: "It would seem that, as he examined the several possibilities, a suspicion crossed his mind: the memory of how he himself had behaved in earlier days made him ask whether someone might be hiding her from the world."

212

spring brought an attack of spring fever: I have been extremely drowsy all day, but very pleasantly so. Taking a message from the drowsiness, I informed myself that a person needs a holiday from time to time, and besides I have company, and a person must be polite to company; and so I did not get very much done on the *Genji*.

I did go over to the Frieze Building for a time in the morning, and looked at Charles Hamilton's comments on the last two chapters. They are very encouraging. He has no significant changes at all to suggest in "Yume no ukihashi,"[54] save that some of the footnotes are pedantic, and there are long sections of "Tenarai" too which he finds – his word – "flawless." And his final comment is, "Begorra, and it is a fine story." So maybe I will be all right, if I can think of a way to make people begin at the end and read backwards.

And that is that for the Uji chapters. Tomorrow I must begin a new phase: checking and unifying the notes, a process long anticipated with some dread.

Monday, November 18: People kept coming in to chat, and I may have been brusque and even surly. Marjorie came bouncing in with a package from a New York remainder house, and said she would wait for me to open it, and with her I was definitely brusque, for I knew what was in it. Pornography, is what.

Lunch with Maeda, after which he went to catch the airport limousine. Another day, another house guest on his way. He said he would come again, and so I suppose I did not mistreat him.

I commenced reworking *Genji* notes, and made my way through the first eight chapters, and found it utterly engrossing work, checking all the numbers, trying to run down elusive poems and poets – and some of them are pretty elusive, for I seem, without having been aware of the fact, to have drawn heavily upon inconspicuous commentaries. That is what scholarship is about: getting utterly lost in the pursuit of buried facts. They may tell you, they who do it, that it is the pursuit of truth; but the real point is getting utterly lost, and forgetting all about such illusory matters as the passage of time.

Dinner at Hanna's. Her other guest was a visiting Polish poet named Edward Strachura. He was difficult to talk to, for he knows little English, but at one point he became eloquent on the weird, unreal quality of dealing with the "socialist" bureaucracy. Writers refer to censors as "they," and censors, perfectly nice people when you sit down at the table with them, also refer to a mysterious "they," responsible for it all.

Thursday, November 21 : Today my sister is fifty. Silver threads among the gold. I awoke feeling fretful and unwilling to arise; but arise I did, and when I had washed myself and had my morning coffee and settled down with the *Genji* notes once more, I felt happy once more. It is extremely tranquilizing work. Perhaps I am a clerk or accountant by nature, or perhaps it is that I have a strong yearning for order; but whatever it is, I do like the business of tidying things up, gathering in loose ends and retrieving lost stitches, solving problems of a severely limited, self-contained nature. When I find that I have inadvertently translated the same poem twice and that the two translations seem strangely unrelated to each other, the discovery is cause less for disquiet than for a pleasant, quiet sort of bemusement, that they should be so different.

To St. Joseph's in the morning. When Dr. Olsen peered inside my ear he gave the discouraging report that the graft has not, or apparently has not, completely succeeded. There seems to be evidence, though he cannot be sure, and I cannot be sure why he cannot be sure, that a small hole has opened up once more. And so, he said cheerfully, perhaps there was after all an infection when, a week or so after the operation, he assured me that there was none. Perhaps he is as blameless as his cheerful, open manner would have us believe, but the feeling does grow that some sort of reformation is needed, something to make our new high priesthood undergo a bout of sincere self-reflection.

Sunday, December 1 : Beautiful, beautiful snow. It started falling heavily in midmorning and is still falling heavily, and there seems to be about a foot on the balconies and walnut trees outside my north windows. I spent a great deal of time through the day lost in the beauty of it when I should have been lost in other things.

Very few people passed, and now and then a car crept by on Huron Street, as if about to give up; and, leaping and plunging and sniffing at the wind, the dogs seemed deliriously happy. It is nice to have the wild reassert itself, though I suppose we would not want that sort of thing all the time. I am among the lovers of the wild who would not do very well in it. Think of having to go out and look for food in all that beautiful snow.

I was at the office some hours before the snow began, and at work on my final reading of the *Genji*. I got through "The Young Gromwell." Speaking of whom or which: yesterday I was glancing at a copy of the Suematsu translation of the early chapters. I laughed to see Murasaki called Violet ("a note came from Violet") and was taken by a rare inspiration. I once considered translating *aoi* as "heartsease." If I return now to that thought and make it operable, why then I can call Aoi Pansy!

The journey back through the snows in the evening seems to have left me all tuckered out. I made myself a spartan meal and lay down on the sofa, and there I found myself at bedtime, a half hour or so ago. I had all sorts of things to do with the evening, but the only thing I actually got done was a bit of dreamy gazing at the snow. It is just as well – such beauty is more important than most things. The marvel of a foot of snow resting silently on a walnut twig.

Monday, December 2: I knew, as I slipped and plunged through the snow in the morning twilight, that it had been a pretty grand snow, but I did not know until I had myself ready for my classes and then looked around for someone to come to them just how grand it had been. There was no one in sight, and queries over the telephone revealed that classes had been called off – which news of course produced another revelation, how very isolated I am.

So there I was with an unexpected holiday ahead of me. Surprisingly, I felt somewhat depressed at the prospect – or perhaps not so surprisingly, since we have had many holidays lately, and for me a holiday is less a day of rest than a day of silence. So there I was, I say, at midmorning, and I had not much of anything to do but push ahead with my final reading of the *Genji*. Though with close and exhausting attention, I am reading with a certain pleasure, as if the thing were not my responsibility. I feel fairly sure that it has an amount of life in it, and there is no way to forestall the nigglers and the exquisite sensibilities who will lament the lack of poetry.

I become aware of inconsistencies which it is probably too late to do anything about. Why do I call Kokiden Kokiden when Rokujō is "the Rokujō lady"? Very well, I am inconsistent.

Tuesday, December 3: It was a most remarkable storm. I continue to marvel at it, and to devour reports upon it. I now learn that the reason why we west of Lake Erie got such a staggering load of snow is that the storm came not from the north and west, as do most storms, but up the Appalachians and across the lake. Begorra, and it was a fine storm.

I am almost through to the exile, almost to the end of the first Iwanami volume. Who knows, at this rate I might just possibly be finished by Christmas. I would have gone yet further had I not spent so much time going over suggestions by last-minute readers of the early chapters. I had expected to cast them off in irritation, but found them useful and interesting. Those who do not playa da game still have a right to maka da rules. (Myself, I thought that Butz's remark was pretty funny, and that it was awfully small and boy-scoutish of Ford to make him apologize. So many of Ford's doings are even so.)

An evening nap was interrupted by a telephone call. It was Hanna, who wanted to know what for me is the single dominant sensual image of Japan. The smell of mildew, I replied.

Saturday, December 7: It was a bleak day, this anniversary of the commencement of My War with the Japanese, and little did I suspect what a long war it would be. There was icy rain through most of the day, and tonight no doubt it will freeze, and so tomorrow we can all go skating.

I continued the reading through of the *Genji* translation and the taking into account of various people's comments upon it, chiefly Johnson's. On the whole my serenity continues unruffled, and that is the important thing. I have a vague feeling, though we are too far along for it to be allowed to ruffle the serenity, that I may be doing what I so tiresomely charge Waley with doing, laying on a rather thick coating of whitewash. I am far less aware, reading rapidly over the translation, than I have been on reading the original, of a difference in the quality of the chapters. So Johnson's hostile remarks about the third chapter, from a slight remove and with these later thoughts on my mind, become curiously reassuring, for they do suggest that not everything has the same bland surface.

I suppose "Asagao"[20] today seemed the most questionable chapter. It seemed in a way the least interesting and in a way the most: the least interesting because it is so futile, having to do with an unsuccessful assault on a lady who does not seem all that worth assaulting in the first place; the most interesting because of its place in the grand development of the tale. Some enthusiasts might say that it looks ahead, foreshadowing the affairs of the first Uji princess, and therefore gives evidence that Murasaki knew what she was doing far in advance. To me this seems highly unlikely. I think rather that it looks backwards, as far, perhaps, as the second chapter. It is the last of the variations on the theme announced in that chapter.

A celebration in the evening. Choo Won has finished, but for details, the Uji chapters, and so I took her and Sibley to dinner, at Haabs in Ypsilanti. She does not like the Uji chapters – reassuring evidence once more, if I choose to see the matter so, that not all my chapters are blandly alike. She thinks that Genji, while he has his faults, has a certain grandeur, while Kaoru and Niou and especially the former are merely small and mean.

Sunday, December 15: Sometimes in the morning before sunrise, when I walk across the campus, the trees are white with frost, a marvel of delicate, cold beauty, as if they too might vanish quite away with the frost, every twig a clean white line against the dark skies. So it was this morning.

So we come to the last week of classes. That it is not a time of complete exhilaration may have to do with an awareness that holidays are approaching. For those who live alone, a deadness settles over everything. It is already beginning to settle. Holidays are traditional times, when the old commune reasserts itself. Living outside the commune is a very new and radical thing, and that it should be punished is quite proper. The thought of all those silent holidays to get through is oppressive all the same.

I continued my final reading of the *Genji*. I did very well, finishing the first "New Herbs" chapter and moving on to the second – and at this rate I might almost be finished by Christmas. The "New Herbs" seem much better than the chapters that precede them, more considerable and substantial, as if after a time of frivolities there were important things to consider once more. "Seem" these several things, I say, because I despair, after all these years of intimate association, of being really objective.

In the afternoon I went shopping, not in the spirit of Christmas generosity, but with the selfish intent of provisioning myself for the passage westward in the new year. State Street was cheerful with Christmas shoppers. Main Street was cheerful with little white lights, but almost without shoppers. It is dying, and that is a pity, since we will need it when we run out of gasoline. I looked in on the pornography shops. Among the peep shows was a rather charming little thing from Thailand, all amiable and busy.

John Farrior is spending the night here. It is good to have him. He was among the consciences of my young days, and that is a role which would have caused many a man to reject me utterly. Harriet came over in the evening, and we went to dinner at the Village Bell, where they reminisced about their days together in the Shanghai American School. Usually reminiscences of years which one did not share are merely a bore, but somehow it all seemed so far away and improbable as to be like a good travel book.

Tuesday, December 17: I read through three more *Genji* chapters, indeed the three which I think I might offer as my favorite succession, my favorite trio in all the long story: "The Flute" and "The Bell Cricket" and "Evening Mist." The last I think perhaps I like best of all the fifty-four, and there can be no doubt that the comedy is more successful by virtue of following "The Bell Cricket," which as we all know Waley cut, and the fact that he did so seems inexplicabler and inexplicabler. I also went over some installments of Charles Hamilton's "Poisoned Dew" that I had skipped over, *jijō ni yotte*, on earlier readings. Some of his remarks are rather biting, some very amusing. When, in "The Bell Cricket," I refer to the Third Princess's garden as "a natural moor," he remarks: "A black bastard?"

In the afternoon I took a cold walk downtown to the Main Street post office to pick up a registered letter. As I came past the pornography shops on Fourth Street, one of them was apparently being raided. I gathered from the cluster of surly damsels among the police gentlemen that prostitution and not printed matter was the reason for the raid.

Friday, December 20: Clear-cut things, however harsh, give to winter beauty and excitement, but this grayness with fretful spits is merely dreary.

I pushed ahead with the Uji chapters, rather slowly, and without enthusiasm. The weather may have had something to do with the case, but I suspect that I again have been working too hard. Things that have moved me on earlier readings, such as Nakanokimi's farewell to Bennokimi on the eve of the departure for the city, or Nakanokimi's request of Kaoru that he take her back to Uji, did not do much for me this time. Kaoru, saying the same thing over and over again at endless length, becomes next to unbearable. And then just at the moment when relief seems absolutely essential it comes. An element of delicate jocularity enters the conversation, and Ukifune does so as well, and it seems possible to continue. A virtuoso performance, if you will, offering relief at the last possible moment; but surely there are less cruel ways to bestow pleasure. I go on thinking that the Uji chapters could have been written only by Murasaki Shikibu, and yet I think that the change in her, keeping so grimly at it and so puritanically, refusing to allow frivolous diversions, is not entirely a lovable one.

Some shopping afterwards, and a trip to the museum to see whether it might have some amusing Christmas presents. I bought a very silly little Egyptian bird, but think I will keep it for myself.

Saturday, December 21: Again we were not permitted to observe the sun, as it hesitated and turned back towards the north. It was a leaden day, though in the evening a quarter moon was mistily visible.

I overslept badly, and oversleeping, even when the evidence is that I need sleep, makes me grouchy and reluctant to be productive. But I informed myself that a full holiday from the *Genji* would be a disaster, and got to work on it. Whether in fact the crisis was that deep I do not know, but I felt as I have felt at times of similar crisis that to falter would mean to stumble and fall for good. It is most surprising that in these circumstances I did not like Ukifune's very own chapter even less than the chapters preceding it, but in fact I was much taken with it. Perhaps the important thing is that Kaoru is not prominently in evidence, and when he is he is an almost comic figure, all censorious and self-righteous, Genji and Yūgiri reduced to a pillar of small-town society. For the rest, the balancing of the comic and the pathetic, Ukifune's nurse and Ukifune herself, is very skillful; and then there are the lower classes, the watchmen so inflexibly eager to do their duty, and Ukifune's woman Ukon, the only really sane one in all the insanity, a little like one of Faulkner's Negroes. Yes, it is a good chapter – and provides disheartening evidence that my feelings about the preceding chapters are founded in objective truth. Well, I shall not worry about them. Let them go and face the cruel public for what they are.

Monday, December 23: The sun was out, and I am happy. I worked upon the Uji chapters with considerably more serenity, and made it through to the last but one, which has always been among my favorites. The last but two I would at times in the past have been prepared to call the worst of the Uji chapters. I liked the former once more, but I liked the latter too. The important thing, surely, is that Kaoru is not offered a helpless lady to whom to plead his unhappiness and his virtue. He figures in "Writing Practice" scarcely at all, and, though I doubt that I have considered the matter in quite that light, it may be his absence that has pleased me. In "The Drake Fly" he can be nasty, behaving rather as Genji did towards Kashiwagi but somehow in a narrower and meaner way; and maybe nastiness is the nearest thing to a human trait that he has. I kept thinking that maybe I should go back over the chapters which he dominates and try to give him at least some verbal distinction, an elegant rhetoric that may get him past the unwary and keep him from being merely tiresome. But it is too late. Let him go, let him go. ("St. James's Infirmary" kept running through my head as I worked, and all of a sudden I see why.)

Late in the afternoon I went slipping and slogging over to the Huckers' for tea. Their new house is in one of the more elegant parts of town. They have had people in for a succession of teas, of which today's was the last, I believe, and whether or not this fact did me honor I do not know. Bob and Laura were there, and the dog barked at me only briefly as I was leaving.

Tuesday, December 24: Snow spits once more, though it was warm and rather a lot of aged snow melted.

I finished reading through the *Genji*, I did, this Christmas Eve. The last chapter seemed to me very good, gently sad and utterly quiet. It is not, however, as good an ending as several spots one can think of along the way. The best of all, perhaps, would have been in "The Wizard," with Genji at the end of a year and, as he puts it, the end of a life. The last paragraph in "The Floating Bridge of Dreams" seems to point ahead, and it is unfortunate that Kaoru should have the last word. One wishes that Ukifune could be left alone to her fate. These thoughts, however, do not make me a proponent of the dual-author theory. Doubts there may be as to whether the "conclusion" is a proper one, and it is perhaps unfortunate that the best of the earlier "conclusions" should fall at exactly the place where the second author is most commonly averred to have taken over; but they are not doubts of a sort that a minor author would have given rise to.

Dinner with Hanna Lerski and Martha at Hanna's. I spent much of the time looking at Hanna's family albums. Prewar Poland. Terribly sad – beautiful, elegant ladies on the eve of the collapse of their world.

Wednesday, December 25: A very silent day. Scarcely any automobiles on the streets, no creature save me stirring all through the Frieze Building. Though I would have liked to be with people – it is the only time of the year when family seems to matter a great deal – I did not let the silence bother me enormously. I cannot deny that I would have liked a bottle of gin, too – and I can easily see why there are so many suicides at Christmas.

I was at the office fairly early, and applied myself to the notes for the Uji chapters. It is work which I enjoy, and therefore good work for a silent Christmas. The mindlessness contains perhaps a measure of Zen.

So now, looking back over the long process of translation, I am uncomfortably aware of two sections that do not seem really finished, the last of the Tamakazura chapters and the chapters between the death of the Eight Prince and the appearance of Ukifune. So they will remain. I doubt that I could change things much at this late date, and as I glance back at random through the vast manuscript my eye keeps lighting on details that do not seem right. I have Genji "feeling" for Yūgao as she lies dying, and that seems a mild reaction indeed; and I have someone else peeking out somewhat ridiculously from a cocoon – it is such details, and no doubt they are legion, that people are likely to notice, and not the more considerable lapses of which I now seem to find myself aware.

Dinner at Bob and Laura's. Choo Won was their other guest, and Bob spent most of the time teaching her to do needlepoint, and that seemed a very cozy way to spend a Christmas night. He gave me a tie dotted with pigs of which the initials are MCP, "Male Chauvinist Pig."

Thursday, December 26: The Frieze Building was a little, a very little, livelier than yesterday. Sandy, the secretary, sat in the office listening to the radio and drawing her wages, and one or two of the lecturers came in; but for the most part The Great Christmas Silence continued. The last time I spent Christmas in Ann Arbor I got drunk, and that, I think, was a good idea.

Through much of the day, looking down over a greensward unpopulated save by squirrels and unlicensed dogs, I worked on the Uji notes. I felt very serene, and dare I say enlightened? – enlightened after the Uji fashion, having put away worldly entanglements, feeling no ambitions and no frustrations. I became aware of numerous little inadequacies – inconsistencies and carelessnesses – which I could worry about if I chose to. I am glad I am not a perfectionist; a perfectionist would, after a day's work of this sort, be going back and seeking to dig up buried remains for purposes of reshaping. But enough, is what I say. There comes a time when an end must be called, and the whole enormous project tied up and put in the mail.

To Detroit with the Johnsons in the evening, to view a hockey game. I marveled through much of the game at how extraordinarily little I remembered from last years's game. My chief recollection was a very general one of a certain wild, surging beauty. There it was again this evening, huge brutes of men soaring about with the most marvelous grace, like angels, and pausing now and then to beat hell out of one another. It was the Red Wings and the Minnesota North Stars that we saw this year, and the encounter was a tie.

Thursday, January 2, 1975: There came in the mail a letter from a young lady at the Shitennōji young ladies' school in Osaka informing me that she and certain of her schoolmates have embarked upon an English translation of the *Genji*. She wishes to know whether they can be of service to me. The airy insouciance with which these people embark upon such projects makes a person feel very small and inadequate.

Again I came very close to finishing the *Genji*, but didn't quite make it. I went over most of Johnson's remaining comments, and rewrote the introduction slightly, and then set about separating the more than five thousand pages into three heaps to make three complete copies. I expected to find this last work, if monotonous, soothing and productive of strong feelings of satisfaction. Instead I found it almost nightmarish. The sheer bulk of the manuscript somehow produced a regression to childhood nightmares, when I was overwhelmed by and asked to do something about figures of astronomical and incomprehensible proportions. By noon the horror had so overcome me that I could do no more, and that was that. Otherwise I think that today would have been the day of the grand completion.

For the rest I spent a goodly amount of time hearing about people's problems and thinking how we escape from major problems by fretting over minor ones. During the recent Democratic convention in Kansas City a lady from, I think, New Jersey likened the President to a person rearranging the deck chairs on the *Titanic*. So it is: we sit on the brink of unimaginable catastrophes, and fret over problems that are not problems at all.

Is "catastrophe" complete and ultimate, so that there can be no plural? I think so, but shall not seek to correct the solecism.

Friday, January 3: The work which yesterday I found so nightmarish I was this morning able to pick up with poise and equanimity, with something like serenity. The trouble yesterday I think was that I felt myself rising to the top of a frenetic phase, and there was the huge pile of paper gradually wearing down, like a kalpa having its time and passing. Anyway, by midmorning the heap had been reduced to nothing, the kalpa had come to its end. There were a couple of other little things to do. For reasons too vague and wispy to be apprehended in words, I had the notion that there was something in error somewhere in a passage in one of the last chapters. So I hunted, and found that a reference to a flower had been omitted. And then I reworked the paragraph of acknowledgements in the introduction. And then I could not think of a single other thing to do save wrap and address the several reams of paper. So I did that. And I was finished.

And with what do I make known that an era has just ended? Why with a ✠ or two.